THE ALDINE EDITION

OF THE BRITISH

POETS

THE POETICAL WORKS OF EDWARD YOUNG

IN TWO VOLUMES

VOL I

THE POETICAL WORKS OF

EDWARD YOUNG

VOLUME I

GREENWOOD PRESS, PUBLISHERS
WESTPORT, CONNECTICUT

Originally published
by Bell and Daldy, London

First Greenwood Reprinting 1970

SBN 8371-2921-4 (SET)
SBN 8371-2922-2 (VOL. 1)

PRINTED IN UNITED STATES OF AMERICA

CONTENTS.

VOLUME I.

In the Sixth Night arguments were drawn, from
Nature, in proof of immortality : here, others are
drawn from Man : from his discontent, p. 138 ; from
his passions and powers, 139 ; from the gradual growth
of reason, 140 ; from his fear of death, 140 ; from
the nature of hope, 141 ; and of virtue, 142, &c. ;
from knowledge, and love, as being the most essential properties of the soul, 145 ; from the order of
creation, 146, &c. ; from the nature of ambition, 148,
&c. Avarice, 151 ; pleasure, 152. A digression on
the grandeur of the passions, 153, &c. Immortality
alone renders our present state intelligible, 154. An
objection from the stoics' disbelief of immortality
answered, 155. Endless questions unresolvable, but
on supposition of our immortality, 156. The natural,
most melancholy, and pathetic complaint of a worthy
man, under the persuasion of no futurity, 157, &c.
The gross absurdities and horrors of annihilation urged

home on Lorenzo, 163, &c. The soul's vast importance, 167, &c.; from whence it arises, 170, &c. The
difficulty of being an infidel, 171; the infamy, 172;
the cause, 173; and the character, 173, of an infidel
state. What true free-thinking is, 174; the necessary punishment of the false, 175. Man's ruin is
from himself, 176. An infidel accuses himself of guilt
and hypocrisy; and that of the worst sort, 177. His
obligation to Christians, 177. What danger he incurs
by virtue, 178. Vice recommended to him, 178. His
high pretences to virtue, and benevolence, exploded,
178. The conclusion, on the nature of faith, 180.
Reason, 180; and Hope, 181; with an apology for
this attempt, 181.

SONNET

WRITTEN AT WELWYN.

MOURN not a leaf that strews the linden shade
Of Welwyn's faded bower; and if the year
Hath touch'd her glittering foliage with the sere
And yellow look of autumn, it hath laid
A fitlier residence for her the maid
Divine Urania.—So let nought appear
Of the world's transitory glories near
This consecrated roof; nor thou upbraid
With thoughtless speech, time's ministers with
      wrong
Done to the Muse's dwelling : not a thing
But blooms immortal here ; to all belong
Perennial verdure, and an endless Spring
Breathed from the Poet's pure celestial Song.

J. M.

Oct. 14th, 1833.

THE LIFE OF EDWARD YOUNG,

BY THE REV. J. MITFORD.

EDWARD YOUNG was born at Upham, in Hampshire, a small and pleasant village standing on elevated ground, near the skirts of the forest, between Bishops Waltham and Winchester.[1] His birth took place in June, 1681. His father was rector of the parish, which preferment he held with his fellowship. His grandfather was John Young, of Woodhay, in Berkshire. In September, 1682, the poet's father was collated to a prebendal stall in the Cathedral of Salisbury, by Bishop Ward. He preached a latin sermon[2] in 1686, before Sprat, who expressed his approbation of it, and his regret that so learned a divine had one of the poorest stalls in the Church. He had a patron in Lord Bradford, to whom he dedicated two volumes of sermons; and by the interest of that nobleman, added to his own merit and reputation, he was appointed chaplain to King William, and preferred to the Deanery of Salisbury. Jacob[3] says, that he was chaplain and clerk of the closet

---

[1] See Wood's Ath. Ox. vol. ii. c. 991, 2. Biog. Brit. Life of Young, note A.

[2] Young Edvd. amoris christiani Mnemoneuticon, sive Concio ad clerum habita in Visitatione Metropolitica Ecclesiæ Cathedralis, Sarum. July 12, 1686. 12mo. The text was John, xiii. 34, 35. a scarce little volume. To this sermon were added some verses, by that excellent poetess, Mrs. Anne Wharton, upon its being translated into English, at the instance of Waller, by W. Atwood, Esq. v. Biog. Brit. art. Young, note c, and Nichols's Anecdotes, vol. i. p. 5, for an account of his works.

[3] Poetical Register, 1723.

to the late Queen Anne, who honoured him by
standing godmother to his son, the poet. The dean
died after a short illness, in 1705, and in his sixty-
third year. Bishop Burnet preached in the cathedral,[1] on the Sunday after his decease, and passed
an impressive encomium on his virtue and holiness.

Our poet was placed by his father on the foundation of Winchester, but no vacancy at New College, Oxford, occurring before he was eighteen,
he became, by the laws of the Society, superan-
nuated. He therefore entered in October, 1703,
as an independent member, and resided at the
Warden's lodgings, till he should be qualified to
stand for a fellowship of All Souls. On the death
of his friend, the Warden, he removed to Corpus
Christi, and was soon appointed to a law-fellowship
at All Souls, by Archbishop Tenison, 1708. On
the 23rd of April, 1714, he took his degree of
Bachelor of Civil Law, and his Doctor's degree
on the 10th of June, 1719.

It is probable that at this time Young was distinguished for superior learning and abilities; for

---

[1] The following inscription is on the tablet in Salisbury
Cathedral, written by the poet to his father's memory:

H. S. E.
Edvardvs Young, L. L. B.
hujus Ecclesiæ Decanus.
Vir cum primis
eruditus, probus, integer.
Summo utique honore dignissimus
utpote qui de Ecclesia Anglicana
cui fidissimo fuit Præsidio
summoque ornamento
quam optime meruit.
Anno Ætatis suæ 63,
obiit 9 Aug.
annoque Domini, 1705.

In the north aisle of Winchester Cathedral are inscriptions
in memory of his daughter and her husband. v. Nichols, i.
p. 6.

when the foundation of the Codrington Library was laid, on the 20th of June, 1716, he was appointed to speak the Latin oration. It was published 'rogatu Hæredis dignissimi,' with an English dedication to the ladies of the Codrington family, which is only distinguished for its false wit, flippancy of style, and affected adulation. The Oration was not admitted by Young into his own edition of his works; and when, in 1741, Curll and Tonson printed theirs, he judiciously advised them to omit it.[1] It is composed in a taste that is anything but classical, abounding in puerile conceits, and written in a latinity often questionable, often incorrect,[2] and never elegant nor pure.

Something has been said on general report of the conduct of Young while at College; and that it did not hold out much promise of the virtues that adorned and dignified the remainder of his life. That he was patronized by Wharton[3] was one of the exceptionable points : but a speech of Pope's to Warburton, which his biographer Ruffhead has preserved, has probably put us in possession of all the truth on that subject that is worth

[1] Young's oration was printed with the one by Digby Coates, the University Orator, at Codrington's interment, in 1716. The books bequeathed to the college were said to be of the value of £6000.

[2] I will quote a passage, the latter part of which has been wrought up again in the Satires.—"Si menti, judices, ignem inditum, si splendidum ingenium, si nominis amplitudinem, si bello vim, si vitam (eheu ! cur amico hanc defuisti ?) brevissimam, si totum denique virum, in exiguo depingendum, uno verbo coarctandum mihi desumpserim, ducem præstantissimum pulveri pyreo ab igne correpto conferre non timerem—*caluit, enituit, insonuit, concussit, abivit.*"

[3] Young's father had been acquainted with Lady Anne Wharton, the first wife of the Marquis of Wharton, who was celebrated by Burnet and Waller for her poetical talents; she added some verses to Dean Young's visitation sermon.

knowing.—" Young," he said, " had much of a sublime genius, though without common sense. So that his genius, having no guide, was perpetually liable to degenerate into bombast. This made him pass a *foolish youth*, the sport of peers and poets; but his having a very good heart, enabled him to support the clerical character, when he assumed it, first with decency, and afterwards with honour." That he was distinguished for his ingenuity and learning[1] above his fellow-students and contemporaries, is known by a complaint of Tindal the atheist, who said, " the other boys I can always answer, because I always know where they have their arguments, which I have read a hundred times : but that fellow Young is continually pestering me with something of his own."

An epistle to the Right Honourable George Lord Lansdowne, in 1712, was Young's first essay in poetry; this he was afterwards willing to forget.[2] The versification is flat, but the diction pure; with occasional specimens of the conceits which he so much indulged in, as when he calls ' soberness' the prose of life, or when he says that ' Isabel's tears water the bays of Southern.' Sometimes he is vague and obscure in his expressions.

[1] The late Dr. Ridley remembered a report current at Oxford, that when Young was composing, he would shut up his windows, and sit by a lamp even at mid-day, nay, that skulls, bones, and instruments of death were among the ornaments of his study.

[2] To Young's own edition of his works, the following advertisement is prefixed :—" I think the following pieces, in four volumes, to be the most excusable of all that I have formerly written : and I wish less apology was needful for these. As there is no recalling what is got abroad, the pieces have been republished. I have revised and corrected, and rendered them as pardonable as was in my power to do." *All the original dedications appear to have been suppressed.*

> But unconfined by bounds of time and place,
> You choose companions from all human race,
> Converse with those the deluge swept away,
> Or those whose midnight is Britannia's day.

The poem concludes with a lamentation on the death of Harrison,[1] the author of Woodstock, and other poems ; who was recommended by Swift to the patronage of Bolingbroke, and who died soon after his return to England from the embassy at Utrecht. There is a passage in it which contains the sentiment afterwards so beautifully introduced and expressed by Gray in his Ode to Vicissitude.

> The Patient thus, when on his bed of Pain,
> No longer he invokes the gods in vain.
> But rises to new life ;—in every field
> He finds Elysium :—rivers nectar yield,
> Nothing so cheap and vulgar but can please,
> And borrow beauties from his late disease.

In 1713, he prefixed a copy of indifferent verses to Addison's Cato ; his poem also on the *Last Day* was given to the public in the same year,[2] though it had been finished by Young as early as 1710, before he was thirty: part of it was printed in the Guardian, May 9th, 1713. It was inscribed to the Queen in a dedication that was afterwards judiciously omitted ; for it was written in a strain of fulsome and hyperbolical flattery.—" It is, madam, (he writes) a prospect truly great to behold you seated on your throne, surrounded with your faithful counsellors, and mighty men of war, issu-

---

[1] Spence's Anecdotes, p. 351, " Harrison had a sweetness of versification even beyond that of Ovid. Dr. Young remembered some lines on a woman debauched by presents, who repented afterwards, and died of grief.

> ————Tarpææ virginis instar,
> Obruitur donis accumulata suis."

See further account of him in note by Dr. Young.

The Vice-Chancellor's imprimatur on this poem, was dated at Oxford, March 19, 1713, see Tatler, vol. v. p. 138.

ing forth commands to your own people, or giving audience to the great princes, and powerful rulers of the earth. But why should we confine your glory here? I am pleased to see you rise from this lower world, soaring above the clouds, passing the first and second heavens, leaving the fixt stars behind you: nor will I lose you there, but keep you still in view through the boundless spaces on the other side of creation, in your journey towards eternal bliss; till I behold the heaven of heavens open, and angels receiving and conveying you still onward from the stretch of my imagination, which tires in her pursuit, and falls back again to the earth."

This poem has received the praise of Johnson, but it must be allowed that the choice of the subject was not judicious; there is also much exaggeration in the language, as

> Leviathans but heave their cumbrous mail.
> It makes a tide, *and wind-bound navies sail.*

and an incongruity of allusion, and want of finish, as

> While other Bourbons rule in other *lands,*
> And (if man's sin forbids not) other *Anne's.*

and the descriptions are often minute and particular, when the subject should have been veiled in general terms, as in the description of the Resurrection:

> Now monuments prove faithful to their trust,
> And render back their long committed dust.
> Now charnels rattle, scattered limbs, and all
> The various bones, obsequious to the call
> Self-mov'd, advance—the neck perhaps to meet
> The distant head, the distant legs the feet,
> Dreadful to view, see through the dusky sky,
> Fragments of bodies in confusion fly,
> To distant regions journeying, there to claim
> Deserted members, and complete the same.

and in another place,

When lo ! a mighty trump, one half conceal'd
In clouds, one half to mortal eye reveal'd,
Shall pour a dreadful note.—

That Young at this time received a stipend as
a writer on the side of the Court, seems to be
proved by some lines in Swift's Rhapsody on
Poetry :

Whence Gay was banish'd in disgrace,
Where Pope will never show his face,
Where Y—— must torture his invention
To flatter knaves, or lose his pension.

That the initial letter was meant for Young, the
biographer observes is proved by other lines in
the same poem,

Attend, ye Popes, and Youngs, and Gays,
And tune your harps, and strew your bays,
Your panegyricks here provide,
You cannot err on flattery's side.

A poem in two books called the " Force of Religion; or, Vanquished Love," was the next production of our author.   It was founded on the execution of Lady Jane Grey,[1] and her husband Lord
Guildford.   This also came into the world under
the shelter of a dedication to the Countess of
Salisbury, highly extolling her beauty and virtue ;
but which having been cancelled by the author, need
not now be revived.   Occasionally the expressions
are flat and too familiar, as

In space confined, the muse forbears to tell,
Deep was her anguish, *but she bore it well.*

On the death of the Queen, in 1714, Young
published a poem which he inscribed to Addison:
it abounded in the most complimentary and somewhat extravagant praises of the new King, and
attributed our military achievements, and the
splendid series of victories won by the British

---

[1] This was chosen as the subject of a tragedy by Webster,
afterwards by Edw. Smith, and Rowe.

Army, not to the skill of the Generals or courage of the troops, but to the prayers and piety of the Queen:

> Argyle and Churchill but the glory share,
> Whilst millions lie subdued by *Anna's prayer.*

The poet has also not forgotten to return thanks for the tenths and first-fruits bestowed by the Queen upon the Church:

> She saw, and grieved to see the mean estate
> Of those who round the hallow'd altars wait;
> She shed her bounty piously profuse,
> And thought it more her own in sacred use.

This poem having performed its transitory purpose, joined the ranks of its suppressed predecessors. From a passage in Young's letter to Richardson,[1] on Original composition, relating to Swift, it appears that he was at one time in Ireland; and it has been supposed that he went with the Marquis of Wharton, in 1717.

In 1719,[2] his tragedy of Busiris was brought on the stage, it was inscribed to the Duke of Newcastle; " because the late instances he had received of his Grace's undeserved and uncommon favour in an affair of some consequence, foreign to the theatre, had taken from him the privilege of choosing a patron." Of the extent or nature of his Grace's benevolence we are not informed; but when Young collected his works, he did not think fit to perpetuate his praise. In the same year

---

[1] Two epigrams, by Young, on Richardson s Grandison, are in the life of the latter, by Mrs. Barbauld, vol. 1, cxxviii, cxliii.

[2] From a passage in the Englishman, it would appear that Young began his theatrical career so early as 1713, v. Biogr. Dict. see a criticism on Busiris and Young's plays, in Biogr. Dramatica, art. Bvsiris. Young received £84 for his play, as appears by an old account book of B. Lintot, a price much larger than was paid to Rowe, either for Jane Shore or Lady Jane Grey.

also appeared a poetical letter from our Author to Mr. Tickell, on the death of Addison.

The tragedy of Busiris is written in language of sufficient elegance, and many of the images and ideas are such as proceed from a truly poetical conception: but at the same time it is one, that like the Cato of Addison, is composed after the artificial rules of criticism, and not from the inspirations of nature and genius. It has no resemblance to the old tragedies of the English stage, but partakes rather of the school of Corneille and Voltaire, and some of our writers who just preceded Young. The language is too often darkened by clouds of declamation; there is little diversity of character, or variety of incident. It is a drama that might have been written by a man only conversant with books, without any stores of observation, any experience of life, or any knowledge of mankind. Busiris is a fine example of the "fierce tyrant in tapestry;" whose speech is declamation, whose passions are his only guide, and whose will is the universal law. When he appears, it is only to boast his unlimited power, to exaggerate the extent of his enormous rule, and to command obedience to his despotic sway. The whole of the sentiments are swollen into a style of Asiatic exaggeration. Violence is opposed to violence, and one ungovernable passion is hurled against another. There are no delicate gradations of feeling, no fine connections of thought, no playful dalliances of the imagination. All is ambition, and jealousy, and hate, and cruelty, in their naked and uncontrolled forms; the mutual recriminations of the wretched accomplices in guilt, the shameless avowal of the most detestable designs, or the unnatural exhibition of the most guilty feelings. The plot is constructed without any great ingenuity of design, and the epilogue is very gross and indecent.

The Paraphrase on Part of the Book of Job was now given to the public; the dedication to the Lord Chancellor Parker appeared only in Tonson's edition. Young speaks in it with satisfaction of his retirement, but the flattering style of his dedication to a patron almost unknown to him, seems to prove that he would not have been very unwilling to leave it. The versification of this poem is flowing, copious, and elegant; but it has a defect which no poetic graces could supply: in dilating the descriptions and reflexions of the original, it has detracted much from its majestic eloquence; the greatness of the subject, and the sublimity of the thoughts required the most severe simplicity of style; every additional ornament is an injury; instead of expressing a sentiment, the poet is employed in painting an image, and the accumulation of figures, and the other poetic decorations, overwhelm the simple grandeur of the whole. How different from the language of the original are expressions like the following:

> Exhausted woe had left him nought to fear,
> But gave him all to grief—

In 1721, Busiris was followed by the celebrated tragedy of the Revenge. In his dedication to the Duke of Wharton, which Young afterwards excluded from his works, he acknowledged great obligations. "Your Grace (he writes) has been pleased to make yourself accessary to the following scenes, not only by suggesting the most beautiful incident in them, but by making all possible provision for the success of the whole." And in another part he openly asserts that his present fortune is derived from the Duke's bounty.[1] Whatever

[1] I, my Lord, whose knowledge of your Grace lies more in private life, can tell them in return of one who can animate his country retirements with a kind of pleasures

this may have been; that it was bestowed with
liberality, and recommended by the delicacy with
which it was given, appears on the authority of
the legal reports. The Duke of Wharton's affairs
being found much embarrassed at his death, among
other legal questions, the Chancellor Hardwicke
had to determine whether two annuities granted
by the Duke to Young were for legal considerations. One was dated March 24th, 1719, and
accounted for his Grace's bounty in a style that
may well be called worthy of a prince:—" considering that the public good is advanced by the
encouragement of learning and the polite arts, and
being pleased therein by the attempts of Dr.Young;
in consideration thereof, and of the love I bear
him, &c." The other was dated 10th July, 1722.
Young, on his examination, swore that he quitted
the family of Lord Exeter, and refused an annuity
of £100 per annum, which had been offered him
for life, if he would have continued tutor to Lord
Burleigh, upon the urgent solicitations of the Duke
and his assurance of providing for him.[1] It ap-

sometimes unknown to persons of distinction in that scene,
who can divide the longest into a variety of polite and
useful studies, and appoint the great men of antiquity their
stated hours to receive, if I may so speak, their audience
of him, who is an excellent master of their history in particular; and observing how Nature in a few years is apt
to come round again, and tread in her own footsteps, has a
happiness in applying the facts and characters of ancient to
modern times, which requires a beautiful mixture of learning and genius, and a mind equally knowing in books and
men; who can carry from his studies such a life into conversation, that wine seems only an interruption to wit, who
has as many subjects to talk of as proper matter on those
subjects, as much wit to adorn that matter, and as many
languages to produce it so adorned as any in the age in
which he lives; and yet so sweet his disposition, that no
one ever wished his abilities less, but such as flattered
themselves with the hope of shining when near him.

[1] At that time of life when the Duke of Wharton's most

peared also that the Duke had given him a bond
for £600, dated 15th March, 1721, in consideration of his taking several journeys and being at
great expenses, in order to be chosen member of
the House of Commons, at the Duke's desire; and
in consideration of his not taking two livings of
£200 and £400, in the gift of All-Souls' College,
on his Grace's promises of advancing him in the
world.   Young's attempt to procure a seat in
Parliament, alluded to in the document above,
was made at Cirencester, where he stood a contested election.   It is said that he possessed con-
siderable talents for oratory, and that when he
took orders, his sermons were distinguished for the
grace and animation of their delivery, as well as
for the elegance of the composition. An anecdote
is mentioned of him, that when preaching in his
turn at St. James's, he perceived that it was not
in his power to command the attention of his
audience :[1] this so affected the feelings of the
preacher, that he leaned back in the pulpit and
burst into tears.   At one period of his life it
appears that he was intimate with Tickell, and
in 1719, they communicated whatever verses
they wrote, even to the least things, to each
other.   Soon after, it was generally known (says
Pope) that Mr. Tickell was publishing the first

vehement ambition was to shine in the House as an orator,
he found he had almost forgotten his Latin, and that it was
necessary with his present views to recover it   He therefore desired Dr. Young to go to Winchendon with him,
where they did nothing but read Tully and talk Latin for six
weeks, at the end of which *the Duke talked Latin like that
of Tully.* The Doctor on some other occasions as well as
this, called him a prodigious genius. ♦ Spence's Anecdotes,
p. 351.

[1] Seward, in his anecdotes, in reporting this circumstance,
says it was owing to the inattention of *George the 2nd,* and
not of the audience in general, v. vol. ii.

book of the Iliad, I met Dr. Young in the street, and upon our falling into that subject, the Doctor expressed a great deal of surprise at Tickell's having such a translation by him so long. He said that it was inconceivable to him, and that there must be some mistake in the matter; that he and Tickell were so intimately acquainted at Oxford, that each used to communicate to the other whatever verses they wrote, even to the least things; that Tickell could not have been busied in so long a work without his knowing something of the matter, and that he had never heard a single word of it till on this occasion. This surprise of Dr. Young, together with what Steele had said against Tickell in relation to this affair, make it highly probable that there was some underhand dealing in that business; and indeed, Tickell himself, who is a very fair worthy man, has since in a manner as good as owned it to me.[1]

The tragedy of "The Revenge" is certainly one of the finest and most successful efforts of our poet's genius. The poetry is often beautiful, the thoughts refined and full of imagination, the images select, and a true poetic feeling pervades the whole. But from this praise something must be taken. The tragedy is written after the inferior model of the French drama; with which Dryden, and others of lesser note, had unfortunately superseded the masculine productions of our *native* stage. On this plan, Addison wrote his Cato, Smith his Phædra, and Gray his fragment of Agrippina. It is true that the incongruities and extravagances of Dryden's prolific muse had been much corrected by the improved taste of the later dramatists; that Rowe had adorned his artificial

---

[1] Spence's Anecdotes, p. 148.

scenes of passion, with pomp of language and elegance of sentiment; and that Otway had once
more invoked Nature from her sanctuary to which
she had fled so long : but, with some bright ex-
ceptions, it is too true, that of the *new* tragedy it
might be said in the language of Johnson,

> And declamation roar'd while passion slept.

In the play of the Revenge, Alonzo is placed in
that artificial situation, which makes the pride of
the French tragedy, and which so often forms the
complicated plot of Dryden, when two conflicting
passions are striving for the mastery, as love for
the mistress, and fidelity to the friend.   The triumph of the poet, is to contrive a perfect equipoise
of contending motives, so as to keep the mind in
a state of agonizing suspense; and when either
motive begins to preponderate[1] to throw additional
weight into the opposite scale.

> The French are delicate, and nicely lead
> Of close intrigue the labyrinthian thread.
> Our genius more affects the grand than fine,
> Our strength can make the great *plain action shine.*
> They raise a *great curiosity indeed,*
> From *his dark maze to see* the hero freed,
> We rouse the affections, and that hero show
> Gasping beneath some formidable blow, &c.[2]

Interest in the bosom of the spectator is presumed
to be excited not by the rapidity of the action, or
the sublimity of the passions, or by the force and
truth of the characters; but to be absorbed in
admiration of ideal excellence and supernatural
virtue; by a conscience that is always superior to
temptation, by artificial and exaggerated profes-
sions of virtue and disinterestedness, and by a lofty

---

[1] See the Revenge, act iv. s. 1.'
[2] Young's Ep. to Lord Lansdowne..

and romantic self-denial, that is a poor substitute for the real feelings and passions of the heart.

The character of Zanga[1] is modelled on that of Iago, and on Mrs. Behn's Abdelazar, but the prototype in Shakespeare is more true to nature than the copy; both as to the motive by which Iago is impelled to his course of guilty action, and to the sentiments and feelings which accompany it. Zanga is a character of higher intellectual power, of nobler birth, of a more active imagination, and a more cultivated mind.[2] How far, under these advantages, and with a greater refinement of thought, his long-cherished and inhuman hatred was as likely to be maintained, and exhibited in all its horrid depravity, as in the more vulgar bosom of the Venetian Moor, and whether its continuance were as natural, is worthy of consideration; perhaps the accumulation of injuries which he sustained, the death of his father, slain by Alonzo's sword, the loss of a kingdom through Alonzo's success, and the indignity of a blow from the same hand, will *poetically* authorize the nature and means of his revenge: but in one respect Young appears to me to have excelled even Shakespeare himself; namely, in founding the credulity of Alonzo on reasons more probable, more ingeniously contrived, and more skilfully maintained than those which overpowered the unsuspicious temper, and over-persuaded the credulous reason of Othello.[3]

---

[1] A speech in the City Nightcap, by R. Davenport, contains the outline of the character of Zanga, v. Dodsley's Old Plays, vol. xi. p. 365.   See Reed's note.

[2] See his Speech, act iv.

[3] See criticism on this play in Biog. Dramatica, that is worthy of attention, it was written by G. Steevens. Young could only get £50 for it.   See Warton's Essay on Pope, ii. p. 147.

Zanga's explanations to his wife, and afterwards
to the audience, of the intended effect of his machinations are not skilful, nor dramatic in their
effect; yet the grandeur of sentiment and situation
in the last scene must be felt by all, especially
when assisted, as the present writer has witnessed,
by the efforts hardly to be surpassed of more than
one of our noble tragic actors ; but, after all, it is
the sublimity of Corneille and not of Shakespeare ;
and the sudden revulsion of feeling in Zanga, accompanied with his repentant reflections, are not
true to nature or to life. The great poetical
merits of the play are obvious; its highly sustained
passion, and its impressive and terrific scenes of
guilt are represented on the stage with wonderful
effect; but it is wanting in lights and shadows,
in scenes of tenderness and repose, and in those
softer colours which the magic pencil of Shakespeare used so skilfully to spread like a sunny haze
over the gloom and passion of the most distressing
history; it is deficient in those fine contrasts that
set off and heighten the terrible and pathetic ;
and even in that chaste and comic humour which,
instead of breaking the continuity of feeling, lets
the mind loose a moment from its painful pressure,
and relieves it, by exhibiting that feeling under a
new aspect, and connected with fresh associations.

The Satires of Young were published separately,
in folio, under the title of The Universal Passion.[1]
The first appeared, in folio, in the year 1725, and
the last was finished in the beginning of 1726.

---

[1] A work, says Dr. J. Warton, that abounds in wit, observation on life, pleasantry, delicacy, urbanity, and the
most well bred raillery, without a single mark of spleen
or ill nature. These are the first characteristical satires in
our language, and are written in an ease and facility of
style very different from this author's other works ; the fifth
and sixth, on the Character of Women, are incomparably

The fifth Satire on Woman was not published till
1727, and the sixth not till 1728, when they were
all collected and introduced with a preface, in
which the author hints that poetry is not favour-
able to preferment or honors. He acquired, however, the sum of three thousand pounds by these
poems; of which Spence, on the authority of
Rawlinson, says two thousand was bestowed by
the Duke of Grafton, and that when one of his
friends exclaimed, " two thousand pounds for a
poem," he said, it was the best bargain he ever
made in his life, for the poem was worth four
thousand. The satires are inscribed by Young to
illustrious names, the Duke of Dorset, Mr. Dod-
ington, Mr. Spencer Compton, and Sir Robert
Walpole. His panegyricks did not go unre-
warded ; for in his poem of Instalment, addressed
to the minister, he acknowledges with gratitude
that he has received the bounty of the crown.

> My breast, Oh ! Walpole, glows with grateful fire ;
> The streams of royal bounty turned by thee
> Refresh the dry domains of poetry.

It is said that Swift pronounced of these satires
that they should be either more angry or more
merry, an observation not made without justice,
but which seems to have arisen from some passages
in Young's preface.

These Satires are the production of a mind rendered acute by observation, enriched by reflection,
and polished with wit. They abound in ingenious
and humorous allusions. They show much know-

the best. The introduction to these two satires, particularly the address to Lady Betty Germain, are perhaps as
elegant as anything in our language. After reading these
pieces, so full of a knowledge of the world, one is at a loss
to know what Mr. Pope could mean by saying, that though
Young was a man of genius, yet that he wanted *common
sense.* Warton, Essay on Pope, vol. ii. p. 148.

ledge of life, experience of society, and acquaintance with that learning that is drawn from books.
Their defects appear to me to consist in their
being too epigrammatic, by which single couplets
sparkle with a brilliancy and point, that concen-
trates the allusion or image within their narrow
bounds, and separates it from the rest of the
poem. Many passages read like a continued string
of epigrams; whereas the good execution of a
poem, as of a painting, looks to each particular part
only as it bears upon the whole; the finish of one
is regulated by another; the colouring of one object, if necessary, is lowered to bring it in harmony
with the rest; and nothing is admitted, which,
heightening the brilliancy of particular passages,
tends to cast over the rest a flat and unnatural hue.
If we were allowed to bring to poetry the language
of a sister art, it might be complained that there
is a *spottiness* in the execution of these satires
disagreeable to a pure and correct taste. Unfortunately joined to this careful and elaborate
polish of some more sparkling passages, we find
an occasional versification careless and unfinished;
some rhymes are defective in exactness and some
are wanting.[1] But the great defect is in the
perpetual exaggeration of the sentiment, which
mars the delicacy of the wit, destroys the justice
of the satire, and forfeits the confidence of the
reader. There is no gradation of censure or of
praise, no middle tint bringing the lights and
shadows into harmony, no diminishing perspective
in the moral view. All objects are equally bright,

---

[1] As an instance of imperfect rhymes, the four following
lines occur consecutively.

> Such heads might make their very bustos *laugh*,
> His daughter's starved, but Cleopatra's *safe*.
> Men overloaded with a large *estate*
> May spill their treasure in a nice *conceit*.

and equally near, and all represented in a distorted and disproportionate size. In the following passage, touching on the distempered taste of those who prefer the gaiety of cities, to rural charms and the society of nature, the poet passes on through different illustrations, all exaggerated, till he ends with a fiction unnatural and absurd.

Such Fulvia's passion for the town—fresh air,
An odd effect, gives vapour to the fair.
Green fields, and shady groves, and crystal springs,
And larks, and nightingales are *odious* things.
But smoke, and dust, and noise, and crowds delight ;
And to be press'd to death transports her quite :
When silver rivulets play thro' flowery meads,
And woodbines give their sweets and limes their shades,
Black kennels' absent odours she regrets,
And stops her nose at beds of violets.

It may be proper to observe, that these satires were published before those of Pope. Goldsmith says " that they were in higher reputation when published, than they stand at present. That Young seems fonder of dazzling than of pleasing, of raising our admiration for his wit than of our dislike of the follies he ridicules."[1] They were followed by the Instalment, addressed to Sir Robert Walpole, which was, with great propriety, afterwards suppressed ; for Burleigh and Godolphin are made to descend from heaven " with purple wings," and stars, and garters, to instal the minister.

The reign of the new king was ushered in by Young with an Ode to Ocean: the hint of it was taken from a passage in the royal speech, which recommended the encouragement of seamen, and the abolition of the forcible means of impressment. Its execution is sufficient to show that Young's strength did not lie in lyric poetry. It

---

[1] Vide Essay on English Poetry, p. 420.

often swells into bombast, and as often falls into
flatness ; the choice of the versification was inju-
dicious, though the author says he borrowed it
from Dryden, as his subject was great, to express
majesty. Prefixed to the original publication was
an Ode to the King Pater Patriæ, and an Essay
on Lyric Poetry ; neither of those are preserved.
The ode, which originally consisted of seventy-
three stanzas, Young reduced in his own edition to
forty-nine.   Among the passages omitted is a
wish that concluded the poem, and which was
contained in thirteen stanzas.   The essay is a
performance of no merit, written with a constant
endeavour to be smart and witty ; in the style of
those who profess to consider learning and dulness
as inseparable ; who wish to unite the fine gentleman to the scholar, and who can find nothing more
to say of the ancient lyric poets, than that the
muse of Pindar is like Sacharissa, and that Sappho
is passionately tender, like Lady ——.

Soon after the appearance of this poem, and
when he had arrived at the age of forty-seven,
Young entered into holy orders. In April, 1728,
he was appointed Chaplain to George the Second.[1]
The tragedy of the Brothers, which was then in
rehearsal, was withdrawn.[2] In this play there are
some beautiful lines, and much that is written
with poetical elegance and force, but the ground-
work to the plot, which is the dissension between
the brothers, is displeasing to the mind. The
guilty machinations of Perseus are too successful,
while the feelings of the reader sympathize with

[1] H. Croft's narrative says 1728, but Davies, in his life
of Garrick, says 1720, and that it was produced thirty-three
years after.
[2] When Young was writing a tragedy, Grafton is said
by Spence, to have sent him a human skull with a candle
in it, as a lamp, and the poet is reported to have used it.

the innocence and the undeserved misfortunes of his brother. Perplexities thicken too closely around the termination of the story, which ordinary prudence could avert, or resolution overcome; and the whole is terminated in a manner so unsatisfactory and unskilful, that the author has appended an historical epilogue[1] to carry on the story towards the conclusion, that lay unfortunately beyond the frame and boundaries of his plot.

There is something affecting in the patient kindness and distress of the king; but on the whole there is not much in this play to excite our sympathy. Young seems, in his dramatic poems, to have delighted most in the delineation of the sterner passions. Pride, revenge, and hatred, and cruelty, are the main-springs of the three plays; and if he has fallen behind his contemporaries or immediate predecessors in the same dramatic school, in the popularity of his productions, it arises not from any inferiority in the execution, but from their having engaged on their side the feelings of pity and love, and opened those sources from which the softer affections of the heart arise.

---

[1] Young's epilogue was never read, the place of it being supplied by one from Mallet, who expresses himself in the following terms :—

> A scheme forsooth to benefit the nation,
> Some queer odd whim of pious *propagation*,
> Lord! talk so *here*! the man must be a widgeon,
> Drury may *propagate*—but not religion.

Alluding to the profits being given to the Society for the Propagation of the Gospel. Young was much offended, nor would suffer it to be printed at the end of his piece. He was scarce less angry with Garrick, at whose instigation it was written, as well as delivered to Mrs. Clive, who spoke it in her broadest manner. The play was very coldly received, see Richardson's Correspondence, vol. vi. p. 246; it did not produce £400. See Young's speech to Richardson on the subject.

Ruffhead, in his life-of Pope, mentions that when Young, quitting the study of the law, took holy orders, he consulted his friend Pope with regard to his theological studies, who perhaps, half seriously and half in banter, recommended the study of Aquinas; but when, Ruffhead adds, that after half a year's silence, when Pope sought out his friend, he arrived just in time to save him from an irretrievable derangement; it is plain that he knew nothing of the work to which he alludes. To whatever results it might have led, it assuredly had no tendency to weaken his reasoning powers, oppress his imagination, or disturb the soundness and serenity of his mind.

In 1728, he published in prose a true Estimate of Human Life, dedicated to the Queen, it was suggested by the King's death, and is in fact a moral essay on the passions, written with point and force, but abounding too much in antithesis of sentiment and expression. It reads somewhat like a commentary on Ecclesiastes,[1] and would need but little decoration to be formed into a poem in blank verse. Young also printed a very long sermon, preached before the House of Commons, January 30th, 1728-9, on the martyrdom of King Charles, entitled, an Apology for Princes, or the Reverence due to Government.

This sermon has little application to Charles, or to the circumstances connected with his death, but is employed in abstract considerations of the duties of princes, and the difficulties of the government. There is always ingenuity of thought and fertility of allusion, but it too much resembles a declamation filled with the commonplaces of a rhetorician, and it reads like a translation glitter-

---

[1] The second course, the counterpart of this estimate, never appeared, though announced in 1728.

ing with the pithy apophthegms and pointed sentences of Seneca. What Young most delighted in, were eloquent expositions of moral duty, and directions for the conduct of life, the government of the passions, and the regulation of the understanding. Of his style and its peculiarities, a short specimen will be sufficient.—" If we cast too an eye on our own account, have we contracted no national guilt? or is the moral world almost reversed, a system of infatuation nigh finished among us? have we not luxurious poverty, avaricious wealth? shame-faced religion, frontless immorality, industrious debauchery, contemplative impiety; corruption in high-place, insolence in low, ambitious shame, and criminal repentance; repentance for omission of sins, that black inversion of the day's duty? Has not sin its commandments, error its creed, hypocrisy its saints, profaneness its confessor, and sensuality its martyr, &c." Young, it is to be presumed, was at this time living on his college fellowship, and the pension of Lord Wharton; anxious for the advancement of his fortune and situation in the world, he addressed a letter to Mrs. Howard, the favorite of the King, which has been assigned, by the editor of Lady Suffolk's letters, to a date lying between 1727 and 1730, yet there seems an objection either to admit this or to advance it to a later year. Young asserts that he is turned of fifty years; yet, if the date of his birth is correctly given, in the year 1730 he could have been but forty-nine. Again he alleges that he has no *preferment*: but in 1731 he took the college living of Welwyn, so that either the preferment he desired may not have been *clerical*, or there is some error in the statement, which it is not easy to rectify. The letter will probably be deemed the most curious one we possess from the poet, considering the language of the petition, and the party to whom it was addressed.—

TO MRS. HOWARD.

MADAM,   Monday Morning.

I KNOW his majesty's goodness to his servants, and his love of justice in general, so well, that I am confident, if his majesty knew my case, I should not have any cause to despair of his gracious favor to me.

> Abilities.
> Good Manners.
> Service.
> Age.
> Want.
> Sufferings ⎫
>   and   ⎬ for his majesty.
> Zeal.   ⎭

These, madam, are the proper points of consideration, in the person that humbly hopes his majesty's favor.

As to *abilities*, all I can presume to say, is, I have done the best I could to improve them.

As to *good manners*, I desire no favor, if any just objection lies against them.

As for *service*, I have been near seven years in his majesty's, and never omitted any duty in it, which few can say.

As for *age*, I am turned of fifty.

As for *want*, I have no manner of preferment.

As for *sufferings*,[1] I have lost £300 per annum, by being in his majesty's service ; as I have shown in a representation which his majesty has been so good to read and consider.

---

[1] I suppose that some college living must have fallen, which Young could not accept, having delayed taking orders

As for *zeal*, I have written nothing without showing my duty to their majesties, and some pieces are dedicated to them.

This, madam, is the short and true state of my case. They that make their court to the ministers, and not to their majesties, succeed better. If my case deserves some consideration, and you can serve me in it, I humbly hope and believe you will. I shall, therefore, trouble you no further, but beg leave to subscribe myself, with truest respect and gratitude,

Yours, &c.

EDWARD YOUNG.

P.S. I have some hope that my Lord Townshend is my friend; if, therefore, soon and before he leaves the court, you had an opportunity of mentioning me with that favor you have been so good to show, I think it would not fail of success; and if not, I shall owe you more than any.

In 1730 he published "Imperium Pelagi," a naval lyric, occasioned by His Majesty's return from Hanover, and the succeeding peace. It was inscribed to the Duke of Chandos, and written in imitation of Pindar, but had the misfortune to fall under the ridicule of Fielding in his Tom Thumb. Young must often have had reason to regret the eagerness and haste with which he cast the unripe productions of his genius before the public: this is another of those numerous poems that in his better judgment and improved taste he was unwilling to own. It consists of one hundred and sixty stanzas, and yet the author apologizes for its brevity. Of the Pindaric manner which he professes to have caught, the following specimen may suffice :—

> Kings, merchants, are in league and love,
> Earth's odours pay soft airs above,

> That o'er the teeming field prolific range ;
> Planets are merchants ; take, return,
> Lustre and heat by traffick burn,
> The whole creation is one vast exchange.

In the same year appeared the Epistle to Pope
on the authors of the age. There is much clever-
ness in the poem, wit, satirical humour, and versification forcible and elegant; but there is an occasional want of finish that is found in all Young's
poetical productions, except, perhaps, the dramatic;
and a singular defect of judgment in uniting the
vulgar and colloquial to the elaborate and refined.

In July, 1730, Young was presented by his college to the Rectory of Welwyn, in Hertfordshire ;
and in May, 1731, he married Lady Elizabeth
Lee, daughter of the Earl of Litchfield, and widow
of Colonel Lee ; a connection that arose from his
father's acquaintance with Lady Ann Wharton, who
was co-heiress of Sir Henry Lee, of Ditchley, in
Oxfordshire.

His next production was the Sea Piece,[1] in two

---

[1] Young is said to have composed an extempore Epigram
on Voltaire, who, when in England, ridiculed Milton's
Allegory of Death and Sin—

> You are so witty, profligate, and thin,
> At once we think thee Milton, death, and sin.

but it probably was manufactured by some Wit, from the
following passage in the dedication to his Sea Piece.

> No stranger, Sir, though born in foreign climes,
> On Dorset downs, when Milton's page
> With sin and death provoked thy rage ;
> Thy rage provoked who soothed with gentle rhymes ?

It is thus given in Spence :—

> Thou'rt so ingenious, profligate, and thin,
> That thou thyself art Milton's Death and Sin.

Voltaire's objection to this episode was, that Death and
Sin were non-existents.

Voltaire, like the French in general, showed the greatest complaisance outwardly, and had the greatest contempt

odes, forming another proof of Young's total ignorance of the true nature of lyrical poetry, though
it did not prove unacceptable to the royal taste.

" My shell, which Clio gave, which Kings applaud."

In 1734 he published The Foreign Address, or
the best Argument for Peace, occasioned by the
British fleet, and the posture of affairs, written in
the character of a sailor. This production is not
in the author's edition. It is memorable for its
description of Friar Bacon, in the eighteenth
stanza, and the invention of Gunpowder :—

> See yon cowl'd Friar in his cell,
> With sulphur, flame, and crucible ;
> And can the charms of gold that saint inspire ?
> O cursed cause ! O curs'd event !
> O wondrous power of *accident !*
> He rivals gods, and sets the globe on fire.

Another quotation, from the thirty-fifth stanza,
will suffice :—

> O could I sing as you have fought,
> I'd raise a monument of thought,
> Bright as the sun !—How you burn at my heart
> How the drums all around
> Soul-rousing resound ;
> Swift drawn from the thigh,
> How the swords flame on high ;
> Now the cannons' deep knell
> Fates of kingdoms foretell !
> How to battle, to battle, sick of feminine art,
> How to battle, to conquest, to glory we dart.

In 1741, after a marriage of ten years, Young
was deprived of his wife; a daughter whom she

---

for us inwardly.   He consulted Dr. Young about his Essay
in English, and begged him to correct any gross faults he
might find in it.   The Doctor set very honestly to work ;
marked the passages most liable to censure ; and when he
went to explain himself about them, Voltaire could not
avoid bursting out a laughing in his face.   Vide Spence's
Anecdotes, p. 375.

had by her former husband, and who was married to Mr. Temple, son of Lord Palmerston, died in 1736, and Mr. Temple four years after. It has generally been believed that Mr. and Mrs. Temple were the Philander and Narcissa of the Night Thoughts ; though some circumstances occur in the poem, at least incompatible with the character of the former. Mrs. Temple died of a consumption, at Lyons, on her way to Nice, and Young accompanied her to the Continent.[1] By his wife he had one son, Frederic, who was living in 1780 ; and whom the inconsiderate opinion of some of Young's Biographers identified with the character of Lorenzo in the Night Thoughts. This heedless assertion is disproved by Mr. Herbert Croft, who showed, from the particular passages which he brought forward, that the description was totally inapplicable, even supposing that other circumstances were not at variance with the supposition ; and also, that when in 1741, the character of the finished Infidel was drawn by the father,[2] the son was only eight years old ; it was also mentioned in the Biographia Britannica, that he was dismissed from college ; but this report was found to be totally void of foundation, and

---

[1] Young was abroad during some part of his life, but any particulars of his journey are not known. In his Seventh Satire, he says,—

When after battle I the field have seen
Spread o'er with ghastly shapes, which once were men.

It is also said, that he once wandered into the camp of the enemy with a classic in his hand, which he was reading intently, and had some difficulty in proving that he was not a spy.

[2] The Biographer asks whether Young might not have had *Wharton* in his eye ? Mr. H. Croft was the friend of the son, and wrote his life of Young to vindicate him from some erroneous remarks to his prejudice. Vide Boswell's Johnson, iv. 59,

rested solely on the authority of Dr. Eyre, the schoolfellow of Young at Winchester.

Of the Night Thoughts,[1] which were published from 1742 to 1744, Young's favourite and most finished poem, it may be said, that they show a mind stored with reading and reflexion, purified by virtuous feelings, and supported by religious hope. There is in them fertility of thought and luxuriance of imagination, an originality in the style, an expansion of sentiment, and an accumulation of argument and illustration, which seems almost boundless. With little or no narrative, and but few touches of personal character, the interest is endeavoured to be maintained by the greatness of the subject, the deep and important reflections, and the copious stores of observation. The poem is filled with wise maxims of moral conduct and religious faith : and the poetical language is well chosen without being very select, or elaborately formed. But there is a want of a clear connexion in the subject ; every image is amplified[2] to the utmost ; every argument expanded and

---

[1] The title of my poem (Night Thoughts) not affected ; for I never compose but at night, except sometimes when I am on horseback. Dr. Young, vide Spence's Anecdotes, p. 378. See what Pope said to Warburton on Young's Night Thoughts, in Warton's Pope, vol. iv. p. 235. Miss Hawkins in her Memoirs, i. p. 170. "The Night Thoughts, on their first appearance, were thought to be the production of Tom Hervey, rather than of Young." Dr. Warton says, that Young wrote his Night Thoughts in direct opposition to Pope's view of life in his Essay on Man, which was an argument to make them satisfied even with their present state without looking at another ; but Young has painted in colours too dark and uncomfortable. W. Harte assured Dr. Warton he had seen the letter which Young wrote to Pope on the subject. Swift speaks of Young sometimes with praise, and sometimes with contempt.

[2] So little sensible are we of our own imperfections, that the very last time I saw Dr. Young, he was severely censuring and ridiculing the false pomp of fustian writers, and

varied, as much as the greatest fertility of the
fancy could effect. The subject is pursued through
every gradation of feeling, and every channel of
thought. There is no selection, no discreet and
graceful reservation ; no mark of that experienced
taste that knows exactly when the purpose has
been effected, and which leaves the rest to be supplied by the imagination of the reader. Reflection
follows on reflection, and thought on thought, in
such close succession, that, as in books of maxims,
one truth obstructs and obliterates another ; an expression, otherwise permanent, is destroyed as
soon as formed ; and we feel, I am afraid, in reading this poem of Young, as we do in the perusal
of Seneca, that no progress, no advancement is
made : we seem to move in a perpetually dazzling
circle of argument and reflection, and analogy,
and metaphor, and illustration, without the power
of passing beyond it ; and it is on this account
that the perusal of both these writers, however
delightful for a season, soon fatigues and dissa-
tisfies the mind. Any one who will compare the
moral writings of Cicero and Seneca in this respect, will soon mark the distinction to which I
allude. Besides, the copiousness of expression
outruns the extent of the matter. The words over-
load the subject ; and the magnificence of language
is not always supported by a corresponding grandeur of thought. There is too great a uniformity
of subject for the length of the poem, to keep
the attention enlivened, the fancy amused, or

the nauseousness of *bombast*. I remember he said that such
torrents of eloquence were *muddy* as well as *noisy*, and that
these *violent* and *tumultuous* authors put him in mind of
a passage of Milton, ii. 539. Some excellent observations
on these poems of Young are to be found in Campbell's
Specimens, vol. vi. p. 43. Dr. Johnson's Criticisms at
the end of Croft's Life must not be overlooked.

even the feelings awake; especially when not
adorned by any peculiar harmony of numbers,
or connected with the progress of a narrative.
In the conclusion of the Centaur not Fabulous,
Young acknowledges his not being able to quit
his subject. " My busy mind (he says) perpetually suggests new hints ; my heart knows not
how to refrain from pursuing them.   The volume
grows upon my hands, till its bulk would defeat
its end; new rays of thought dart in upon me,
which, like cross lights, confound and perplex
each other." The flow of his versification was
with Young of secondary importance, and made
subservient to the vigorous enforcement of the
subject.[1]   Nothing can be well more inartificial,
or inharmonious ; it is cut up into short sentences,
and terminates with the pause at the end of the line.
Very seldom can it boast of that flowing harmony
and those modulated cadences which other poets
have produced ; and which in Milton and among
those of later times, have arisen to the highest excellence, and afforded the most exquisite delight.
The high strain of religious feeling, and elevated
language, is often debased by vulgar or satirical
expressions, as " the same old slabbered tale,"—
" peruse the parson'd page,' or when he says

> Walk thoughtful on the silent solemn shore
> Of that vast ocean it must sail too soon,
> *And put good works aboard.*

When he calls God " the great Philanthropist,"

---

[1] As to Dr. Young (says Aaron Hill in a letter), I know
and love the merit of his moral meanings, but am sorry that
he *overflows his banks,* and will not remind himself, when
he has said enough upon a subject, that it is then high
time to stop.   He has beauties scattered up and down his
Complaints, that had he not so separated them by lengths of
cooling intervals, had been capable of carrying into future
ages such a fire, as few past men ever equalled.   Vide
Richardson's Corresp. 102.

it surely is in a taste that cannot be approved;
and such lines as the following—

When later there's less time to play the fool—

are out of harmony with the grave and sacred
character of the poem. I remember once (said
Warburton) reading a poem called the *Night
Thoughts* to Mr. Pope, where the poet was always
on the strain and labouring for expression : " This
is a strange man," said he, " he seems to think
with the apothecaries that *Album Græcum* is
better than an ordinary stool."

In 1745, Young wrote Reflexions on the Public
Situation of the kingdom, addressed to the Duke
of Newcastle; it was originally printed as the conclusion of the Night Thoughts, though very pro-
perly he did not include it in the collection of his
other works; the mediocrity of its execution has
consigned it to a deserved oblivion.

In 1753, the tragedy of the Brothers,[1] which
had lain by him above thirty years, appeared on
the stage. Young had intended to apply the
profits of this play to the Society for the Propagation of the Gospel, but as they fell much short
of his expectations, he made up the sum of a
thousand pounds from his own pocket.

His next performance was the ' Centaur not Fabulous,' in six letters to a friend, on the life in
vogue ; the conclusion is dated November 29th,
1754 ; the character of Altamont has been given,
whether justly or not, to the notorious Lord Euston,[2] a man whose name has only reached posterity,

---

[1] See an account of the ' Brothers ' when it was rehearsed,
and of the line,—" I will speak to you in thunder," in the
life of A. Bellamy, vol. ii. 144.

[2] On Lord Euston, see H. Walpole's letters to H. Mann,
vol. i. p. 8, 14, 21, 290. This work (the Centaur not Fabulous) was much ridiculed, and *Young called a madman.*
See Lady Echlin's Letters to Richardson, vol. v. p. 70.

from the unusual load of infamy with which it is
covered. This work is written with vigour, animation, and eloquence; expounding the doctrines
of moral truth, with elegance of illustration and
power of argument. It is full of imagery, yet
abounds too much in poetical allusions, and those
decorations which the fertility of Young's imagination so easily supplied. There is also the same
want of harmony in this, as in Young's poetical
works.[1] Parts read like the Night Thoughts before they were modelled into verse, and parts have
the wit and epigrammatic point which seem the
rude materials of his lively and pungent satires.

In 1756, Dr. Joseph Warton paid a very just
and elegant tribute to the poetical reputation of
Young, by dedicating to him his entertaining and
learned Essay on Pope. The choice was one of
discrimination as well as affection. Young was at
that time the only survivor of that brotherhood of
poets who had adorned and delighted the preceding ages, and among whom Pope shone with such
unrivalled lustre. He had been the friend, the
admirer, and the companion of the poet whom
Warton illustrated; and he was now reposing in
a calm and dignified age, with a genius still
undimmed, and an activity of mind that preserved its power to the last. Young, it is believed,
approved the opinions which Warton advanced;
and he must, in common with all other readers,
have admired the elegance and variety of learning
with which they were illustrated and sustained

[1] A book called 'Eliza,' erroneously attributed to Dr.
Young, and included in a publication of his works, was
written by Mrs. Charlotte Lennox, v. Nichol's Illustrations,
viii. p. 435. In Richardson's Correspondence, vol. ii. p. 35,
is a poem by Young, 'The Sailor's Song to the South,'
occasioned by the rumour of a war; but I do not know
when it was written, it is in the same style as his *other
lyrics.*

In 1758, he published a sermon preached before the King, at Kensington, in the month of June. The argument was drawn from the circumstances of Christ's death, for the truth of his religion. His majesty did not probably approve much prolixity of discourse, for the sermon is unusually short, and written with less rhetorical amplification and metaphorical ornament than was usual with our poet. There is a curious correspondence between him and Mr. Richardson,[1] on the dedication to this discourse.

The letter in prose, on Original Composition,[2] addressed to Richardson, the author of Clarissa, appeared in 1759. There is in it much sound criticism, many valuable observations, and a spirit and eloquence which betrayed none of the infirmities of age. In 1762, a short time before his death, and when he was upwards of fourscore, he printed his poem of Resignation ; here for the first time, a decay of his powers is manifested.— " Ætas extrema multum etiam eloquentiæ demsit, dum fessa mente retinet silentii impatientiam."[3] He says that it was not intended for publication, but that imperfect copies having got abroad, he was obliged to publish something, lest a copy still more imperfect should fall into the press. It is in fact little else than the subject of the Night Thoughts again worked up, but with a flatness of expression, and a feebleness of execution, which may be expected and pardoned in a bard of four-

[1] See Richardson's letters, vol. ii. p. 48—53.
[2] One of Mr. Warburton's remarks was, that the *character of an original writer* was not confined to subject, but extends to manner, by this distinction, I presume, securing his friend Pope's originality. But he mentioned this with so much good humour, that I should have been glad to have heard you both on the subject.—Richardson to Young, v. Correspondence, ii. 56.
[3] Tacitus, speaking of Domitius Afer.

score. The origin of the poem is thus given by Mrs. Montagu.

Observing that Mrs. Boscawen, in the midst of her grief for the loss of the Admiral, derived consolation from the perusal of the Night Thoughts, Mrs. Montagu pressed a visit to the author. From conversing with Young, Mrs. Boscawen derived further consolation, and to that visit the public is indebted for the poem. Mrs. Montagu added that Young's unbounded genius appeared to greater advantage in the companion than in the author : that in him the christian was a character still more inspired, more enraptured, and more sublime than the poet, and that in his ordinary conversation

> Letting down the golden chain from high,
> He drew his audience upward to the sky.

His friend Richardson died while the poem was being printed, and his death is alluded to in terms of sorrow and affection, while he lectures his hoary friend, Voltaire, on the publication of Candide.

> Why close a life so justly fam'd
> With such bold trash as this ?
> This for renown ! yes, such as makes
> Obscurity a bliss

Indeed, the philosopher of Ferney is scolded, admonished, and warned through the greater part of the poem.[1] Young was now anxious that his poetical career should be closed ; and in his will, dated

---

[1] May this enable couch'd Voltaire
> To see that—all is right,
> His eye, by flash of wit struck blind,
> Restoring to its sight.

> If so, all's well—who much have err'd,
> That much have been forgiven ;
> I speak with joy, with joy he'll hear
> *Voltaires* are now in heaven.

February, 1760, he desires his executors,[1] that all his manuscript books and writings, except his book of accounts, should be burned; and in September, 1764, he added a codicil to his will, wherein he made it his dying entreaty to his housekeeper, to whom he left a thousand pounds,[2] that all his manuscripts might be destroyed as soon as he was dead, which would greatly oblige her deceased friend. In April, 1765, he closed his long and virtuous life. He had performed no duty for the last three or four years,[3] but retained his intellects to the last; he left the chief part of his property to his son.

The curious reader (says Herbert Croft) of Young's life will naturally inquire to what it was owing that though he lived almost forty years after he took orders, which included one whole

[1] His executors were his curate, Rev. John Jones, and his sister's son, a clergyman, of Hampshire.—v. Nichol's Anec. i. 634.

[2] In his will, Young left a legacy to his *friend*, Henry Steevens, a hatter, at the temple gate; and he had applied this term to his footman, John Baker, in an epitaph on him. Young and his housekeeper were ridiculed in a novel published by Kidgell, in 1755, called the Card, under the name of Dr. Elves and Mrs. Fusby. After the death of his wife, Young entrusted his housekeeper with the whole management of his household affairs, and she is said to have attained too great an ascendency over him when his faculties began to decay. Mrs. Hallowes was the widow of a clergyman, and a person of great respectability; she is called the *governante* by Richardson, and in his correspondence are some letters addressed to her, showing her acquaintance with him and the ladies of his family. She died in 1780, see Monthly Mag. Jan. 1816, vol. xli. No. 284, p. 390; Aug. 1816, p. 31, vol. xlii. No 287. Some observations on the moral character of Young are in Gent. Mag. Dec. 1816, p. 511.

[3] The whole duty of the parish is now on my hands, the doctor not being able to do anything therein, or neither has he for about two years past. Rev. J. Jones to Dr. Birch Jan. 1764, v. Nichol's Anec. i. 627.

reign, uncommonly long, and part of another, he was never thought worthy of the least preferment. The author of the Night Thoughts ended his days upon a living which came to him from his college without any favour, and to which he probably had an eye when he entered the church. To satisfy curiosity of this kind is at this time far from easy. The parties themselves know not often at the instant why they are neglected, or why they are preferred. The neglect of Young is by some ascribed to his having attached himself to the Prince of Wales, and to his having preached an offensive sermon at St. James's. It has been told me that he had two hundred a year in the late reign, by the patronage of Walpole, and that whenever any one reminded the king of Young, the only answer was—he has a pension.[1] It appears by the following letter from Secker, that he had solicited preferment from him.

Deanery of St. Paul's, July 8, 1758.

GOOD DR. YOUNG,

I HAVE long wondered that more suitable return of your great merit hath not been taken by persons in power ; but how to remedy the omission

---

[1] And Young must torture his invention
   To flatter knaves, or lose his pension.—SWIFT

The observations of Madame Klopstock are too honest to be omitted, and could only have proceeded from one, who living in Hamburgh, knew not courts. " And our dear Dr. Young has been so ill! but he is better, I thank God, along with you. Oh! that his dear instructive life may be extended! *if it is not against his own wishes.* I read lately in the newspapers, that Dr. Young was made Bishop of Bristol. I must think it is another Young. How could the king make him *only bishop, and Bishop of Bristol, while the place of Canterbury is vacant.* I think the king knows not at all that there is a Young who illustrates his reign."— v. Richardson's Corresp. v. iii. p. 152.

I see not. No encouragement hath ever been
given to me to mention things of this nature to
his majesty, and, therefore, in all likelihood, the
only consequence of doing it would be weakening
the little influence which else I may probably
have on some other occasions. Your fortune and
your reputation set you above the need of advancement, and your sentiments above that concern for it, on your own account, which on that
of the public is sincerely felt by your brother

THO. CANT.

At the age of fourscore, in the year 1761, he
was appointed clerk of the closet to the Princess
Dowager. Herbert Croft considers that his party
and politics stood in the way of his preferment,
perhaps the real cause may be found in his seek-
ing it through a channel where the influence was
much less than general estimation had considered
it; and looking to the favourites of the court,
rather than to the patronage of the ministers. In
the following year, viz. 1762, he writes to a
friend,[1] that his sight is so far gone, that he borrows a hand to write his letter.

Of Young's domestic habits but little is known.
When Mr. H. Croft went to Welwyn, in the
expectation of gathering from his housekeeper
some information, he found that she had just been
buried. A foreigner of the name of Tscharner
in a letter to the great Haller, informs him that
he spent four days with the poet at Welwyn,
" that he lived in ease and comfort, that every
thing about him showed the man, each individual

---

[1] See letter to Rev. T. Newcome, of Hackney, in Nichol's Anec. ii. 698. It was feared at one time that Young
would lose his sight, see Richardson's Correspondence,
vol. v. p. 142, 145, on his appointment to the princess.
See the Bishop of Sodor and Man's Letter, vol. v. p. 150.

being placed by rule: all was neat without art, he was very pleasant in conversation and extremely polite." As so little has been discovered of Young's personal history, or the habits of his life, circumstances that are very minute and unimportant, have been eagerly picked up and thought worthy of being recorded. It was his habit, it appears, like that of the late Dr. Farmer, in reading to fold down the leaf where any particular passage delighted him. Many of his books Mr. Croft asserts to have been so swelled beyond the real bulk by such marks of approbation, that they would hardly shut. Mr. Boswell says he has seen some volumes of Young's copy of the Rambler, in which he marked the passages which he thought particularly excellent, by folding down a corner of the page, and such as he rated in a supereminent degree, are marked by double folds. An entertaining instance of his absence of mind, or inattention is mentioned in Spence:—" Tonson and Lintot were both candidates for printing some work of Dr. Young's. He answered both their letters on the same morning, and in his hurry misdirected them. When *Lintot* opened that which came to him, he found it begin,—that ' Bernard Lintot is so great a scoundrel, that,' &c. It must have been very amusing to have seen him in his rage, he was a great sputtering fellow."[1] To the same entertaining volume we are indebted for another anecdote of our poet.—" There was a club held at the King's Head in Pall Mall, that arrogantly called itself ' The World.' Lord Stanhope then (now Lord Chesterfield), Lord Herbert, &c. were members. Epigrams were proposed to be written on the glasses by each member after dinner. Once

---

[1] Spence's Anecdotes, p. 355.

when Dr. Young was invited there, the Doctor would have declined writing because he had no diamond; Lord Stanhope lent him his, and he wrote immediately,—

> " Accept a miracle instead of wit,
> See two dull lines with Stanhope's pencil writ."[1]

Of Young's eccentricity Pope has given the following ludicrous, and, of course, exaggerated account.—" My supper was as singular as my dinner: it was with a great *poet* and *ode-maker*, that is a great poet out of his wits or out of his way; he came to me very hungry, not for want of a dinner (for that I should make no jest of), but having forgot to dine; he fell most furiously on the broiled relics of a shoulder of mutton, commonly called a blade-bone; he professed he never tasted so exquisite a thing, begged me to tell him what joint it was, wondered he had never heard the name of this joint, or seen it at other tables, and desired to know how he might direct his butcher to cut out the same for the future; and yet this man, so ignorant in modern butchery, has cut up half-a-dozen heroes, and quartered five or six miserable lives in every tragedy he has written."[2]

Dr. Young rose betimes, says the author of his life (in the Biographia Dramatica), and obliged his domestics to join with him in the duty of morning prayer. He read but little; while his health permitted him to walk abroad, he preferred a solitary ramble in his church-yard to exercise with a companion on a more cheerful spot. He was moderate in his meals, and rarely drank wine except when he was ill, being, as he said, unwilling to waste the succour of sickness on the stability of health; after a slight refreshment, he

---

[1] Spence, p. 378.
[2] Pope's Letters, vol. xiv. p. 164.

retired to bed at eight in the evening, although he might have guests in his house who wished to prolong his stay among them to a late hour. He lived at a moderate expense, rather inclining to parsimony[1] than profusion: for he expended annually little more than the half of his income, the world and he having reciprocally turned their backs on each other. Whether his temper had disinclined him to conciliate friends, or he had survived their affection, we are not informed, but his curate at Welwyn being appointed his sole executor, it should seem as if he had resolved to accompany the fortune a son was to inherit, with as few tokens of regard and confidence as a father could bestow. The amount of his wealth cannot be ascertained but by its heir; the executor having purposely transferred every part of it, without casting up the total sum, that he might thereby avoid giving answers to the questions or those whose curiosity exceeds their manners.

A few of his observations that he threw out in conversation have been preserved.[2] Dr. Young, says Pope, observed to me that Shakespeare's style, when the hearts and manners of men are the subject, was always good: his bad lines generally where they were not concerned. 1759.[3]

In the Iliad you are fully engaged in the part you are reading: in the Odyssey you are always wishing for the event; the latter is masterly in raising that appetite which is particular to romance, the other is full in each part. One always affords the pleasure of expectation, the other of fruition.

On my saying, says Spence, that old Cato, in

[1] Young allowed his curate, the Rev. John Jones, £20 a-year. Nichol's Anecdotes, i. p. 617.
[2] Spence's Anecdotes, p. 174.
[3] Spence's Anecdotes, p. 333.

Cicero's delightful treatise on Old Age, always mentioned planting as the greatest pleasure for it; Dr. Young observed that he thought he could mention a greater,—the looking back on a life well spent. [1] He said of Atterbury that he was an admirable orator both in the pulpit and the House of Lords; one of the best he ever heard. Richardson he considered as a truly great natural genius, as great and supereminent in *his* way, as were Shakespeare and Milton in theirs. When asked whether Dr. S. Clarke was of a free open disposition in discourse,—" That no man was more so," he said, " civil, obliging, and modest, and far from reservedness, when there was a proper occasion for freedom in conversation."

Dr. Johnson told us (says Mr. Boswell) that the first time he saw Dr. Young was at the house of Mr. Richardson, the author of Clarissa. He was sent for that the Doctor might read to him his Conjectures on Original Composition, which he did, and Johnson made his remarks, and he was surprised to find Young receive as novelties what he thought very common maxims. He said he believed Young was not a great scholar, nor had studied regularly the art of writing : that there were very fine things in his Night Thoughts, though you could not find twenty lines together without some extravagance. He rehearsed two passages from his Love of Fame : the characters of *Brunetta* and *Stella*, which he praised highly. He said Young pressed him much to come to Welwyn; he always intended it, but never went. The cause of quarrel between Young and his son was, that his son insisted he should turn away a clergyman's widow, who lived with him, and who, having acquired great influence over the father,

---

[1] Spence's Anecdotes, p. 354.

was saucy to the son. Dr. Johnson said she could not conceal her resentment at him for saying to Young, that " an old man should not resign himself to the management of anybody."[1]

Mr. Langton who frequently visited him, informs me that there was an air of benevolence in his manner, but that he could obtain from him less information than he could hope to receive from one who had lived so much in intercourse with the brightest men of what has been called the Augustan age of England; and that he showed a degree of eager curiosity concerning the common occurrences that were then passing, which appeared somewhat remarkable in a man of such intellectual stores, of such an advanced age, and who had retired from life with declared disappointment in his expectations. An instance, at once, of his pensive turn of mind and his cheerfulness of temper, appeared in a little story which he himself told to Mr. Langton, when they were walking in his garden.—" Here (said he) I had put a handsome sun-dial, with this inscription : ' Eheu fugaces,' which, speaking with a smile, was sadly verified, for by the next morning my dial had been carried off." [2]When Dr. Johnson, in his way to Scotland, called at Welwyn, in 1781, his biographer says, he went into the garden, where he found a gravel walk, on each side of which was a row of trees[3] planted by Dr. Young, which formed a handsome gothic arch. We sat some time in the summer-house, on the outside wall of which we inscribed—Ambulantes in horto audibant vocem Dei ; and, in reference to a brook by which it was situated,—vivendi recte qui prorogat horam. I said to Mr. Young that I had

---

[1] Boswell's Tour to the Hebrides, p. 275.
[2] Boswell's Life of Johnson, iv. 60.
[3] The Rev. Samuel Johnes Knight, rector of Welwyn,

been told his father was cheerful. " Sir, (said he) he was too well-bred a man not to be cheerful in company, but he was gloomy when alone; he never was cheerful after my mother's death, and he had met with many disappointments."

[1] The most authentic account, however, of Young, in his declining years, is to be drawn from some letters of his curate and executor, Mr. Jones. In the year 1762, three years before Young's death, he writes to Dr. Birch,—" the old gentleman, I may venture to tell you freely, seems to me to be in a pretty odd way of late, moping, dejected, self-willed, and as if surrounded with some perplexing circumstances. Though I visit him pretty frequently for short intervals, I say very little to his affairs, not choosing to be a party concerned, especially in cases of so intricate and tender a nature. There is much mystery in

---

erected an urn at the entrance of the avenue of limes, in the garden of Welwyn, with the following inscription :

Ut umbra æstiva qua ipse delectabatur
Posteri fruerentur,
Has arbores sic in ordine consevit
Ecclesiæ municipalis quondam sacerdos
Edvardus Young,
Amœni et perelegantis ingenii poeta
Facetiarumque lepore
Ac sententiarum gravitate
Perinde nobilis
Qui cum vitæ esset sanctitas summa
Comitasque par.
Vitia insectabatur, non homines,
Errantes emendabat, non castigabat.

———

Hoc grati animi monumentum
Successorei alter in Ecclesia curandum posuit
Samuel Johnes, A. S. MDCCCXII.
Titulum dedit familiaris
Et consanguineus amicissimus,
R. P. Knight.

Nicho.'s Anecdotes, vol. i. p. 620.

almost all his temporal affairs, as well as in many
of his speculative opinions. Whoever lives in this
neighbourhood to see his exit, will probably hear
and see some very strange things,—time will show
—I am afraid, not greatly to his credit. There is
thought to be an immovable obstruction to his happiness within his walls, as well as another without
them; but the former is the more powerful, and
like to continue so. He has this day been trying
anew to engage me to stay with him; no lucrative
views can tempt me to sacrifice my liberty or my
health to such measures as are proposed here, nor
do I like to have to do with persons whose word
and honour cannot be depended upon;—so much for
this very odd and unhappy life." Again, in the
same year, he writes—"How are matters altered
since my letter to you of the 25th post. You remember what I suggested to you about my resolution of leaving Welwyn, of which I had given very
early notice to the worthy Doctor, that he might
have sufficient time to provide. After repeated
trials and repeated disappointments, though seven or
eight offered, he thought proper to apply to me anew;
and, though lucrative motives could not, earnest
importunities did prevail with me at last to cheer
up his dejected heart, by promising to continue
with him for some time longer at least.   *   *   *
By the way, I privately intimated to you, that the
Doctor is in various respects a very unhappy man.
Few know him so much as I do in these respects,
and have often observed with concern. If he
would be advised by some who wish him well, he
might yet be happy, though his state of health is
lately much altered for the worse." In the letter,
January 1st, 1763, he adds,—"The mismanage-
ment too well known unhappily continues, and,
still more unhappily, seems to be increasing, to
the grief of friends, and, I need not say, to the

ridicule of others, who are not a few. What a
pity! what a loss! but no notice will be taken,
nor can it well be offered. *Penuriousness* and *ob-
stinacy* are two bad things, and a disregard to
the general judgment and friendly wishes of the
wiser part of mankind, another. There seems
to be no hope so long as the ascendency is so
great. My ancient gentleman here is still full of
trouble,[1] which moves and concerns, though it
move only the secret laughter of many, and some
untoward surmises in favour of him and his household. The loss of a very large sum of money is
talked of, whereof this vill and neighbourhood
are full; some disbelieve; others say, " It is no
wonder, when about eighteen or more servants
are sometimes taken and dismissed in the course
of a year." The gentleman himself is allowed by
all to be far more harmless and easy in his family
than some one else who hath too much hand in
it.[2] This, among many others, was one reason
for my late notice to quit." On the 2nd April,

---

[1] Young, when in health, was a man of very social habits, and the animating soul of every company with whom
he intermixed; addicted to horticultural pursuits. My
younger brother practised as a surgeon at Welwyn, and by
his enquiries on the spot collected many curious and some
afflicting anecdotes, concerning the bard at his advanced
age,—v. Maurice's Memoirs of an Author, vol. i. 19. Dr.
Warton says, that Young was one of the most amiable and
benevolent of men, most exemplary in his life and sincere in
his religion. Nobody ever said more brilliant things in conversation. The late Lord Melcomb informed me that when
he and Voltaire were on a visit to his lordship, at Eastbury,
the English poet was far superior to the French in the variety and novelty of his bon mots and repartees, and Lord
Melcomb was himself a good judge of wit and humour,—v.
Essay on Pope, vol. ii. 148; *but Voltaire was conversing
in English*. Mrs. Carter said she was much disappointed
in Young's conversation; it appeared to her, light, trifling,
and full of puns.—v. Censura Lit. viii. 201.
[2] Mrs. Hallows, the good Doctor's housekeeper.

1765, he writes to the same correspondent,—
" Dr. Young is very ill, attended by two physicians.[1] Having mentioned this young gentleman,
Dr. Young's son, I would acquaint you next that
he came hither this morning, having been sent
for, I am told, by the direction of Mrs. Hallows.[2]
Indeed she intimated to me as much herself; and
if this be so, I must say it is one of the most prudent acts she ever did, or could have done in such
a case as this, as it may be the means of preventing much confusion after the death of the Doctor.
I have had some little discourse with the son, he
seems much affected, and I believe really is so.
He earnestly wishes his father might be pleased
to ask after him, for you must know, he has not
yet done this, nor is in my opinion like to do it;
and it has been said further, that upon a like
application made to him on the behalf of his son,

[1] Dr. Cotton, of St. Albans, and Dr. Yates, of Hertford.
[2] A correspondent in the Gentleman's Magazine says,
that Dr. Young's housekeeper was the daughter of a Rector of All-Hallows, Hertford, and upon the marriage of
Miss Catherine Lee, was invited by the Doctor, who knew
her family, to his house. She had some fortune of her own,
perhaps very small, as her father left many children. She
was advanced in years, was a woman of piety and good
sense, improved by reading, and was always treated by
the Doctor and his guests, even those of the highest rank,
with the politeness and respect due to a gentlewoman.
The legacy that he bequeathed to her, was not more than
might be due to one whom he had never degraded by paying wages. Why she did not strictly comply with his last injunctions to destroy his manuscripts, I cannot pretend to
say, and can only lament that she did not; perhaps, as Mr.
Young was in the house, she might fancy she had not the
power. In a letter from Young to Richardson, 1758, he
desires him to send, by the carrier, the *parcel of sermons*
which were packed up when I was in town, that I may
commit them to the flames. See one of the last letters Young
ever wrote, in Gent. Mag. (Feb. 1797) dated Nov. 25,
1762.

he desired that no more might be said to him
about it. How true this may be I cannot as yet be
certain, all I shall say is, it seems not improbable.
[1] Mrs. Hallows has fitted up a suitable apartment in
the house for Mr. Young, where I suppose he will
continue till some further event.   I heartily wish
the ancient man's heart may prove tender towards
his son, though, knowing him so well, I can scarce
hope to hear such desirable news. He took to his
bed yesterday, about eleven in the forenoon, and
hath not been up since.   I called soon after my
coming here, but did not see him; he was then in
a doze.   I imagine his further stay on earth can
be of no long duration."   On the 13th of April,
after Young's death, Mr. Jones writes thus,—
" I have now the pleasure to acquaint you, that
the late Dr. Young, though he had for many
years kept his son at a distance from him, yet has
now at last left him all his possessions, after the
payment of certain legacies; so that the young
gentleman, who bears a fair character and behaves
well, as far as I can hear or see, will, I hope,
soon enjoy and make a prudent use of a very
handsome fortune.   The father on his death-bed,
and since my return from London, was applied to
in the tenderest manner by one of the physicians,
and by another person, to admit the son into his
presence, to make submission, intreat forgiveness,
and obtain his blessing. • As for an interview
with his son, he intimated that he chose to decline
it, as his spirits were then low and his nerves

---

[1] In Gent. Mag. May, 1790. " At her lodgings at
Hertford, aged upwards of eighty, Mrs. Hallows, many
years housekeeper to the late Dr. Young, author of the
Night Thoughts, &c." If this date is correct, what becomes of the truth of Herbert Croft's Narrative, who affirms that she died in 1780 ? two days before he arrived at
Hertford.

weak. With regard to the next particular, he
said " I heartily forgive him;" and upon mention
of the last, he gently lifted up his hand, and
letting it gently fall, pronounced these words,
" God bless him."   After about a fortnight's
illness, and enduring excessive pains,[1] he expired,
a little before eleven of the clock, on the night of
Good Friday last, the 5th instant; and was de-
cently buried yesterday, about six in the afternoon,
in the chancel of this church, close by the remains
of his lady, under the communion table. The
clergy, who are the trustees for his charity school,
and one or two more, attending the funeral: the
last office at interment being performed by me,
&c."[2]

The following inscription was placed over the
grave of Young,[3] by the direction of his son, but
whether it was his composition, I am unable to
say :

M. S.

Optimi Parentis

Hujus Ecclesiæ Rect:

Et Elizabethæ

Fœm : prænob :

Conjugi ejus præstantissimæ

Pio et gratissimo animo

Hoc marmor posuit,

F. Y.

Filius superstes.

[1] I find, says Mr. Jones, that opiates are frequently ad-
ministered to him, I suppose to render him less susceptible
of pain. His intellects, I am told, are still clear, though
what effect the frequent use of opiates may by degrees have
upon him, I know not.

[2] For the particulars of Young's funeral, see Gent. Mag.
vol. xxxv. p. 198.

[3] Highmore painted the only portrait of Young known
to exist. See Gent. Mag. Sept. 1817, p. 209; and Meme's
Hist. of Sculpture, p. 216.

THE COMPLAINT, OR NIGHT
THOUGHTS.

NIGHT THOUGHTS.

THE COMPLAINT.

PREFACE.

As the occasion of this poem was real, not fictitious, so the method pursued in it was rather imposed, by what spontaneously arose in the author's mind on that occasion, than meditated or designed; which will appear very probable from the nature of it: for it differs from the common mode of poetry, which is, from long narrations to draw short morals. Here, on the contrary, the narrative is short, and the morality arising from it makes the bulk of the poem. The reason of it is, that the facts mentioned did naturally pour these moral reflections on the thought of the writer.

NIGHT I.

ON LIFE, DEATH, AND IMMORTALITY.

TO THE RIGHT HONOURABLE ARTHUR ONSLOW, ESQ. SPEAKER OF
THE HOUSE OF COMMONS.

TIR'D Nature's sweet restorer, balmy sleep!
He, like the world, his ready visit pays
Where fortune smiles; the wretched he forsakes;
Swift on his downy pinion flies from woe,
And lights on lids unsullied with a tear.
 From short (as usual) and disturb'd repose,
I wake: how happy they, who wake no more!
Yet that were vain, if dreams infest the grave.

I wake, emerging from a sea of dreams
Tumultuous; where my wreck'd desponding thought,
From wave to wave of fancied misery,
At random drove, her helm of reason lost.
Tho' now restor'd, 'tis only change of pain,
(A bitter change!) severer for severe.
The day too short for my distress; and night,
Ev'n in the zenith of her dark domain,
Is sunshine to the colour of my fate.

　　Night, sable goddess! from her ebon throne,
In rayless majesty, now stretches forth
Her leaden sceptre o'er a slumb'ring world.
Silence, how dead! and darkness, how profound!
Nor eye, nor list'ning ear, an object finds;
Creation sleeps.　'Tis as the gen'ral pulse
Of life stood still, and nature made a pause;
An awful pause! prophetic of her end.
And let her prophecy be soon fulfill'd;
Fate! drop the curtain; I can lose no more.

　　Silence and darkness! solemn sisters! twins
From ancient night, who nurse the tender thought
To reason, and on reason build resolve,
(That column of true majesty in man)
Assist me: I will thank you in the grave;
The grave, your kingdom: there this frame shall fall
A victim sacred to your dreary shrine.
But what are ye?——
　　Thou, who didst put to flight
Primeval silence, when the morning stars,
Exulting, shouted o'er the rising ball;
O Thou, whose word from solid darkness struck
That spark, the sun; strike wisdom from my soul;
My soul, which flies to Thee, her trust, her treasure,
As misers to their gold, while others rest.

Thro' this opaque of nature, and of soul,
This double night, transmit one pitying ray,
To lighten, and to cheer.   O lead my mind,
(A mind that fain would wander from its woe)
Lead it thro' various scenes of life and death;
And from each scene, the noblest truths inspire
Nor less inspire my conduct, than my song;
Teach my best reason, reason; my best will
Teach rectitude; and fix my firm resolve
Wisdom to wed, and pay her long arrear:
Nor let the phial of thy vengeance, pour'd
On this devoted head, be pour'd in vain.

The bell strikes one.   We take no note of time
But from its loss.   To give it then a tongue
Is wise in man.   As if an angel spoke,
I feel the solemn sound.   If heard aright,
It is the knell of my departed hours:
Where are they?   With the years beyond the flood.
It is the signal that demands dispatch :
How much is to be done?   My hopes and fears
Start up alarm'd, and o'er life's narrow verge
Look down.—On what? a fathomless abyss;
A dread eternity! how surely mine !
And can eternity belong to me,
Poor pensioner on the bounties of an hour?

How poor, how rich, how abject, how august,
How complicate, how wonderful, is man !
How passing wonder He, who made him such !
Who centred in our make such strange extremes !
From diff'rent natures marvellously mixt,
Connexion exquisite of distant worlds !
Distinguish'd link in being's endless chain !
Midway from nothing to the deity !
A beam ethereal, sullied, and absorpt !

Tho' sullied, and dishonour'd, still divine !
Dim miniature of greatness absolute !
An heir of glory ! a frail child of dust !
Helpless immortal ! insect infinite !
A worm! a god!—I tremble at myself,
And in myself am lost ! at home a stranger,
Thought wanders up and down, surpris'd, aghast
And wond'ring at her own : how reason reels !
O what a miracle to man is man,
Triumphantly distress'd ! what joy, what dread!
Alternately transported, and alarm'd !
What can preserve my life ? or what destroy ?
An angel's arm can't snatch me from the grave ;
Legions of angels can't confine me there.
   'Tis past conjecture ; all things rise in proof :
While o'er my limbs sleep's soft dominion spread :
What though my soul fantastic measures trod
O'er fairy fields ; or mourn'd along the gloom
Of pathless woods ; or down the craggy steep
Hurl'd headlong, swam with pain the mantled pool ;
Or scal'd the cliff ; or danc'd on hollow winds,
With antic shapes, wild natives of the brain ?
Her ceaseless flight, tho' devious, speaks her nature
Of subtler essence than the trodden clod ;
Active, aerial, tow'ring, unconfin'd,
Unfetter'd with her gross companion's fall.
Ev'n silent night proclaims my soul immortal :
Ev'n silent night proclaims eternal day.
For human weal, heaven husbands all events ;
Dull sleep instructs, nor sport vain dreams in vain.
   Why then their loss deplore, that are not lost ?
Why wanders wretched thought their tombs around,
In infidel distress ?   Are angels there ?
Slumbers, rak'd up in dust, ethereal fire ?

They live ! they greatly live a life on earth
Unkindled, unconceiv'd ; and from an eye
Of tenderness let heavenly pity fall
On me, more justly number'd with the dead.
This is the desart, this the solitude :
How populous, how vital, is the grave !
This is creation's melancholy vault,
The vale funereal, the sad cypress gloom ;
The land of apparitions, empty shades !
All, all on earth is shadow, all beyond
Is substance ; the reverse is folly's creed :
How solid all, where change shall be no more !
 This is the bud of being, the dim dawn,
The twilight of our day, the vestibule ;
Life's theatre as yet is shut, and death,
Strong death, alone can heave the massy bar,
This gross impediment of clay remove,
And make us embryos of existence free.
From real life, but little more remote
Is he, not yet a candidate for light,
The future embryo, slumb'ring in his sire.
Embryos we must be, till we burst the shell,
Yon ambient azure shell, and spring to life,
The life of gods, O transport ! and of man.
 Yet man, fool man ! here buries all his thoughts ;
Inters celestial hopes without one sigh.
Prisoner of earth, and pent beneath the moon,
Here pinions all his wishes ; wing'd by heaven
To fly at infinite ; and reach it there,
Where seraphs gather immortality,
On life's fair tree, fast by the throne of God.
What golden joys ambrosial clust'ring glow,
In his full beam, and ripen for the just,
Where momentary ages are no more !

Where time, and pain, and chance, and death expire!
And is it in the flight of threescore years,
To push eternity from human thought,
And smother souls immortal in the dust?
A soul immortal, spending all her fires,
Wasting her strength in strenuous idleness,
Thrown into tumult, raptur'd, or alarm'd,
At aught this scene can threaten or indulge,
Resembles ocean into tempest wrought,
To waft a feather, or to drown a fly.

Where falls this censure? It o'erwhelms myself;
How was my heart incrusted by the world!
O how self-fetter'd was my grov'ling soul!
How, like a worm, was I wrapt round and round
In silken thought, which reptile fancy spun,
Till darken'd reason lay quite clouded o'er
With soft conceit of endless comfort here,
Nor yet put forth her wings to reach the skies!

Night-visions may befriend (as sung above):
Our waking dreams are fatal. How I dreamt
Of things impossible! (Could sleep do more?)
Of joys perpetual in perpetual change!
Of stable pleasures on the tossing wave!
Eternal sunshine in the storms of life!
How richly were my noon-tide trances hung
With gorgeous tapestries of pictur'd joys!
Joy behind joy, in endless perspective!
Till at death's toll, whose restless iron tongue
Calls daily for his millions at a meal,
Starting I woke, and found myself undone.
Where now my frenzy's pompous furniture?
The cobweb'd cottage, with its ragged wall
Of mould'ring mud, is royalty to me!
The spider's most attenuated thread

Is cord, is cable, to man's tender tie
On earthly bliss; it breaks at every breeze.
  O ye blest scenes of permanent delight!
Full above measure! lasting, beyond bound!
A perpetuity of bliss is bliss.
Could you, so rich in rapture, fear an end,
That ghastly thought would drink up all your joy,
And quite unparadise the realms of light.
Safe are you lodged above these rolling spheres;
The baleful influence of whose giddy dance
Sheds sad vicissitude on all beneath.
Here teems with revolutions every hour;
And rarely for the better; or the best,
More mortal than the common births of fate.
Each moment has its sickle, emulous
Of time's enormous scythe, whose ample sweep
Strikes empires from the root; each moment plays
His little weapon in the narrower sphere
Of sweet domestic comfort, and cuts down
The fairest bloom of sublunary bliss.
  Bliss! sublunary bliss!—proud words, and vain!
Implicit treason to divine decree!
A bold invasion of the rights of heaven!
I clasp'd the phantoms, and I found them air.
O had I weigh'd it ere my fond embrace!
What darts of agony had miss'd my heart!
  Death! great proprietor of all! 'tis thine
To tread out empire, and to quench the stars.
The sun himself by thy permission shines;
And, one day, thou shalt pluck him from his sphere.
Amid such mighty plunder, why exhaust
Thy partial quiver on a mark so mean?
Why thy peculiar rancour wreak'd on me?
Insatiate archer! could not one suffice?

Thy shaft flew thrice; and thrice my peace was slain;
And thrice, ere thrice yon moon had fill'd her horn.
O Cynthia! why so pale? Dost thou lament
Thy wretched neighbour? Grieve to see thy wheel
Of ceaseless change outwhirl'd in human life?
How wanes my borrow'd bliss! from fortune's smile
Precarious courtesy! not virtue's sure,
Self-given, solar ray of sound delight.

    In ev'ry varied posture, place, and hour,
How widow'd ev'ry thought of ev'ry joy!
Thought, busy thought! too busy for my peace!
Thro' the dark postern of time long elaps'd,
Led softly, by the stillness of the night,
Led, like a murderer, (and such it proves!)
Strays (wretched rover!) o'er the pleasing past;
In quest of wretchedness perversely strays;
And finds all desart now; and meets the ghosts
Of my departed joys; a num'rous train!
I rue the riches of my former fate;
Sweet comfort's blasted clusters I lament;
I tremble at the blessings once so dear;
And ev'ry pleasure pains me to the heart.

    Yet why complain? or why complain for one?
Hangs out the sun his lustre but for me,
The single man? Are angels all beside?
I mourn for millions: 'Tis the common lot;
In this shape, or in that, has fate entail'd
The mother's throes on all of woman born,
Not more the children, than sure heirs, of pain.

    War, famine, pest, volcano, storm, and fire,
Intestine broils, oppression, with her heart
Wrapt up in triple brass, besiege mankind.
God's image disinherited of day,
Here, plung'd in mines, forgets a sun was made.

There, beings deathless as their haughty lord,
Are hammer'd to the galling oar for life ;
And plough the winter's wave, and reap despair.
Some, for hard masters, broken under arms,
In battle lopt away, with half their limbs,
Beg bitter bread thro' realms their valour sav'd,
If so the tyrant, or his minion, doom.
Want, and incurable disease, (fell pair !)
On hopeless multitudes remorseless seize
At once ; and make a refuge of the grave.
How groaning hospitals eject their dead !
What numbers groan for sad admission there !
What numbers, once in fortune's lap high-fed,
Solicit the cold hand of charity !
To shock us more, solicit it in vain !
Ye silken sons of pleasure ! since in pains
You rue more modish visits, visit here,
And breathe from your debauch : give, and reduce
Surfeit's dominion o'er you : But so great
Your impudence, you blush at what is right.

Happy ! did sorrow seize on such alone.
Not prudence can defend, or virtue save ;
Disease invades the chastest temperance ;
And punishment the guiltless ; and alarm,
Thro' thickest shades, pursues the fond of peace.
Man's caution often into danger turns,
And, his guard falling, crushes him to death.
Not happiness itself makes good her name !
Our very wishes give us not our wish.
How distant oft the thing we dote on most,
From that for which we dote, felicity !
The smoothest course of nature has its pains ;
And truest friends, thro' error, wound our rest
Without misfortune, what calamities !

And what hostilities, without a foe !
Nor are foes wanting to the best on earth.
But endless is the list of human ills,
And sighs might sooner fail, than cause to sigh.
   A part how small of the terraqueous globe
Is tenanted by man ! the rest a waste,
Rocks, desarts, frozen seas, and burning sands :
Wild haunts of monsters, poisons, stings, and death
Such is earth's melancholy map ! But, far
More sad ! this earth is a true map of man.
So bounded are its haughty lord's delights
To woe's wide empire ; where deep troubles toss,
Loud sorrows howl, invenom'd passions bite,
Rav'nous calamities our vitals seize,
And threat'ning fate wide opens to devour.
   What then am I, who sorrow for myself ?
In age, in infancy, from others' aid
Is all our hope ; to teach us to be kind.
That, nature's first, last lesson to mankind ;
The selfish heart deserves the pain it feels,
More gen'rous sorrow, while it sinks, exalts ;
And conscious virtue mitigates the pang.
Nor virtue, more than prudence, bids me give
Swoln thought a second channel ; who divide,
They weaken too, the torrent of their grief.
Take then, O world ! thy much-indebted tear :
How sad a sight is human happiness,
To those whose thought can pierce beyond an hour.
O thou ! whate'er thou art, whose heart exults !
Wouldst thou I should congratulate thy fate ?
I know thou wouldst ; thy pride demands it from me.
Let thy pride pardon, what thy nature needs,
The salutary censure of a friend.
Thou happy wretch ! by blindness thou art blest ;

By dotage dandled to perpetual smiles.
Know, smiler! at thy peril art thou pleas'd;
Thy pleasure is the promise of thy pain.
Misfortune, like a creditor severe,
But rises in demand for her delay;
She makes a scourge of past prosperity,
To sting thee more, and double thy distress.

    Lorenzo, fortune makes her court to thee,
Thy fond heart dances, while the syren sings.
Dear is thy welfare; think me not unkind;
I would not damp, but to secure thy joys.
Think not that fear is sacred to the storm:
Stand on thy guard against the smiles of fate.
Is heaven tremendous in its frowns? Most sure;
And in its favours formidable too:
Its favours here are trials, not rewards;
A call to duty, not discharge from care;
And should alarm us, full as much as woes;
Awake us to their cause and consequence;
And make us tremble, weigh'd with our desert;
Awe nature's tumult, and chastise her joys,
Lest while we clasp, we kill them; nay, invert
To worse than simple misery, their charms.
Revolted joys, like foes in civil war,
Like bosom friendships to resentment sour'd,
With rage envenom'd rise against our peace.
Beware what earth calls happiness; beware
All joys, but joys that never can expire.
Who builds on less than an immortal base,
Fond as he seems, condemns his joys to death.

    Mine died with thee, Philander! thy last sigh
Dissolved the charm; the disenchanted earth
Lost all her lustre. Where her glitt'ring towers?
Her golden mountains, where? all darken'd down

To naked waste; a dreary vale of tears:
The great magician's dead! Thou poor, pale piece
Of out-cast earth, in darkness! what a change
From yesterday! Thy darling hope so near,
(Long-labour'd prize!) O how ambition flush'd
Thy glowing cheek! Ambition truly great,
Of virtuous praise.   Death's subtle seed within,
(Sly, treach'rous miner!) working in the dark,
Smil'd at thy well-concerted scheme, and beckon'd
The worm to riot on that rose so red,
Unfaded ere it fell; one moment's prey!

    Man's foresight is conditionally wise;
Lorenzo; wisdom into folly turns
Oft, the first instant, its idea fair
To labouring thought is born. How dim our eye!
The present moment terminates our sight;
Clouds, thick as those on doomsday, drown the next;
We penetrate, we prophesy in vain.
Time is dealt out by particles; and each,
Ere mingled with the streaming sands of life,
By fate's inviolable oath is sworn
Deep silence, "Where eternity begins."

    By nature's law, what may be, may be now;
There's no prerogative in human hours.
In human hearts what bolder thought can rise,
Than man's presumption on to-morrow's dawn?
Where is to-morrow? In another world.
For numbers this is certain; the reverse
Is sure to none; and yet on this perhaps,
This peradventure, infamous for lies,
As on a rock of adamant, we build
Our mountain hopes; spin out eternal schemes,
As we the fatal sisters could out-spin,
And, big with life's futurities, expire.

Not ev'n Philander had bespoke his shroud.
Nor had he cause; a warning was denied:
How many fall as sudden, not as safe!
As sudden, tho' for years admonish'd home.
Of human ills the last extreme beware,
Beware, Lorenzo! a slow sudden death.
How dreadful that deliberate surprise!
Be wise to-day; 'tis madness to defer;
Next day the fatal precedent will plead;
Thus on, till wisdom is push'd out of life.
Procrastination is the thief of time;
Year after year it steals, till all are fled,
And to the mercies of a moment leaves
The vast concerns of an eternal scene.
If not so frequent, would not this be strange?
That 'tis so frequent, this is stranger still.
    Of man's miraculous mistakes, this bears
The palm, " That all men are about to live,"
For ever on the brink of being born.
All pay themselves the compliment to think
They one day shall not drivel: and their pride
On this reversion takes up ready praise;
At least, their own; their future selves applauds;
How excellent that life they ne'er will lead!
Time lodg'd in their own hands is folly's vails;
That lodg'd in fate's, to wisdom they consign;
The thing they can't but purpose, they postpone;
'Tis not in folly, not to scorn a fool;
And scarce in human wisdom to do more.
All promise is poor dilatory man,
And that thro' ev'ry stage: when young, indeed,
In full content we, sometimes, nobly rest,
Unanxious for ourselves; and only wish,
As duteous sons, our fathers were more wise.

At thirty man suspects himself a fool;
Knows it at forty, and reforms his plan;
At fifty chides his infamous delay,
Pushes his prudent purpose to resolve;
In all the magnanimity of thought
Resolves; and re-resolves; then dies the same.
And why? Because he thinks himself immortal.
All men think all men mortal, but themselves;
Themselves, when some alarming shock of fate
Strikes thro' their wounded hearts the sudden dread;
But their hearts wounded, like the wounded air,
Soon close; where past the shaft, no trace is found.
As from the wing no scar the sky retains;
The parted wave no furrow from the keel;
So dies in human hearts the thought of death.
Ev'n with the tender tear which nature sheds
O'er those we love, we drop it in their grave.
Can I forget Philander? That were strange!
O my full heart—But should I give it vent,
The longest night, tho' longer far, would fail,
And the lark listen to my midnight song.

The spritely lark's shrill matin wakes the morn;
Grief's sharpest thorn hard pressing on my breast
I strive, with wakeful melody, to cheer
The sullen gloom, sweet Philomel! like thee,
And call the stars to listen: every star
Is deaf to mine, enamour'd of thy lay.
Yet be not vain; there are, who thine excel,
And charm thro' distant ages: wrapt in shade,
Pris'ner of darkness! to the silent hours,
How often I repeat their rage divine,
To lull my griefs, and steal my heart from woe!
I roll their raptures, but not catch their fire.
Dark, tho' not blind, like thee, Mæonides!

Or, Milton! thee; ah could I reach your strain!
Or his, who made Mæonides our own.
Man too he sung: immortal man I sing;
Oft bursts my song beyond the bounds of life;
What, now, but immortality can please?
O had he press'd his theme, pursu'd the track,
Which opens out of darkness into day!
O had he, mounted on his wing of fire,
Soar'd where I sink, and sung immortal man!
How had it blest mankind, and rescu'd me!

NIGHT II.

ON TIME, DEATH, AND FRIENDSHIP.

TO THE RIGHT HONOURABLE THE EARL OF WILMINGTON

" When the cock crew, he wept"—smote by that
    eye,
Which looks on me, on all: that power, who bids
This midnight sentinel, with clarion shrill,
Emblem of that which shall awake the dead,
Rouse souls from slumber, into thoughts of Heaven
Shall I too weep? Where then is fortitude?
And, fortitude abandoned, where is man?
I know the terms on which he sees the light;
He that is born, is listed; life is war;
Eternal war with woe. Who bears it best,
Deserves it least.—On other themes I'll dwell.
Lorenzo! let me turn my thoughts on thee,
And thine, on themes may profit; profit there,
Where most thy need. Themes, too, the genuine
    growth

Of dear Philander's dust. He, thus, though dead,
May still befriend—what themes ? Time's won-
       drous price,
Death, friendship, and Philander's final scene.
So could I touch these themes, as might obtain
Thine ear, nor leave thy heart quite disengaged,
The good deed would delight me ; half impress
On my dark cloud an Iris ; and from grief
Call glory—dost thou mourn Philander's fate ?
I know thou say'st it : Says thy life the same ?
He mourns the dead, who lives as they desire.
Where is that thrift, that avarice of time,
(O glorious avarice !) thought of death inspires,
As rumour'd robberies endear our gold ?
O time ! than gold more sacred ; more a load
Than lead, to fools ; and fools reputed wise.
What moment granted man without account ?
What years are squander'd, wisdom's debt unpaid ?
Our wealth in days, all due to that discharge.
Haste, haste, he lies in wait, he's at the door,
Insidious Death ! should his strong hand arrest,
No composition sets the prisoner free.
Eternity's inexorable chain
Fast binds ; and vengeance claims the full arrear.
How late I shuddered on the brink ! how late
Life called for her last refuge in despair !
That time is mine, O Mead ! to thee I owe ;
Fain would I pay thee with eternity.
But ill my genius answers my desire ;
My sickly song is mortal, past thy cure.
Accept the will ;—that dies not with my strain.

    For what calls thy disease, Lorenzo ? not
For Esculapian, but for moral aid.
Thou think'st it folly to be wise too soon.

Youth is not rich in time, it may be poor;
Part with it as with money, sparing; pay
No moment, but in purchase of its worth;
And what its worth, ask death-beds; they can tell.
Part with it as with life, reluctant; big
With holy hope of nobler time to come;
Time higher aim'd, still nearer the great mark
Of men and angels; virtue more divine.

   Is this our duty, wisdom, glory, gain?
(These heaven benign in vital union binds)
And sport we like the natives of the bough,
When vernal suns inspire? amusement reigns
Man's great demand: to trifle is to live:
And is it then a trifle, too, to die?

   Thou say'st I preach, Lorenzo! 'tis confest.
What, if for once, I preach thee quite awake?
Who wants amusement in the flame of battle?
Is it not treason, to the soul immortal,
Her foes in arms, eternity the prize?
Will toys amuse, when med'cines cannot cure?
When spirits ebb, when life's enchanting scenes
Their lustre lose, and lessen in our sight,
As lands, and cities with their glitt'ring spires,
To the poor shatter'd bark, by sudden storm
Thrown off to sea, and soon to perish thère?
Will toys amuse? No: thrones will then be toys,
And earth and skies seem dust upon the scale.

   Redeem we time?—Its loss we dearly buy.
What pleads Lorenzo for his high-priz'd sports?
He pleads time's num'rous blanks; he loudly pleads
The straw-like trifles on life's common stream.
From whom those blanks and trifles, but from thee?
No blank, no trifle, nature made, or meant.
Virtue, or purpos'd virtue, still be thine;

This cancels thy complaint at once, this leaves
In act no trifle, and no blank in time.
This greatens, fills, immortalizes all;
This, the blest art of turning all to gold;
This, the good heart's prerogative to raise
A royal tribute from the poorest hours;
Immense revenue! ev'ry moment pays.
If nothing more than purpose in thy power;
Thy purpose firm, is equal to the deed:
Who does the best his circumstance allows,
Does well, acts nobly; angels could no more.
Our outward act, indeed, admits restraint;
'Tis not in things o'er thought to domineer;
Guard well thy thought; our thoughts are heard in
   On all important time, thro' ev'ry age,   [heaven.
Tho' much, and warm, the wise have urg'd; the
Is yet unborn, who duly weighs an hour.   [man
" I've lost a day"——the prince who nobly cried
Had been an emperor without his crown;
Of Rome? say, rather, lord of human race:
He spoke, as if deputed by mankind.
So should all speak: so reason speaks in all:
From the soft whispers of that God in man,
Why fly to folly, why to phrensy fly,
For rescue from the blessing we possess?
Time the supreme!—Time is eternity;
Pregnant with all eternity can give;
Pregnant with all, that makes archangels smile.
Who murders time, he crushes in the birth
A power ethereal, only not ador'd.
   Ah! how unjust to nature, and himself;
Is thoughtless, thankless, inconsistent man!
Like children babbling nonsense in their sports,
We censure nature for a span too short;

That span too short, we tax as tedious too;
Torture invention, all expedients tire,
To lash the ling'ring moments into speed,
And whirl us (happy riddance!) from ourselves.
Art, brainless art! our furious charioteer
(For nature's voice unstifled would recall)
Drives headlong tow'rds the precipice of death;
Death, most our dread; death thus more dreadful
O what a riddle of absurdity!   [made:
Leisure is pain; takes off our chariot wheels;
How heavily we drag the load of life!
Blest leisure is our curse; like that of Cain,
It makes us wander; wander earth around
To fly that tyrant, thought.   As Atlas groan'd
The world beneath, we groan beneath an hour.
We cry for mercy to the next amusement;
The next amusement mortgages our fields;
Slight inconvenience! prisons hardly frown,
From hateful time if prisons set us free.
Yet when death kindly tenders us relief,
We call him cruel; years to moments shrink,
Ages to years.   The telescope is turn'd.
To man's false optics (from his folly false)
Time, in advance, behind him hides his wings,
And seems to creep, decrepit with his age;
Behold him, when past by; what then is seen,
But his broad pinions swifter than the winds?
And all mankind, in contradiction strong,
Rueful, aghast! cry out on his career.
   Leave to thy foes these errors, and these ills;
To nature just, their cause and cure explore.
Not short heaven's bounty, boundless our expense;
No niggard, nature; men are prodigals.
We waste, not use our time; we breathe, not live.

Time wasted is existence, us'd is life.
And bare existence, man, to live ordain'd,
Wrings, and oppresses with enormous weight.
And why? since time was giv'n for use, not waste,
Injoin'd to fly; with tempest, tide, and stars,
To keep his speed, nor ever wait for man;
Time's use was doom'd a pleasure: waste, a pain;
That man might feel his error, if unseen:
And, feeling, fly to labour for his cure;
Not, blund'ring, split on idleness for ease.
Life's cares are comforts; such by heaven design'd;
He that has none, must make them, or be wretched.
Cares are employments; and without employ
The soul is on a rack; the rack of rest,
To souls most adverse; action all their joy.
    Here then, the riddle, mark'd above, unfolds;
Then time turns torment, when man turns a fool.
We rave, we wrestle, with great nature's plan;
We thwart the Deity; and 'tis decreed,
Who thwart his will, shall contradict their own.
Hence our unnatural quarrels with ourselves;
Our thoughts at enmity; our bosom-broils;
We push time from us, and we wish him back;
Lavish of lustrums, and yet fond of life;
Life we think long, and short; death seek, and shun;
Body and soul, like peevish man and wife,
United jar, and yet are loth to part.
    Oh the dark days of vanity! while here,
How tasteless! and how terrible, when gone!
Gone! they ne'er go; when past, they haunt us still;
The spirit walks of ev'ry day deceas'd;
And smiles an angel, or a fury frowns.
Nor death, nor life delight us. If time past,
And time possest, both pain us, what can please?

That which the Deity to please ordain'd,
Time us'd. The man who consecrates his hours
By vig'rous effort, and an honest aim,
At once he draws the sting of life and death;
He walks with nature; and her paths are peace.
    Our error's cause and cure are seen : see next
Time's nature, origin, importance, speed;
And thy great gain from urging his career.—
All-sensual man, because untouch'd, unseen,
He looks on time as nothing. Nothing else
Is truly man's; 'tis fortune's.—Time's a god.
Hast thou ne'er heard of Time's omnipotence?
For, or against, what wonders he can do!
And will: to stand blank neuter he disdains.
Not on those terms was time (heaven's stranger!) sent
On his important embassy to man.
Lorenzo! no: on the long-destin'd hour,
From everlasting ages growing ripe,
That memorable hour of wondrous birth,
When the dread sire, on emanation bent,
And big with nature, rising in his might,
Call'd forth creation (for then time was born),
By godhead streaming thro' a thousand worlds;
Not on those terms, from the great days of heaven
From old eternity's mysterious orb,
Was time cut off, and cast beneath the skies;
The skies, which watch him in his new abode,
Measuring his motions by revolving spheres;
That horologe machinery divine.   [play,
Hours, days, and months, and years, his children
Like num'rous wings around him, as he flies ·
Or, rather, as unequal plumes, they shape
His ample pinions, swift as darted flame,
To gain his goal, to reach his ancient rest,

And join anew eternity his sire;
In his immutability to nest,
When worlds, that count his circles now, unhing'd,
(Fate the loud signal sounding) headlong rush
To timeless night and chaos, whence they rose.
  Why spur the speedy?   Why with levities
New wing thy short, short day's too rapid flight?
Know'st thou, or what thou dost, or what is done?
Man flies from time, and time from man; too soon
In sad divorce this double flight must end:
And then, where are we? where, Lorenzo! then
Thy sports? thy pomps?—I grant thee, in a state
Not unambitious; in the ruffled shroud,
Thy Parian tomb's triumphant arch beneath.
Has death his fopperies?   Then well may life
Put on her plume, and in her rainbow shine.
Ye well-array'd! ye lilies of our land!
Ye lilies male! who neither toil, nor spin,
(As sister lilies might) if not so wise
As Solomon, more sumptuous to the sight!
Ye delicate! who nothing can support,
Yourselves most insupportable! for whom
The winter rose must blow, the sun put on
A brighter beam in Leo; silky-soft
Favonius breathe still softer, or be chid;
And other worlds send odours, sauce, and song,
And robes, and notions, fram'd in foreign looms!
O ye Lorenzos of our age! who deem
One moment unamus'd, a misery
Not made for feeble man! who call aloud
For ev'ry bawble drivel'd o'er by sense;
For rattles, and conceits of ev'ry cast,
For change of follies, and relays of joy,
To drag your patient through the tedious length

Of a short winter's day—say, sages ! say,
Wit's oracles ! say, dreamers of gay dreams !
How will you weather an eternal night,
Where such expedients fail ?

   O treach'rous conscience ! while she seems to sleep
On rose and myrtle, lull'd with siren song ;
While she seems, nodding o'er her charge, to drop
On headlong appetite the slacken'd rein,
And give us up to license, unrecall'd,
Unmark'd ;—see, from behind her secret stand,
The sly informer minutes ev'ry fault,
And her dread diary with horror fills.
Not the gross act alone employs her pen ;
She reconnoitres Fancy's airy band,
A watchful foe ! the formidable spy,
List'ning, o'erhears the whispers of our camp :
Our dawning purposes of heart explores,
And steals our embryos of iniquity.
As all-rapacious usurers conceal
Their doomsday-book from all-consuming heirs ;
Thus, with indulgence most severe, she treats
Us spendthrifts of inestimable time ;
Unnoted, notes each moment misapplied ;
In leaves more durable than leaves of brass,
Writes our whole history ; which death shall read
In ev'ry pale delinquent's private ear ;
And judgment publish ; publish to more worlds
Than this ; and endless age in groans resound.
Lorenzo, such that sleeper in thy breast !
Such is her slumber ; and her vengeance such
For slighted counsel ; such thy future peace !
And think'st thou still thou canst be wise too soon ?

   But why on time so lavish is my song ?
On this great theme kind nature keeps a school,

To teach her sons herself. Each night we die,
Each morn are born anew : Each day, a life !
And shall we kill each day ? If trifling kills ;
Sure vice must butcher. O what heaps of slain
Cry out for vengeance on us ! Time destroy'd
Is suicide, where more than blood is spilt.
Time flies, death urges, knells call, heaven invites,
Hell threatens : All exerts ; in effort, all ;
More than creation labours !—labours more ?
And is there in creation, what, amidst
This tumult universal, wing'd dispatch ;
And ardent energy, supinely yawns ?——
Man sleeps ; and man alone ; and man, whose fate,
Fate irreversible, intire, extreme,
Endless, hair-hung, breeze-shaken, o'er the gulf
A moment trembles ; drops ! and man, for whom
All else is in alarm ! Man, the sole cause
Of this surrounding storm ! and yet he sleeps,
As the storm rock'd to rest.—Throw years away ?
Throw empires, and be blameless. Moments seize ;
Heaven's on their wing : A moment we may wish,
When worlds want wealth to buy. Bid day stand still,
Bid him drive back his car, and reimport
The period past, regive the given hour.
Lorenzo, more than miracles we want ;
Lorenzo—O for yesterdays to come !
    Such is the language of the man awake ;
His ardour such, for what oppresses thee.
And is his ardour vain, Lorenzo ? No ;
That more than miracle the gods indulge ;
To-day is yesterday return'd ; return'd
Full power'd to cancel, expiate, raise, adorn,
And reinstate us on the rock of peace.
Let it not share its predecessor's fate ;

Nor, like its elder sisters, die a fool.
Shall it evaporate in fume? Fly off
Fuliginous, and stain us deeper still?
Shall we be poorer for the plenty pour'd?
More wretched for the clemencies of heaven?
　Where shall I find him? Angels! tell me where.
You know him: he is near you: point him out:
Shall I see glories beaming from his brow?
Or trace his footsteps by the rising flowers?
Your golden wings, now hov'ring o'er him, shed
Protection; now, are waving in applause
To that blest son of foresight! lord of fate!
That awful independent on to-morrow!
Whose work is done; who triumphs in the past;
Whose yesterdays look backwards with a smile;
Nor, like the Parthian, wound him as they fly;
That common, but opprobrious lot! past hours,
If not by guilt, yet wound us by their flight,
If folly bounds our prospect by the grave,
All feeling of futurity benumb'd;
All god-like passion for eternals quencht;
All relish of realities expir'd;
Renounc'd all correspondence with the skies;
Our freedom chain'd; quite wingless our desire;
In sense dark-prison'd all that ought to soar;
Prone to the centre; crawling in the dust;
Dismounted ev'ry great and glorious aim;
Embruted ev'ry faculty divine;
Heart-buried in the rubbish of the world.
The world, that gulf of souls, immortal souls,
Souls elevate, angelic, wing'd with fire
To reach the distant skies, and triumph there
On thrones, which shall not mourn their masters
　　chang'd,

Tho' we from earth ; ethereal, they that fell.
Such veneration due, O man, to man.
    Who venerate themselves, the world despise.
For what, gay friend ! is this escutcheon'd world,
Which hangs out death in one eternal night ?
A night, that glooms us in the noon-tide ray,
And wraps our thought, at banquets, in the shroud.
Life's little stage is a small eminence,
Inch-high the grave above ; that home of man,
Where dwells the multitude : We gaze around ;
We read their monuments ; we sigh ; and while
We sigh, we sink ; and are what we deplor'd ;
Lamenting, or lamented, all our lot !
    Is death at distance ? No : He has been on thee ;
And giv'n sure earnest of his final blow.
Those hours that lately smil'd, where are they now ?
Pallid to thought, and ghastly ! drown'd, all drown'd
In that great deep, which nothing disembogues !
And, dying, they bequeath'd thee small renown.
The rest are on the wing : How fleet their flight !
Already has the fatal train took fire ;
A moment, and the world's blown up to thee ;
The sun is darkness, and the stars are dust.
    'Tis greatly wise to talk with our past hours ;
And ask them, what report they bore to heaven ;
And how they might have borne more welcome news.
Their answers form what men experience call ;
If wisdom's friend, her best ; if not, worst foe.
O reconcile them ! kind experience cries,
" There's nothing here, but what as nothing weighs ;
The more our joy, the more we know it vain ;
And by success are tutor'd to despair."
Nor is it only thus, but must be so.
Who knows not this, tho' gray, is still a child.

Loose then from earth the grasp of fond desire,
Weight anchor, and some happier clime explore.
  Art thou so moor'd thou canst not disengage,
Nor give thy thoughts a ply to future scenes?
Since, by life's passing breath, blown up from earth,
Light, as the summer's dusk, we take in air
A moment's giddy flight, and fall again;
Join the dull mass, increase the trodden soil,
And sleep, till earth herself shall be no more;
Since then (as emmets, their small world o'erthrown)
We, sore-amazed, from out earth's ruins crawl,
And rise to fate extreme of foul or fair,
As man's own choice (controller of the skies!)
As man's despotic will, perhaps one hour,
(O how omnipotent is time!) decrees;
Should not each warning give a strong alarm?
Warning, far less than that of bosom torn
From bosom, bleeding o'er the sacred dead!
Should not each dial strike us as we pass,
Portentous, as the written wall, which struck,
O'er midnight bowls, the proud Assyrian pale,
Ere-while high-flusht, with insolence and wine?
Like that, the dial speaks; and points to thee,
Lorenzo! loth to break thy banquet up:
" O man, thy kingdom is departing from thee;
And, while it lasts, is emptier than my shade."
Its silent language such: Nor need'st thou call
Thy Magi, to decipher what it means.
Know, like the Median, fate is in thy walls:
Dost ask, How? Whence? Belshazzar-like, amaz'd?
Man's make incloses the sure seeds of death;
Life feeds the murderer: Ingrate! he thrives
On her own meal, and then his nurse devours.
  But here, Lorenzo, the delusion lies;

That solar shadow, as it measures life,
It life resembles too : life speeds away
From point to point, tho' seeming to stand still.
The cunning fugitive is swift by stealth :
Too subtle is the movement to be seen ;
Yet soon man's hour is up, and we are gone.
Warnings point out our danger; gnomons, time :
As these are useless when the sun is set :
So those, but when more glorious reason shines.
Reason should judge in all ; in reason's eye,
That sedentary shadow travels hard.
But such our gravitation to the wrong,
So prone our hearts to whisper what we wish,
'Tis later with the wise than he's aware :
A Wilmington goes slower than the sun :
And all mankind mistake their time of day ;
Ev'n age itself.   Fresh hopes are hourly sown
In furrow'd brows.   To gentle life's descent
We shut our eyes, and think it is a plain.
We take fair days in winter, for the spring ;
And turn our blessings into bane.   Since oft
Man must compute that age he cannot feel,
He scarce believes he's older for his years.
Thus, at life's latest eve, we keep in store
One disappointment sure, to crown the rest ;
The disappointment of a promis'd hour.
    On this, or similar, Philander ! thou
Whose mind was moral, as the preacher's tongue ;
And strong, to wield all science, worth the name ;
How often we talk'd down the summer's sun,
And cool'd our passions by the breezy stream !
How often thaw'd and shorten'd winter's eve,
By conflict kind, that struck out latent truth,
Best found, so sought ; to the recluse more coy !

Thoughts disentangle passing o'er the lip ;
Clean runs the thread ; if not, 'tis thrown away,
Or kept to   up nonsense for a song ;
Song, fashionably fruitless ; such as stains
The fancy, and unhallow'd passion fires ;
Chiming her saints to Cytherea's fane.

Know'st thou, Lorenzo ! what a friend contains?
As bees mixt nectar draw from fragrant flow'rs,
So men from friendship, wisdom, and delight ;
'Twins tied by nature, if they part, they die.
Hast thou no friend to set thy mind abroach ?
Good sense will stagnate. Thoughts shut up want air,
And spoil, like bales unopen'd to the sun.
Had thought been all, sweet speech had been denied ;
Speech, thought's canal ! speech, thought's criterion
        too !
Thought in the mine, may come forth gold, or dross ;
When coin'd in words, we know its real worth.
If sterling, store it for thy future use ;
'Twill buy thee benefit ; perhaps, renown.
Thought, too, deliver'd, is the more possest ;
Teaching, we learn ; and giving, we retain
The births of intellect ; when dumb, forgot.
Speech ventilates our intellectual fire ;
Speech burnishes our mental magazine ;
Brightens, for ornament ; and whets, for use.
What numbers, sheath'd in erudition, lie,
Plung'd to the hilts in venerable tomes,
And rusted in ; who might have borne an edge,
And play'd a sprightly beam, if born to speech ;
If born blest heirs of half their mother's tongue !
'Tis thought's exchange, which, like th' alternate
        push
Of waves conflicting, breaks the learned scum,

And defecates the student's standing pool.
    In contemplation is his proud resource?
'Tis poor, as proud, by converse unsustain'd.
Rude thought runs wild in contemplation's field;
Converse, the menage, breaks it to the bit
Of due restraint; and emulation's spur
Gives graceful energy, by rivals aw'd.
'Tis converse qualifies for solitude;
As exercise, for salutary rest.
By that untutor'd, contemplation raves;
And nature's fool, by wisdom's is undone.
    Wisdom, tho' richer than Peruvian mines,
And sweeter than the sweet ambrosial hive,
What is she, but the means of happiness?
That unobtain'd, than folly more a fool;
A melancholy fool, without her bells.
Friendship, the means of wisdom, richly gives
The precious end, which makes our wisdom wise.
Nature, in zeal for human amity,
Denies, or damps, an undivided joy.
Joy is an import; joy is an exchange;
Joy flies monopolists: it calls for two;
Rich fruit! heaven-planted! never pluckt by one.
Needful auxiliars are our friends, to give
To social man true relish of himself.
Full on ourselves, descending in a line,
Pleasure's bright beam is feeble in delight:
Delight intense, is taken by rebound;
Reverberated pleasures fire the breast.
    Celestial happiness, whene'er she stoops
To visit earth, one shrine the goddess finds,
And one alone, to make her sweet amends
For absent heaven—the bosom of a friend;
Where heart meets heart, reciprocally soft,

Each other's pillow to repose divine.
Beware the counterfeit: in passion's flame
Hearts melt, but melt like ice, soon harder froze.
True love strikes root in reason; passion's foe:
Virtue alone entenders us for life:
I wrong her much—entenders us for ever:
Of friendship's fairest fruits, the fruit most fair
Is virtue kindling at a rival fire,
And, emulously, rapid in her race.
O the soft enmity! endearing strife!
This carries friendship to her noon-tide point,
And gives the rivet of eternity.

From friendship, which outlives my former themes,
Glorious survivor of old time and death!
From friendship, thus, that flow'r of heavenly seed,
The wise extract earth's most Hyblean bliss,
Superior wisdom, crown'd with smiling joy.

But for whom blossoms this Elysian flower?
Abroad they find, who cherish it at home.
Lorenzo! pardon what my love extorts,
An honest love, and not afraid to frown.
Tho' choice of follies fasten on the great,
None clings more obstinate than fancy, fond
That sacred friendship is their easy prey;
Caught by the wafture of a golden lure,
Or fascination of a high-born smile.
Their smiles, the great, and the coquet, throw out
For others' hearts, tenacious of their own;
And we no less of ours, when such the bait.
Ye fortune's cofferers! ye pow'rs of wealth!
Can gold gain friendship? Impudence of hope!
As well mere man an angel might beget.
Love, and love only, is the loan for love.
Lorenzo! pride repress; nor hope to find

A friend, but what has found a friend in thee.
All like the purchase; few the price will pay;
And this makes friends such miracles below.
    What if (since daring on so nice a theme)
I show thee friendship delicate, as dear,
Of tender violations apt to die?
Reverse will wound it; and distrust, destroy.
Deliberate on all things with thy friend.
But since friends grow not thick on ev'ry bough,
Nor ev'ry friend unrotten at the core;
First, on thy friend, delib'rate with thyself;
Pause, ponder, sift; not eager in the choice,
Nor jealous of the chosen; fixing, fix;
Judge before friendship, then confide till death.
Well, for thy friend; but nobler far for thee;
How gallant danger for earth's highest prize!
A friend is worth all hazards we can run.
" Poor is the friendless master of a world:
A world in purchase for a friend is gain."
    So sung he, (angels hear that angel sing!
Angels from friendship gather half their joy)
So sung Philander, as his friend went round
In the rich ichor, in the gen'rous blood
Of Bacchus, purple god of joyous wit,
A brow solute, and ever-laughing eye.
He drank long health, and virtue, to his friend;
His friend, who warm'd him more, who more inspir'd.
Friendship's the wine of life; but friendship new
(Not such was his) is neither strong, nor pure.
O! for the bright complexion, cordial warmth,
And elevating spirit, of a friend,
For twenty summers ripening by my side;
All feculence of falsehood long thrown down;
All social virtues rising in his soul;

As crystal clear; and smiling, as they rise!
Here nectar flows; it sparkles in our sight;
Rich to the taste, and genuine from the heart.
High-flavour'd bliss for gods! on earth how rare
On earth how lost!—Philander is no more.

Think'st thou the theme intoxicates my song?
Am I too warm?—too warm I cannot be.
I lov'd him much; but now I love him more.
Like birds, whose beauties languish, half-conceal'd,
Till, mounted on the wing, their glossy plumes
Expanded shine with azure, green, and gold;
How blessings brighten as they take their flight!
His flight Philander took; his upward flight,
If ever soul ascended.   Had he dropt,
(That eagle genius!) O had he let fall
One feather as he flew; I, then, had wrote,
What friends might flatter; prudent foes forbear;
Rivals scarce damn; and Zoilus reprieve.
Yet what I can, I must: it were profane
To quench a glory lighted at the skies,
And cast in shadows his illustrious close.
Strange! the theme most affecting, most sublime
Momentous most to man, should sleep unsung!
And yet it sleeps, by genius unawak'd,
Painim or Christian; to the blush of wit.
Man's highest triumph! man's profoundest fall!
The death-bed of the just! is yet undrawn
By mortal hand; it merits a divine:
Angels should paint it, angels ever there;
There, on a post of honour, and of joy.

Dare I presume, then? But Philander bids;
And glory tempts, and inclination calls——
Yet am I struck; as struck the soul, beneath
Aerial groves' impenetrable gloom;

Or, in some mighty ruin's solemn shade;
Or, gazing by pale lamps on high-born dust,
In vaults; thin courts of poor unflatter'd kings;
Or, at the midnight altar's hallow'd flame.
It is religion to proceed: I pause——
And enter, aw'd, the temple of my theme.
Is it his death-bed? No: it is his shrine:
Behold him, there, just rising to a god.

The chamber where the good man meets his fate,
Is privileg'd beyond the common walk
Of virtuous life, quite in the verge of heaven.
Fly, ye profane! If not, draw near with awe,
Receive the blessing, and adore the chance,
That threw in this Bethesda your disease;
If unrestor'd by this, despair your cure.
For here, resistless demonstration dwells;
A death-bed's a detector of the heart.
Here tir'd dissimulation drops her masque,
Thro' life's grimace, that mistress of the scene!
Here real, and apparent, are the same.
You see the man; you see his hold on heaven;
If sound his virtue; as Philander's, sound.
Heaven waits not the last moment; owns her friends
On this side death; and points them out to men,
A lecture, silent, but of sov'reign pow'r!
To vice, confusion; and to virtue, peace.

Whatever farce the boastful hero plays,
Virtue alone has majesty in death;
And greater still, the more the tyrant frowns.
Philander! he severely frown'd on thee.
" No warning giv'n! Unceremonious fate!
A sudden rush from life's meridian joy!
A wrench from all we love! from all we are!
A restless bed of pain! a plunge opaque

Beyond conjecture ! feeble Nature's dread !
Strong Reason's shudder at the dark unknown !
A sun extinguisht ! a just opening grave !
And oh ! the last, last, what ? (can words express ?
Thought reach it ?) the last—silence of a friend !"
Where are those horrors, that amazement, where,
This hideous group of ills, which singly shock,
Demand from man ?—I thought him man till now.

Thro' nature's wreck, thro' vanquisht agonies,
(Like the stars struggling thro' this midnight gloom)
What gleams of joy ? what more than human
        peace ?
Where, the frail mortal ? the poor abject worm ?
No, not in death, the mortal to be found.
His conduct is a legacy for all.
Richer than Mammon's for his single heir.
His comforters he comforts ; great in ruin,
With unreluctant grandeur, gives, not yields
His soul sublime ; and closes with his fate.

How our hearts burnt within us at the scene !
Whence this brave bound o'er limits fixt to man
His God sustains him in his final hour !
His final hour brings glory to his God !
Man's glory heaven vouchsafes to call her own.
We gaze, we weep ; mixt tears of grief and joy !
Amazement strikes ! devotion bursts to flame !
Christians adore ! and infidels believe !

As some tall tow'r, or lofty mountain's brow,
Detains the sun, illustrious from its height ;
While rising vapours, and descending shades,
With damps, and darkness, drown the spacious vale ;
Undampt by doubt, undarken'd by despair,
Philander, thus, augustly rears his head,
At that black hour, which gen'ral horror sheds

On the low level of th' inglorious throng :
Sweet peace, and heavenly hope, and humble joy,
Divinely beam on his exalted soul ;
Destruction gild, and crown him for the skies,
With incommunicable lustre, bright.

NIGHT III.

NARCISSA.

TO HER GRACE THE DUCHESS OF P——.

" Ignoscenda quidem, scirent si ignoscere manes."—VIRGIL.

FROM dreams, where thought in fancy's maze runs
To reason, that heaven-lighted lamp in man, [mad,
Once more I wake ; and at the destin'd hour,
Punctual as lovers to the moment sworn,
I keep my assignation with my woe.
    O ! lost to virtue, lost to manly thought,
Lost to the noble sallies of the soul !
Who think it solitude, to be alone.
Communion sweet ! communion large and high !
Our reason, guardian angel, and our God !
Then nearest these, when others most remote ;
And all, ere long, shall be remote, but these.
How dreadful, then, to meet them all alone,
A stranger ! unacknowledg'd ! unapprov'd !
Now woo them ; wed them ; bind them to thy breast ;
To win thy wish, creation has no more.
Or if we wish a fourth, it is a friend—
But friends, how mortal ! dang'rous the desire.
    Take Phœbus to yourselves, ye basking bards !
Inebriate at fair fortune's fountain-head ;
And reeling thro' the wilderness of joy ;

Where sense runs savage, broke from reason's chain,
And sings false peace, till smother'd by the pall.
My fortune is unlike; unlike my song;
Unlike the deity my song invokes.
I to Day's soft-eyed sister pay my court,
(Endymion's rival!) and her aid implore;
Now first implor'd in succour to the Muse.

    Thou, who didst lately borrow[1] Cynthia's form,
And modestly forego thine own! O thou,
Who didst thyself, at midnight hours, inspire!
Say, why not Cynthia patroness of song?
As thou her crescent, she thy character
Assumes; still more a goddess by the change.

    Are there demurring wits, who dare dispute
This revolution in the world inspir'd?
Ye train Pierian! to the lunar sphere,
In silent hour, address your ardent call
For aid immortal; less her brother's right.
She, with the spheres harmonious, nightly leads
The mazy dance, and hears their matchless strain,
A strain for gods, denied to mortal ear.
Transmit it heard, thou silver queen of heaven!
What title, or what name, endears thee most?
Cynthia! Cyllene! Phœbe!—or dost hear
With higher gust, fair P——d of the skies!
Is that the soft inchantment calls thee down,
More pow'rful than of old Circean charm?
Come; but from heavenly banquets with thee bring
The soul of song, and whisper in my ear
The theft divine; or in propitious dreams
(For dreams are thine) transfuse it thro' the breast
Of thy first votary——but not thy last;
If, like thy namesake, thou art ever kind.

[1] At the Duke of Norfolk's masquerade.

And kind thou wilt be ; kind on such a theme ;
A theme so like thee, a quite lunar theme,
Soft, modest, melancholy, female, fair !
A theme that rose all pale, and told my soul,
'Twas Night; on her fond hopes perpetual night ;
A night which struck a damp, a deadlier damp,
Than that which smote me from Philander's tomb
Narcissa follows, ere his tomb is clos'd.
Woes cluster ; rare are solitary woes ;
They love a train, they tread each other's heel ,
Her death invades his mournful right, and claims
The grief that started from my lids for Him :
Seizes the faithless, alienated tear,
Or shares it, ere it falls.   So frequent death,
Sorrow he more than causes, he confounds ;
For human sighs his rival strokes contend,
And make distress, distraction.   Oh Philander !
What was thy fate ?   A double fate to me ;
Portent, and pain ! a menace, and a blow !
Like the black raven hov'ring o'er my peace,
Not less a bird of omen, than of prey.
It called Narcissa long before her hour ;
It called her tender soul, by break of bliss,
From the first blossom, from the buds of joy ;
Those few our noxious fate unblasted leaves
In this inclement clime of human life.

　　Sweet harmonist ! and beautiful as sweet !
And young as beautiful ! and soft as young !
And gay as soft ! and innocent as gay !
And happy (if aught happy here) as good !
For fortune fond had built her nest on high.
Like birds quite exquisite of note and plume,
Transfixt by fate (who loves a lofty mark)
How from the summit of the grove she fell,

And left it unharmonious ! All its charm
Extinguisht in the wonders of her song !
Her song still vibrates in my ravisht ear,
Still melting there, and with voluptuous pain
(O to forget her !) thrilling thro' my heart !

    Song, beauty, youth, love, virtue, joy ! this group
Of bright ideas, flowers of paradise,
As yet unforfeit ! in one blaze we bind,
Kneel, and present it to the skies ; as all
We guess of heaven : and these were all her own.
And she was mine ; and I was—was !—most blest !—
Gay title of the deepest misery !
As bodies grow more pond'rous, robb'd of life ;
Good lost weighs more in grief, than gain'd, in joy.
Like blossom'd trees o'erturn'd by vernal storm,
Lovely in death the beauteous ruin lay ;
And if in death still lovely, lovelier there ;
Far lovelier ! pity swells the tide of love.
And will not the severe excuse a sigh ?
Scorn the proud man that is asham'd to weep ;
Our tears indulg'd, indeed deserve our shame.
Ye that e'er lost an angel ! pity me.

    Soon as the lustre languisht in her eye,
Dawning a dimmer day on human sight ;
And on her cheek, the residence of spring,
Pale omen sat ; and scatter'd fears around
On all that saw (and who would cease to gaze,
That once had seen ?) with haste, parental haste,
I flew, I snatch'd her from the rigid north,
Her native bed, on which bleak boreas blew,
And bore her nearer to the sun ; the sun
(As if the sun could envy) checkt his beam,
Denied his wonted succour ; nor with more
Regret beheld her drooping, than the bells

Of lilies; fairest lilies, not so fair!
   Queen lilies! and ye painted popu!ace!
Who dwell in fields, and lead ambrosial lives;
In morn and ev'ning dew, your beauties bathe,
And drink the sun; which gives your cheeks to glow,
And out-blush (mine excepted) ev'ry fair;
You gladlier grew, ambitious of her hand,
Which often cropt your odours, incense meet
To thought so pure! Ye lovely fugitives!
Coeval race with man! for man you smile;
Why not smile at him too? You share indeed
His sudden pass; but not his constant pain.
   So man is made, nought ministers delight,
By what his glowing passions can engage;
And glowing passions, bent on aught below,
Must, soon or late, with anguish turn the scale;
And anguish, after rapture, how severe!
Rapture? Bold man! who tempts the wrath divine,
By plucking fruit denied to mortal taste,
While here, presuming on the rights of heaven.
For transport dost thou call on ev'ry hour,
Lorenzo?   At thy friend's expense be wise;
Lean not on earth; 'twill pierce thee to the heart;
A broken reed, at best; but, oft, a spear;
On its sharp point peace bleeds, and hope expires.
   Turn, hopeless thought! turn from her :—
         thought repell'd
Resenting rallies, and wakes ev'ry woe.
Snatch'd ere thy prime! and in thy bridal hour!
And when kind fortune, with thy lover, smil'd!
And when high flavour'd thy fresh op'ning joys!
And when blind man pronounc'd thy bliss complete!
And on a foreign shore; where strangers wept!
Strangers to thee; and, more surprising still,

Strangers to kindness, wept : their eyes let fall
Inhuman tears : strange tears ! that trickled down
From marble hearts ! obdurate tenderness !
A tenderness that call'd them more severe ;
In spite of nature's soft persuasion, steel'd ;
While nature melted, superstition rav'd ;
That mourn'd the dead ; and this denied a grave.
　Their sighs incens'd ; sighs foreign to the will !
Their will the tiger suck'd, outrag'd the storm.
For oh ! the curst ungodliness of zeal !
While sinful flesh relented, spirit nurst
In blind infallibility's embrace,
The sainted spirit petrified the breast ;
Denied the charity of dust, to spread
O'er dust ! a charity their dogs enjoy.
What could I do ? What succour ? What resource ?
With pious sacrilege, a grave I stole ;
With impious piety, that grave I wrong'd ;
Short in my duty ; coward in my grief !
More like her murderer, than friend, I crept,
With soft-suspended step, and muffled deep
In midnight darkness, whisper'd my last sigh.
I whisper'd what should echo thro' their realms ;
Nor writ her name, whose tomb should pierce the
　　　skies.
Presumptuous fear ! How durst I dread her foes,
While nature's loudest dictates I obey'd ?
Pardon necessity, blest shade ! Of grief
And indignation rival bursts I pour'd ;
Half execration mingled with my prayer ;
Kindled at man, while I his God ador'd ;
Sore grudg'd the savage land her sacred dust ;
Stampt the curst soil ; and with humanity
(Denied Narcissa) wisht them all a grave.

Glows my resentment into guilt ? What guilt
Can equal violations of the dead ?
The dead how sacred ! Sacred is the dust
Of this heaven-labour'd form, erect, divine !
This heaven-assum'd majestic robe of earth,
He deign'd to wear, who hung the vast expanse
With azure bright, and cloth'd the sun in gold.
When ev'ry passion sleeps that can offend ;
When strikes us ev'ry motive that can melt ;
When man can wreak his rancour uncontroll'd,
That strongest curb on insult and ill-will ;
Then, spleen to dust ? the dust of innocence ?
An angel's dust ?—This Lucifer transcends ;
When he contended for the patriarch's bones,
'Twas not the strife of malice, but of pride ;
The strife of pontiff pride, not pontiff gall.

Far less than this is shocking in a race
Most wretched, but from streams of mutual love ;
And uncreated, but for love divine ;
And, but for love divine, this moment, lost,
By fate resorb'd, and sunk in endless night.
Man hard of heart to man ! Of horrid things
Most horrid ! 'Mid stupendous, highly strange !
Yet oft his courtesies are smoother wrongs ;
Pride brandishes the favours He confers,
And contumelious his humanity :
What then his vengeance ? Hear it not, ye stars !
And thou, pale moon ! turn paler at the sound ;
Man is to man the sorest, surest ill.
A previous blast foretells the rising storm ;
O'erwhelming turrets threaten ere they fall ;
Volcanos bellow ere they disembogue ;
Earth trembles ere her yawning jaws devour ;
And smoke betrays the wide-consuming fire :

Ruin from man is most conceal'd when near,
And sends the dreadful tidings in the blow.
Is this the flight of fancy? Would it were!
Heaven's sovereign saves all beings, but himself,
That hideous sight, a naked human heart.

Fir'd is the muse? And let the muse be fir'd:
Who not inflam'd, when what he speaks, he feels,
And in the nerve most tender, in his friends?
Shame to mankind! Philander had his foes;
He felt the truths I sing, and I in him.
But he, nor I, feel more: Past ills, Narcissa!
Are sunk in thee, thou recent wound of heart!
Which bleeds with other cares, with other pangs;
Pangs num'rous, as the num'rous ills that swarm'd
O'er thy distinguish'd fate, and, clust'ring there
Thick as the locusts on the land of Nile,
Made death more deadly, and more dark the grave.
Reflect (if not forgot my touching tale)
How was each circumstance with aspics arm'd?
An aspic, each! and all, a hydra woe:
What strong Herculean virtue could suffice?——
Or is it virtue to be conquer'd here?
This hoary cheek a train of tears bedews;
And each tear mourns its own distinct distress;
And each distress, distinctly mourn'd, demands
Of grief still more, as heighten'd by the whole.
A grief like this proprietors excludes:
Not friends alone such obsequies deplore;
They make mankind the mourner; carry sighs
Far as the fatal fame can wing her way;
And turn the gayest thought of gayest age,
Down their right channel, through the vale of death.

The vale of death! that husht Cimmerian vale,
Where darkness, brooding o'er unfinisht fates,

With raven wing incumbent, waits the day
(Dread day!) that interdicts all future change!
That subterranean world, that land of ruin!
Fit walk, Lorenzo, for proud human thought!
There let my thought expatiate, and explore
Balsamic truths, and healing sentiments,
Of all most wanted, and most welcome, here.
For gay Lorenzo's sake, and for thy own,
My soul! " the fruits of dying friends survey;
Expose the vain of life; weigh life and death;
Give death his eulogy; thy fear subdue;
And labour that first palm of noble minds,
A manly scorn of terror from the tomb."

This harvest reap from thy Narcissa's grave.
As poets feign'd from Ajax' streaming blood
Arose, with grief inscrib'd, a mournful flow'r;
Let wisdom blossom from my mortal wound.
And first, of dying friends; what fruit from these?
It brings us more than triple aid; an aid
To chase our thoughtlessness, fear, pride, and guilt.

Our dying friends come o'er us like a cloud,
To damp our brainless ardours; and abate
That glare of life, which often blinds the wise.
Our dying friends are pioneers, to smooth
Our rugged pass to death; to break those bars
Of terror and abhorrence, nature throws
Cross our obstructed way; and, thus to make
Welcome, as safe, our port from ev'ry storm.
Each friend by fate snatch'd from us, is a plume
Pluckt from the wing of human vanity,
Which makes us stoop from our aerial heights,
And, dampt with omen of our own decease,
On drooping pinions of ambition lower'd,
Just skim earth's surface, ere we break it up,

O'er putrid earth to scratch a little dust,
And save the world a nuisance.   Smitten friends
Are angels sent on errands full of love ;
For us they languish, and for us they die :
And shall they languish, shall they die, in vain ?
Ungrateful, shall we grieve their hov'ring shades,
Which wait the revolution in our hearts ?
Shall we disdain their silent, soft address ;
Their posthumous advice, and pious pray'r ?
Senseless, as herds that graze their hallow'd graves,
Tread under-foot their agonies and groans ;
Frustrate their anguish, and destroy their deaths?

   Lorenzo ! no ; the thought of death indulge ;
Give it its wholesome empire ! let it reign,
That kind chastiser of thy soul in joy !
Its reign will spread thy glorious conquests far,
And still the tumults of thy ruffled breast :
Auspicious era ! golden days, begin !
The thought of death shall, like a god, inspire.
And why not think on death ?   Is life the theme
Of ev'ry thought ? and wish of ev'ry hour ?
And song of ev'ry joy ?   Surprising truth !
The beaten spaniel's fondness not so strange.
To wave the num'rous ills that seize on life
As their own property, their lawful prey ;
Ere man has measur'd half his weary stage,
His luxuries have left him no reserve,
No maiden relishes, unbroacht delights ;
On cold serv'd repetitions he subsists,
And in the tasteless present chews the past ;
Disgusted chews, and scarce can swallow down.
Like lavish ancestors, his earlier years
Have disinherited his future hours,
Which starve on orts, and glean their former field.

Live ever here, Lorenzo!—shocking thought!
So shocking, they who wish, disown it too;
Disown from shame, what they from folly crave.
Live ever in the womb, nor see the light?
For what live ever here?—With lab'ring step
To tread our former footsteps? Pace the round
Eternal? To climb life's worn, heavy wheel,
Which draws up nothing new? To beat, and beat
The beaten track? To bid each wretched day
The former mock? To surfeit on the same,
And yawn our joys? Or thank a misery
For change, tho' sad? To see what we have seen?
Hear, till unheard, the same old slabber'd tale?
To taste the tasted, and at each return
Less tasteful? O'er our palates to decant
Another vintage? Strain a flatter year,
Thro' loaded vessels, and a laxer tone?
Crazy machines to grind earth's wasted fruits!
Ill-ground, and worse concocted! Load, not life!
The rational foul kennels of excess!
Still-streaming thoroughfares of dull debauch!
Trembling each gulp, lest death should snatch the
    Such of our fine ones is the wish refin'd! [bowl.
So would they have it: elegant desire!
Why not invite the bellowing stalls, and wilds?
But such examples might their riot awe.
Thro' want of virtue, that is, want of thought,
(Tho' on bright thought they father all their flights)
To what are they reduc'd? To love and hate,
The same vain world; to censure, and espouse,
This painted shrew of life, who calls them fool
Each moment of each day; to flatter bad
Thro' dread of worse; to cling to this rude rock
Barren to them, of good, and sharp with ills,

And hourly blacken'd with impending storms,
And infamous for wrecks of human hope——
Scar'd at the gloomy gulf, that yawns beneath,
Such are their triumphs ! such their pangs of joy !
    'Tis time, high time, to shift this dismal scene.
This hugg'd, this hideous state, what art can cure ?
One only ; but that one, what all may reach ;
Virtue—she, wonder-working goddess ! charms
That rock to bloom ; and tames the painted shrew,
And what will more surprise, Lorenzo ! gives
To life's sick, nauseous iteration, change ;
And straitens nature's circle to a line.
Believ'st thou this, Lorenzo ? lend an ear,
A patient ear, thou'lt blush to disbelieve.
    A languid, leaden, iteration reigns,
And ever must, o'er those, whose joys are joys
Of sight, smell, taste : the cuckoo-seasons sing
The same dull note to such as nothing prize,
But what those seasons, from the teeming earth
To doating sense indulge.   But nobler minds,
Which relish fruits unripen'd by the sun,
Make their days various ; various as the dyes
On the dove's neck, which wanton in his rays.
On minds of dove-like innocence possest,
On lighten'd minds, that bask in virtue's beams,
Nothing hangs tedious, nothing old revolves
In that, for which they long ; for which they live.
Their glorious efforts, wing'd with heavenly hope,
Each rising morning sees still higher rise ;
Each bounteous dawn its novelty presents
To worth maturing, new strength, lustre, fame ;
While nature's circle, like a chariot-wheel
Rolling beneath their elevated aims,
Makes their fair prospect fairer ev'ry hour ;

Advancing virtue, in a line to bliss;
Virtue, which Christian motives best inspire!
And bliss, which Christian schemes alone ensure!
And shall we then, for virtue's sake, commence
Apostates? and turn infidels for joy?
A truth it is, few doubt, but fewer trust,
" He sins against this life, who slights the next."
What is this life? How few their fav'rite know!
Fond in the dark, and blind in our embrace,
By passionately loving life, we make
Lov'd life unlovely; hugging her to death.
We give to time eternity's regard;
And, dreaming, take our passage for our port.
Life has no value as an end, but means;
An end deplorable! a means divine!
When 'tis our all, 'tis nothing; worse than nought;
A nest of pains: when held as nothing, much:
Like some fair hum'rists, life is most enjoy'd,
When courted least; most worth, when disesteem'd;
Then 'tis the seat of comfort, rich in peace;
In prospect richer far; important! awful!
Not to be mention'd, but with shouts of praise!
Not to be thought on, but with tides of joy!
The mighty basis of eternal bliss!
Where now the barren rock? the painted shrew?
Where now, Lorenzo! life's eternal round?
Have I not made my triple promise good?
Vain is the world; but only to the vain.
To what compare we then this varying scene,
Whose worth ambiguous rises, and declines?
Waxes, and wanes? (in all propitious, night
Assists me here) compare it to the moon;
Dark in herself, and indigent; but rich
In borrow'd lustre from a higher sphere.

When gross guilt interposes, lab'ring earth,
O'ershadow'd, mourns a deep eclipse of joy;
Her joys, at brightest, pallid, to that font
Of full effulgent glory, whence they flow
 Nor is that glory distant: Oh Lorenzo!
A good man, and an angel! these between
How thin the barrier! What divides their fate?
Perhaps a moment, or perhaps a year;
Or, if an age, it is a moment still;
A moment, or eternity's forgot.
Then be, what once they were, who now are gods;
Be what Philander was, and claim the skies.
Starts timid nature at the gloomy pass?
The soft transition call it; and be cheer'd:
Such it is often, and why not to thee?
To hope the best, is pious, brave, and wise;
And may itself procure, what it presumes.
Life is much flatter'd, death is much traduc'd;
Compare the rivals, and the kinder crown.
"Strange competition!"—True, Lorenzo! strange!
So little life can cast into the scale.
 Life makes the soul dependent on the dust;
Death gives her wings to mount above the spheres.
Thro' chinks, styl'd organs, dim life peeps at light;
Death bursts th' involving cloud, and all is day;
All eye, all ear, the disembodied power.
Death has feign'd evils, nature shall not feel;
Life, ills substantial, wisdom cannot shun.
Is not the mighty mind, that son of heaven!
By tyrant life dethron'd, imprison'd, pain'd?
By death enlarg'd, ennobled, deified?
Death but entombs the body; life the soul.
 Is death then guiltless? How he marks his way
With dreadful waste of what 'eserves to shine!

Art, genius, fortune, elevated power!
With various lustres these light up the world,
Which death puts out, and darkens human race."
I grant, Lorenzo! this indictment just:
The sage, peer, potentate, king, conqueror!
Death humbles these; more barb'rous life, the man.
Life is the triumph of our mould'ring clay;
Death, of the spirit infinite! divine!
Death has no dread, but what frail life imparts;
Nor life true joy, but what kind death improves.
No bliss has life to boast, till death can give
Far greater; life's a debtor to the grave,
Dark lattice! letting in eternal day.

　Lorenzo! blush at fondness for a life,
Which sends celestial souls on errands vile,
To cater for the sense; and serve at boards,
Where ev'ry ranger of the wilds, perhaps
Each reptile, justly claims our upper hand.
Luxurious feast! a soul, a soul immortal,
In all the dainties of a brute bemir'd!
Lorenzo! blush at terror for a death,
Which gives thee to repose in festive bowers,
Where nectars sparkle, angels minister,
And more than angels share, and raise, and crown,
And eternize, the birth, bloom, bursts of bliss.
What need I more? O death, the palm is thine.

　Then welcome, death! thy dreaded harbingers,
Age and disease; disease, tho' long my guest;
That plucks my nerves, those tender strings of life;
Which, pluckt a little more, will toll the bell,
That calls my few friends to my funeral;
Where feeble nature drops, perhaps, a tear,
While reason and religion, better taught,
Congratulate the dead, and crown his tomb

With wreath triumphant. Death is victory;
It binds in chains the raging ills of life:
Lust and ambition, wrath and avarice,
Dragg'd at his chariot-wheel, applaud his power.
That ills corrosive, cares importunate,
Are not immortal too, O death! is thine.
Our day of dissolution!—name it right;
'Tis our great pay-day; 'tis our harvest, rich
And ripe: What tho' the sickle, sometimes keen,
Just scars us as we reap the golden grain?
More than thy balm, O Gilead! heals the wound.
Birth's feeble cry, and death's deep dismal groan,
Are slender tributes low-taxt nature pays
For mighty gain: the gain of each, a life!
But O! the last the former so transcends,
Life dies, compar'd; life lives beyond the grave.

And feel I, death! no joy from thought of thee?
Death, the great counsellor, who man inspires
With ev'ry nobler thought, and fairer deed!
Death, the deliverer, who rescues man!
Death, the rewarder, who the rescu'd crowns!
Death, that absolves my birth; a curse without it!
Rich death, that realizes all my cares,
Toils, virtues, hopes; without it a chimera!
Death, of all pain the period, not of joy;
Joy's source, and subject, still subsist unhurt;
One, in my soul; and one, in her great sire;
Tho' the four winds were warring for my dust.
Yes, and from winds, and waves, and central night,
Tho' prison'd there, my dust too I reclaim,
(To dust when drop proud nature's proudest spheres)
And live intire. Death is the crown of life:
Were death denied, poor man would live in vain;
Were death denied, to live would not be life;

Were death denied, ev'n fools would wish to die.
Death wounds to cure : we fall; we rise; we reign!
Spring from our fetters; fasten in the skies;
Where blooming Eden withers in our sight :
Death gives us more than was in Eden lost.
This king of terrors is the prince of peace.
When shall I die to vanity, pain, death?
When shall I die ?—When shall I live for ever?

NIGHT IV.

THE CHRISTIAN TRIUMPH:

CONTAINING OUR ONLY CURE FOR THE FEAR OF DEATH ; AND
PROPER SENTIMENTS OF HEART ON THAT INESTIMABLE
BLESSING. TO THE HONOURABLE MR. YORKE.

A MUCH indebted muse, O Yorke ! intrudes.
Amid the smiles of fortune, and of youth,
Thine ear is patient of a serious song.
How deep implanted in the breast of man
The dread of death ! I sing its sov'reign cure.
    Why start at death? Where is he? Death arriv'd,
Is past; not come, or gone, he's never here.
Ere hope, sensation fails ; black-boding man
Receives, not suffers, death's tremendous blow.
The knell, the shroud, the mattock, and the grave;
The deep damp vault, the darkness, and the worm;
These are the bugbears of a winter's eve,
The terrors of the living, not the dead.
Imagination's fool, and error's wretch,
Man makes a death, which nature never made;

Then on the point of his own fancy falls;
And feels a thousand deaths, in fearing one.

But were death frightful, what has age to fear?
If prudent, age should meet the friendly foe,
And shelter in his hospitable gloom.
I scarce can meet a monument, but holds
My younger; ev'ry date cries—" Come away."
And what recalls me? Look the world around,
And tell me what: The wisest cannot tell.
Should any born of woman give his thought
Full range, on just dislike's unbounded field;
Of things, the vanity; of men, the flaws;
Flaws in the best; the many, flaw all o'er;
As leopards, spotted, or, as Ethiops, dark;
Vivacious ill; good dying immature;
(How immature, Narcissa's marble tells!)
And at his death bequeathing endless pain;
His heart, tho' bold, would sicken at the sight,
And spend itself in sighs, for future scenes.

But grant to life (and just it is to grant
To lucky life) some perquisites of joy;
A time there is, when, like a thrice-told tale,
Long-rifled life of sweet can yield no more,
But from our comment on the comedy,
Pleasing reflections on parts well-sustain'd,
Or purpos'd emendations where we fail'd,
Or hopes of plaudits from our candid judge,
When, on their exit, souls are bid unrobe,
Toss fortune back her tinsel, and her plume,
And drop this mask of flesh behind the scene.

With me, that time is come; my world is dead;
A new world rises, and new manners reign:
Foreign comedians, a spruce band! arrive,
To push me from the scene, or hiss me there.

What a pert race starts up! the strangers gaze,
And I at them; my neighbour is unknown;
Nor that the worst: ah me! the dire effect
Of loit'ring here, of death defrauded long;
Of old so gracious (and let that suffice),
My very master knows me not.——

Shall I dare say, peculiar is the fate?
I've been so long remember'd, I'm forgot.
An object ever pressing dims the sight,
And hides behind its ardour to be seen.
When in his courtiers' ears I pour my plaint,
They drink it as the nectar of the great;
And squeeze my hand, and beg me come to-morrow.
Refusal! canst thou wear a smoother form?

Indulge me, nor conceive I drop my theme:
Who cheapens life, abates the fear of Death:
Twice told the period spent on stubborn Troy,
Court favour, yet untaken, I besiege;
Ambition's ill-judg'd effort to be rich.
Alas! ambition makes my little less;
Embitt'ring the possess'd: Why wish for more?
Wishing, of all employments, is the worst;
Philosophy's reverse; and health's decay!
Were I as plump as stall'd theology,
Wishing would waste me to this shade again.
Were I as wealthy as a south-sea dream,
Wishing is an expedient to be poor.
Wishing, that constant hectic of a fool;
Caught at a court; purg'd off by purer air,
And simpler diet; gifts of rural life!

Blest be that hand divine, which gently laid
My heart at rest, beneath this humble shed.
The world's a stately bark, on dang'rous seas,
With pleasure seen, but boarded at our peril;

Here, on a single plank, thrown safe ashore,
I hear the tumult of the distant throng,
As that of seas remote, or dying storms:
And meditate on scenes, more silent still;
Pursue thy theme, and fight the fear of Death.
Here, like a shepherd gazing from his hut,
Touching his reed, or leaning on his staff,
Eager ambition's fiery chace I see;
I see the circling hunt, of noisy men,
Burst law's inclosure, leap the mounds of right,
Pursuing, and pursu'd, each other's prey;
As wolves, for rapine; as the fox, for wiles;
Till Death, that mighty hunter, earths them all.

Why all this toil for triumphs of an hour?
What tho' we wade in wealth, or soar in fame?
Earth's highest station ends in " Here he lies:"
And " dust to dust" concludes her noblest song.
If this song lives, posterity shall know
One, tho' in Britain born, with courtiers bred,
Who thought ev'n gold might come a day too late;
Nor on his subtle death-bed plann'd his scheme
For future vacancies in church or state;
Some avocation deeming it———to die,
Unbit by rage canine of dying rich;
Guilt's blunder! and the loudest laugh of hell.

O my coevals! remnants of yourselves!
Poor human ruins, tott'ring o'er the grave!
Shall we, shall aged men, like aged trees,
Strike deeper their vile root, and closer cling,
Still more enamour'd of this wretched soil?
Shall our pale, wither'd hands, be still stretch'd out,
Trembling, at once, with eagerness and age?
With av'rice, and convulsions, grasping hard?
Grasping at air! for what has earth beside?

Man wants but little ; nor that little, long ;
How soon must he resign his very dust,
Which frugal nature lent him for an hour !
Years unexperienc'd rush on numerous ills ;
And soon as man, expert from time, has found
The key of life, it opes the gates of death.

When in this vale of years I backward look,
And miss such numbers, numbers too of such,
Firmer in health, and greener in their age,
And stricter on their guard, and fitter far
To play life's subtle game, I scarce believe
I still survive : and am I fond of life,
Who scarce can think it possible, I live ?
Alive by miracle ! or, what is next,
Alive by Mead ! if I am still alive,
Who long have buried what gives life to live,
Firmness of nerve, and energy of thought.
Life's lee is not more shallow, than impure,
And vapid ; sense and reason show the door,
Call for my bier, and point me to the dust.

O thou great arbiter of life and death !
Nature's immortal, immaterial sun !
Whose all-prolific beam late call'd me forth
From darkness, teeming darkness, where I lay
The worm's inferior, and, in rank, beneath
The dust I tread on, high to bear my brow,
To drink the spirit of the golden day,
And triumph in existence ; and could know
No motive, but my bliss ; and hast ordain'd
A rise in blessing ! with the patriarch's joy,
Thy call I follow to the land unknown ;
I trust in thee, and know in whom I trust ;
Or life, or death, is equal ; neither weighs :
All weight in this —O let me live to thee !

Tho' nature's terrors, thus, may be represt;
Still frowns grim Death; guilt points the tyrant's
     spear.
And whence all human guilt? From death forgot.
Ah me! too long I set at nought the swarm
Of friendly warnings, which around me flew;
And smil'd, unsmitten: small my cause to smile!
Death's admonitions, like shafts upwards shot,
More dreadful by delay, the longer ere
They strike our hearts, the deeper is their wound;
O think how deep, Lorenzo! here it stings:
Who can appease its anguish? How it burns!
What hand the barb'd, invenom'd thought can draw?
What healing hand can pour the balm of peace?
And turn my sight undaunted on the tomb?

    With joy,—with grief, that healing hand I see;
Ah! too conspicuous! it is fix'd on high.
On high?—What means my phrensy? I blaspheme;
Alas! how low! how far beneath the skies!
The skies it form'd; and now it bleeds for me—
But bleeds the balm I want—yet still it bleeds;
Draw the dire steel—ah no! the dreadful blessing
What heart or can sustain, or dares forego?
There hangs all human hope: that nail supports
The falling universe: that gone, we drop;
Horror receives us, and the dismal wish
Creation had been smother'd in her birth—
Darkness his curtain, and his bed the dust;
When stars and sun are dust beneath his throne!
In heaven itself can such indulgence dwell?
O what a groan was there! A groan not his.
He seiz'd our dreadful right; the load sustain'd;
And heav'd the mountain from a guilty world.
A thousand worlds, so bought, were bought too dear;

Sensations new in angels' bosoms rise;
Suspend their song; and make a pause in bliss.
  O for their song; to reach my lofty theme
Inspire me, night! with all thy tuneful spheres;
Whilst I with seraphs share seraphic themes,
And show to men the dignity of man;
Lest I blaspheme my subject with my song.
Shall Pagan pages glow celestial flame,
And Christian languish? On our hearts, not heads,
Falls the foul infamy: my heart! awake.
What can awake thee, unawak'd by this,
" Expended deity on human weal?"
Feel the great truths, which burst the tenfold night
Of heathen error, with a golden flood
Of endless day: to feel, is to be fir'd;
And to believe, Lorenzo! is to feel.
  Thou most indulgent, most tremendous pow'r!
Still more tremendous, for thy wond'rous love!
That arms, with awe more awful, thy commands;
And foul transgression dips in sev'nfold night;
How our hearts tremble at thy love immense!
In love immense, inviolably just!
Thou, rather than thy justice should be stain'd,
Did'st stain the cross; and work of wonders far
The greatest, that thy dearest far might bleed.
  Bold thought! shall I dare speak it, or repress?
Should man more execrate, or boast, the guilt
Which rous'd such vengeance? which such love
        inflam'd?   [arms,
O'er guilt (how mountainous!) with out-stretcht
Stern justice, and soft-smiling love embrace,
Supporting, in full majesty, thy throne,
When seem'd its majesty to need support,
Or that, or man, inevitably lost:

What, but the fathomless of thought divine,
Could labour such expedient from despair,
And rescue both? Both rescue! both exalt!
O how are both exalted by the deed!
The wondrous deed! or shall I call it more?
A wonder in Omnipotence itself!
A mystery no less to gods than men!

    Not, thus, our infidels th' eternal draw
A God all o'er, consummate, absolute,
Full-orb'd, in his whole round of rays complete:
They set at odds heaven's jarring attributes;
And, with one excellence, another wound;
Maim heaven's perfection, break its equal beams,
Bid mercy triumph over—God himself,
Undeified by their opprobrious praise:
A God all mercy, is a God unjust.

    Ye brainless wits! ye baptiz'd infidels!
Ye worse for mending! wash'd to fouler stains!
The ransom was paid down; the fund of heaven,
Heaven's inexhaustible, exhausted fund,
Amazing, and amaz'd, pour'd forth the price,
All price beyond: tho' curious to compute,
Archangels fail'd to cast the mighty sum:
Its value vast, ungraspt by minds create,
For ever hides, and glows, in the Supreme.

    And was the ransom paid? It was: and paid
(What can exalt the bounty more?) for you.
The sun beheld it—no, the shocking scene
Drove back his chariot: midnight veil'd his face;
Not such as this; not such as nature makes;
A midnight nature shudder'd to behold;
A midnight new! a dread eclipse (without
Opposing spheres) from her Creator's frown!
Sun! didst thou fly thy Maker's pain? or start

At that enormous load of human guilt,
Which bow'd his blessed head; o'erwhelm'd his cross;
Made groan the centre; burst earth's marble womb,
With pangs, strange pangs! deliver'd of her dead?
Hell howl'd; and heaven that hour let fall a tear;
Heaven wept, that men might smile! Heaven bled,
    that man
Might never die!——

    And is devotion virtue? 'Tis compell'd:
What heart of stone but glows at thoughts like these?
Such contemplations mount us; and should mount
The mind still higher; nor ever glance on man,
Unraptur'd, uninflam'd.—Where roll my thoughts
To rest from wonders? Other wonders rise;
And strike where'er they roll: my soul is caught:
Heaven's sovereign blessings, clust'ring from the
    cross,
Rush on her, in a throng, and close her round,
The pris'ner of amaze!—In his blest life,
I see the path, and, in his death, the price,
And in his great ascent, the proof supreme
Of immortality.—And did he rise?
Hear, O ye nations! hear it, O ye dead!
He rose! he rose! He burst the bars of death.
Lift up your heads, ye everlasting gates!
And give the king of glory to come in.
Who is the king of glory? He who left
His throne of glory, for the pang of death:
Lift up your heads, ye everlasting gates!
And give the king of glory to come in.
Who is the king of glory? He who slew
The rav'nous foe, that gorg'd all human race!
The king of glory, he, whose glory fill'd
Heaven with amazement at his love to man;

And with divine complacency beheld
Pow'rs most illumin'd, wilder'd in the theme.

    The theme, the joy, how then shall man sustain?
Oh the burst gates! crush'd sting! demolish'd
        throne!   [heaven!
Last gasp! of vanquish'd death. Shout earth and
This sum of good to man. Whose nature, then,
Took wing, and mounted with him from the tomb!
Then, then, I rose; then first humanity
Triumphant past the crystal ports of light,
(Stupendous guest!) and seiz'd eternal youth,
Seiz'd in our name. E'er since, 'tis blasphemous
To call man mortal. Man's mortality   [tion
Was, then, transferr'd to death; and heaven's dura-
Unalienably seal'd to this frail frame,
This child of dust—man, all-immortal! hail;
Hail, heaven! all lavish of strange gifts to man!
Thine all the glory; man's the boundless bliss.

    Where am I rapt by this triumphant theme,
On Christian joy's exulting wing, above
Th' Aonian mount!—Alas! small cause for joy!
What if to pain immortal? If extent
Of being, to preclude a close of woe?
Where, then, my boast of immortality?
I boast it still, tho' cover'd o'er with guilt;
For guilt, not innocence, his life he pour'd;
'Tis guilt alone can justify his death;
Nor that, unless his death can justify
Relenting guilt in heaven's indulgent sight.
If, sick of folly, I relent; he writes
My name in heaven, with that inverted spear
(A spear deep-dipt in blood!) which pierc'd his side,
And open'd there a font for all mankind,
Who strive, who combat crimes to drink, and live:

This, only this, subdues the fear of death.
   And what is this ?—Survey the wondrous cure:
And at each step, let higher wonder rise !
" Pardon for infinite offence ! and pardon
Thro' means that speak its value infinite !
A pardon bought with blood ! with blood divine !
With blood divine of him, I made my foe !
Persisted to provoke ! tho' woo'd, and aw'd,
Blest, and chastis'd, a flagrant rebel still !
A rebel, 'midst the thunders of his throne !
Nor I alone ! a rebel universe !
My species up in arms ! not one exempt !
Yet for the foulest of the foul, he dies,
Most joy'd, for the redeem'd from deepest guilt !
As if our race were held of highest rank ;
And Godhead dearer, as more kind to man !"
   Bound, ev'ry heart ! and ev'ry bosom, burn !
O what a scale of miracles is here !
Its lowest round, high planted on the skies ;
Its tow'ring summit lost beyond the thought
Of man or angel ! O that I could climb
The wonderful ascent, with equal praise !
Praise ! flow for ever, (if astonishment
Will give thee leave) my praise ! for ever flow ;
Praise ardent, cordial, constant, to high heaven
More fragrant, than Arabia sacrific'd,
And all her spicy mountains in a flame.
   So dear, so due to heaven, shall praise descend,
With her soft plume (from plausive angel's wing
First pluck'd by man) to tickle mortal ears,
Thus diving in the pockets of the great ?
Is praise the perquisite of ev'ry paw,
Tho' black as hell, that grapples well for gold ?
Oh love of gold ! thou meanest of amours !

Shall praise her odours waste on virtue's dead,
Embalm the base, perfume the stench of guilt,
Earn dirty bread by washing Æthiops fair,
Removing filth, or sinking it from sight,
A scavenger in scenes, where vacant posts,
Like gibbets yet untenanted, expect
Their future ornaments ? From courts and thrones,
Return, apostate praise ! thou vagabond !
Thou prostitute ! to thy first love return,
Thy first, thy greatest, once unrival'd theme.

There flow redundant; like Meander flow,
Back to thy fountain ; to that parent pow'r,
Who gives the tongue to sound, the thought to soar,
The soul to be. Men homage pay to men,
Thoughtless beneath whose dreadful eye they bow
In mutual awe profound, of clay to clay,
Of guilt to guilt; and turn their back on thee,
Great sire ! whom thrones celestial ceaseless sing;
To prostrate angels, an amazing scene !
O the presumption of man's awe for man !—
Man's author ! end ! restorer ! law ! and judge !
Thine, all; day thine, and thine this gloom of night,
With all her wealth, with all her radiant worlds :
What, night eternal, but a frown from thee ?
What heaven's meridian glory, but thy smile ?
And shall not praise be thine, not human praise ?
While heaven's high host on hallelujahs live ?

O may I breathe no longer, than I breathe
My soul in praise to him, who gave my soul,
And all her infinite of prospect fair,
Cut thro' the shades of hell, great love ! by thee
Oh most adorable ! most unador'd !   [end ?
Where shall that praise begin which ne'er should
Where'er I turn, what claim on all applause !

How is night's sable mantle labour'd o'er,
How richly wrought with attributes divine ! [pomp,
What wisdom shines ! what love !   This midnight
This gorgeous arch, with golden worlds inlay'd !
Built with divine ambition ! nought to thee ;
For others this profusion : Thou, apart,
Above ! beyond ! Oh tell me, mighty mind !
Where art thou ? Shall I dive into the deep ?
Call to the sun, or ask the roaring winds,
For their creator ?   Shall I question loud
The thunder, if in that th' Almighty dwells ?
Or holds he furious storms in streighten'd reins,
And bids fierce whirlwinds wheel his rapid car ?
　　What mean these questions?—Trembling I re-
　　　　tract ;
My prostrate soul adores the present God :
Praise I a distant deity ? He tunes
My voice (if tun'd) ; the nerve, that writes, sustains :
Wrapp'd in his being, I resound his praise :
But tho' past all diffus'd, without a shore,
His essence ; local is his throne (as meet),
To gather the disperst (as standards call
The listed from afar) : to fix a point,
A central point, collective of his sons,
Since finite ev'ry nature but his own.
　　The nameless he, whose nod is nature's birth ;
And nature's shield, the shadow of his hand ;
Her dissolution, his suspended smile !
The great first-last ! pavilion'd high he sits
In darkness from excessive splendour born,
By gods unseen, unless thro' lustre lost.
His glory, to created glory, bright,
As that to central horrors ; he looks down
On all that soars ; and spans immensity.

Tho' night unnumber'd worlds unfolds to view,
Boundless creation! what art thou? A beam,
A mere effluvium of his majesty:
And shall an atom of this atom-world
Mutter in dust and sin, the theme of heaven?
Down to the centre should I send my thought
Thro' beds of glitt'ring ore, and glowing gems,
Their beggar'd blaze wants lustre for my lay;
Goes out in darkness: if, on tow'ring wing,
I send it through the boundless vault of stars!
The stars, tho' rich, what dross their gold to thee,
Great! good! wise! wonderful! eternal king!
If to those conscious stars thy throne around,
Praise ever-pouring, and imbibing bliss;
And ask their strain; they want it, more they want,
Poor their abundance, humble their sublime.
Languid their energy, their ardour cold,
Indebted still, their highest rapture burns;
Short of its mark, defective, tho' divine. [alone;
    Still more—This theme is man's, and man's
Their vast appointments reach it not: they see
On earth a bounty not indulg'd on high;
And downward look for heaven's superior praise!
First-born of ether! high in fields of light!
View man, to see the glory of your God!
Could angels envy, they had envied here;
And some did envy; and the rest, tho' gods,
Yet still gods unredeem'd (there triumphs man,
Tempted to weigh the dust against the skies)
They less would feel, tho' more adorn, my theme.
They sung creation (for in that they shar'd);
How rose in melody, that child of love!
Creation's great superior, man! is thine;
Thine is redemption; they just gave the key:

vol. i.   v

'Tis thine to raise, and eternize, the song ;
Tho' human, yet divine ; for should not this
Raise man o'er man, and kindle seraphs here ?
Redemption ! 'twas creation more sublime ;
Redemption ! 'twas the labour of the skies ;
Far more than labour—It was death in heaven.
A truth so strange ! 'twere bold to think it true ;
If not far bolder still, to disbelieve.

    Here pause, and ponder : Was there death in
        heaven ?   [blow ?
What then on earth ? On earth, which struck the
Who struck it ? Who ?—O how is man enlarg'd,
Seen thro' this medium ! How the pigmy tow'rs !
How counterpois'd his origin from dust !
How counterpois'd, to dust his sad return !
How voided his vast distance from the skies !
How near he presses on the seraph's wing !
Which is the seraph ? Which the born of clay ?
How this demonstrates, thro' the thickest cloud
Of guilt, and clay condenst, the son of heaven !
The double son ; the made, and the re-made !
And shall heaven's double property be lost ?
Man's double madness only can destroy.
To man the bleeding cross has promis'd all ;
The bleeding cross has sworn eternal grace ;
Who gave his life, what grace shall he deny ?
O ye ! who, from this rock of ages, leap,
Apostates, plunging headlong in the deep !
What cordial joy, what consolation strong,
Whatever winds arise, or billows roll,
Our int'rest in the master of the storm !
Cling there, and in wreck'd nature's ruins smile ;
While vile apostates tremble in a calm.

    Man ! know thyself. All wisdom centres there ;

To none man seems ignoble, but to man ;
Angels that grandeur, men o'erlook, admire :
How long shall human nature be their book,
Degen'rate mortal ! and unread by thee ?
The beam dim reason sheds shows wonders there;
What high contents ! Illustrious faculties !
But the grand comment, which displays at full
Our human height, scarce sever'd from divine,
By heaven compos'd, was publish'd on the cross.
  Who looks on that, and sees not in himself
An awful stranger, a terrestrial god ?
A glorious partner with the deity
In that high attribute, immortal life ?
If a god bleeds, he bleeds not for a worm :
I gaze, and, as I gaze, my mounting soul
Catches strange fire, eternity ! at thee ;
And drops the world—or rather, more enjoys :
How chang'd the face of nature ! how improv'd !
What seem'd a chaos, shines a glorious world,
Or, what a world, an Eden ; heighten'd all !
It is another scene ! another self !
And still another, as time rolls along ;
And that a self far more illustrious still.
Beyond long ages, yet roll'd up in shades
Unpierc'd by bold conjecture's keenest ray,
What evolutions of surprising fate !
How nature opens, and receives my soul
In boundless walks of raptur'd thought ! where gods
Encounter and embrace me ! What new births
Of strange adventure, foreign to the sun,
Where what now charms, perhaps, whate'er exists,
Old time, and fair creation, are forgot !
  Is this extravagant ? Of man we form
Extravagant conception, to be just:

Conception unconfin'd wants wings to reach him:
Beyond its reach, the godhead only, more.
He, the great Father ! kindled at one flame
The world of rationals ; one spirit pour'd
From spirit's awful fountain ! pour'd himself
Thro' all their souls ; but not in equal stream,
Profuse, or frugal, of th' inspiring God,
As his wise plan demanded ; and when past
Their various trials, in their various spheres,
If they continue rational, as made,
Resorbs them all into himself again ;
His throne their centre, and his smile their crown.
    Why doubt we, then, the glorious truth to sing,
Tho' yet unsung, as deem'd, perhaps, too bold ?
Angels are men of a superior kind ;
Angels are men in lighter habit clad,
High o'er celestial mountains wing'd in flight ;
And men are angels, loaded for an hour,
Who wade this miry vale, and climb with pain,
And slipp'ry step, the bottom of the steep.
Angels their failings, mortals have their praise ;
While here, of corps ethereal, such enroll'd,
And summon'd to the glorious standard soon,
Which flames eternal crimson thro' the skies.
Nor are our brothers thoughtless of their kin,
Yet absent ; but not absent from their love.
Michael has fought our battles ; Raphael sung
Our triumphs ; Gabriel on our errands flown,
Sent by the sovereign : and are these, O man !
Thy friends, thy warm allies ? And thou (shame
        burn
The cheek to cinder !) rival to the brute ?
    Religion's all.   Descending from the skies
To wretched man, the goddess in her left

Holds out this world, and, in her right, the next;
Religion! the sole voucher man is man;
Supporter sole of man above himself;
Ev'n in this night of frailty, change, and death,
She gives the soul a soul that acts a god.
Religion! providence! an after-state!
Here is firm footing; here is solid rock!
This can support us; all is sea besides;
Sinks under us; bestorms, and then devours.
His hand the good man fastens on the skies,
And bids earth roll, nor feels her idle whirl.

As when a wretch, from thick, polluted air,
Darkness, and stench, and suffocating damps,
And dungeon-horrors, by kind fate, discharg'd
Climbs some fair eminence, where ether pure
Surrounds him, and Elysian prospects rise,
His heart exults, his spirits cast their load;
As if new-born, he triumphs in the change;
So joys the soul, when from inglorious aims,
And sordid sweets, from feculence and froth
Of ties terrestrial, set at large, she mounts
To reason's region, her own element,
Breathes hopes immortal, and affects the skies.

Religion! thou the soul of happiness;
And, groaning Calvary, of thee! there shine
The noblest truths; there strongest motives sting;
There sacred violence assaults the soul;
There, nothing but compulsion is forborne.
Can love allure us? or can terror awe?
He weeps!—the falling drop puts out the sun;
He sighs—the sigh earth's deep foundation shakes.
If in his love so terrible, what then
His wrath inflam'd? his tenderness on fire?
Like soft, smooth oil, out-blazing other fires

Can prayer, can praise avert it?—Thou, my all!
My theme! my inspiration! and my crown!
My strength in age! my rise in low estate!
My soul's ambition, pleasure, wealth!—my world!
My light in darkness! and my life in death!
My boast thro' time! bliss thro' eternity!
Eternity, too short to speak thy praise!
Or fathom thy profound of love to man!
To man of men the meanest, ev'n to me;
My sacrifice! my God!—what things are these!
  What then art thou? by what name shall I call
    thee?
Knew I the name devout archangels use,
Devout archangels should the name enjoy,
By me unrival'd; thousands more sublime,
None half so dear, as that, which, tho' unspoke
Still glows at heart: O how omnipotence
Is lost in love! Thou great philanthropist!
Father of angels! but the friend of man!
Like Jacob, fondest of the younger born!
Thou, who didst save him, snatch the smoking brand
From out the flames, and quench it in thy blood!
How art thou pleas'd, by bounty to distress!
To make us groan beneath our gratitude,
Too big for birth! to favour, and confound;
To challenge, and to distance all return!
Of lavish love stupendous heights to soar,
And leave praise panting in the distant vale!
Thy right too great, defrauds thee of thy due;
And sacrilegious our sublimest song.
But since the naked will obtains thy smile,
Beneath this monument of praise unpaid,
And future life symphonious to my strain,
(That noblest hymn to heaven!) for ever lie

Intomb'd my fear of death! and ev'ry fear,
The dread of ev'ry evil, but thy frown.

Whom see I yonder, so demurely smile?
Laughter a labour, and might break their rest
Ye quietists, in homage to the skies!
Serene! of soft address! who mildly make
An unobtrusive tender of your hearts,
Abhorring violence! who halt indeed;
But, for the blessing, wrestle not with heaven!
Think you my song too turbulent? too warm?
Are passions, then, the pagans of the soul?
Reason alone baptiz'd? alone ordain'd
To touch things sacred? Oh for warmer still!
Guilt chills my zeal, and age benumbs my pow'rs;
Oh for an humbler heart, and prouder song!
Thou, my much-injur'd theme! with that soft eye,
Which melted o'er doom'd Salem, deign to look
Compassion to the coldness of my breast;
And pardon to the winter in my strain.

Oh ye cold-hearted, frozen, formalists!
On such a theme, 'tis impious to be calm;
Passion is reason, transport temper, here.
Shall heaven, which gave us ardour, and has shown
Her own for man so strongly, not disdain
What smooth emollients in theology,
Recumbent virtue's downy doctors preach,
That prose of piety, a lukewarm praise?
Rise odours sweet from incense uninflam'd?
Devotion, when lukewarm, is undevout;
But when it glows, its heat is struck to heaven;
To human hearts her golden harps are strung;
High heaven's orchestra chants amen to man.

Hear I, or dream I hear, their distant strain,
Sweet to the soul, and tasting strong of heaven,

Soft- wafted on celestial pity's plume,
Thro' the vast spaces of the universe,
To cheer me in this melancholy gloom?
Oh, when will death (now stingless), like a friend,
Admit me of their choir?   O, when will death
This mould'ring, old, partition-wall throw down?
Give beings, one in nature, one abode?
Oh death divine! that giv'st us to the skies!
Great future! glorious patron of the past,
And present! when shall I thy shrine adore?
From nature's continent, immensely wide,
Immensely blest, this little isle of life,
This dark, incarcerating colony,
Divides us.   Happy day! that breaks our chain,
That manumits; that calls from exile home;
That leads to nature's great metropolis,
And re-admits us, thro' the guardian hand
Of elder brothers, to our Father's throne;
Who hears our Advocate, and, thro' his wounds
Beholding man, allows that tender name.
'Tis this makes Christian triumph a command:
'Tis this makes joy a duty to the wise;
'Tis impious in a good man to be sad.
    See thou, Lorenzo! where hangs all our hope!
Touch'd by the cross, we live; or, more than die;
That touch which touch'd not angels; more divine
Than that which touch'd confusion into form,
And darkness into glory; partial touch!
Ineffably pre-eminent regard!
Sacred to man, and sov'reign thro' the whole
Long golden chain of miracles, which hangs
From heav'n thro' all duration, and supports
In one illustrious, and amazing plan,
Thy welfare, nature! and thy God's renown;

That touch, with charm celestial, heals the soul
Diseas'd, drives pain from guilt, lights life in death,
Turns earth to heaven, to heavenly thrones trans-
     forms
The ghastly ruins of the mould'ring tomb.

    Dost ask me when? When he who died returns;
Returns, how chang'd! where then the man of woe?
In glory's terrors all the godhead burns;
And all his courts, exhausted by the tide
Of deities triumphant in his train,
Leave a stupendous solitude in heaven;
Replenisht soon, replenisht with increase
Of pomp, and multitude; a radiant band
Of angels new; of angels from the tomb.

    Is this by fancy thrown remote? and rise
Dark doubts between the promise, and event?
I send thee not to volumes for thy cure;
Read Nature; Nature is a friend to truth;
Nature is christian; preaches to mankind;
And bids dead matter aid us in our creed.
Hast thou ne'er seen the comet's flaming flight?
Th' illustrious stranger passing, terror sheds
On gazing nations, from his fiery train
Of length enormous, takes his ample round
Thro' depths of ether; coasts unnumber'd worlds
Of more than solar glory; doubles wide
Heaven's mighty cape; and then revisits earth,
From the long travel of a thousand years.
Thus, at the destin'd period, shall return
He, once on earth, who bids the comet blaze:
And, with him, all our triumph o'er the tomb.

    Nature is dumb on this important point;
Or hope precarious in low whisper breathes;
Faith speaks alo:d, distinct; ev'n adders hear;

But turn, and dart into the dark again.
Faith builds a bridge across the gulf of death,
To break the shock blind nature cannot shun,
And lands thought smoothly on the farther shore.
Death's terror is the mountain faith removes ;
That mountain barrier between man and peace.
'Tis faith disarms destruction ; and absolves
From ev'ry clam'rous charge the guiltless tomb.
　　Why disbelieve ? Lorenzo !—" Reason bids,
All-sacred reason."—Hold her sacred still ;
Nor shalt thou want a rival in thy flame :
All-sacred reason ! source, and soul, of all
Demanding praise, on earth, or earth above !
My heart is thine : deep in its inmost folds,
Live thou with life ; live dearer of the two.
Wear I the blessed cross, by fortune stampt
On passive nature, before thought was born ?
My birth's blind bigot ! fir'd with local zeal !
No ; reason re-baptiz'd me when adult ;
Weigh'd true, and false, in her impartial·scale ;
My heart became the convert of my head ;
And made that choice, which once was but my fate.
" On argument alone my faith is built :"
Reason pursu'd is faith ; and, unpursu'd
Where proof invites, 'tis reason, then, no more :
And such our proof, that, or our faith, is right,
Or reason lies, and heaven design'd it wrong :
Absolve we this ? What, then, is blasphemy ?
　　Fond as we are, and justly fond, of faith,
Reason, we grant, demands out first regard ;
The mother honour'd, as the daughter dear.
Reason the root, fair faith is but the flower ;
The fading flower shall die ; but reason lives
Immortal, as her father in the skies.

When faith is virtue, reason makes it so.
Wrong not the christian; think not reason yours:
'Tis reason our great master holds so dear;
'Tis reason's injur'd rights his wrath resents;
'Tis reason's voice obey'd his glories crown;
To give lost reason life, he pour'd his own:
Believe, and show the reason of a man;
Believe, and taste the pleasure of a God;
Believe, and look with triumph on the tomb:
Thro' reason's wounds alone thy faith can die;
Which dying, tenfold terror gives to death,
And dips in venom his twice-mortal sting.

Learn hence what honours, what loud pæans, due
To those, who push our antidote aside;
Those boasted friends to reason, and to man,
Whose fatal love stabs ev'ry joy, and leaves
Death's terror heighten'd, gnawing on his heart.
Those pompous sons of reason idolized
And vilified at once; of reason dead,
Then deified, as monarchs were of old;
What conduct plants proud laurels on their brow?
While love of truth thro' all their camp resounds,
They draw pride's curtain o'er the noon-tide ray,
Spike up their inch of reason, on the point
Of philosophic wit, call'd argument;
And then, exulting in their taper, cry,
" Behold the sun:" and, Indian-like, adore.

Talk they of morals? O thou bleeding love!
Thou maker of new morals to mankind!
The grand morality is love of thee.
As wise as Socrates, if such they were,
(Nor will they 'bate of that sublime renown)
As wise as Socrates, might justly stand
The definition of a modern fool.

A christian is the highest style of man :
And is there, who the blessed cross wipes off,
As a foul blot from his dishonour'd brow ?
If angels tremble, 'tis at such a sight :
The wretch they quit, desponding of their charge,
More struck with grief or wonder, who can tell ?
    Ye sold to sense ! ye citizens of earth !
(For such alone the christian banner fly)
Know ye how wise your choice, how great your gain ?
Behold the picture of earth's happiest man :
" He calls his wish, it comes ; he sends it back,
And says, he call'd another ; that arrives,
Meets the same welcome ; yet he still calls on ;
Till one calls him, who varies not his call,
But holds him fast, in chains of darkness bound,
Till nature dies, and judgment sets him free ;
A freedom far less welcome than his chain."
    But grant man happy ; grant him happy long ;
Add to life's highest prize her latest hour ;
That hour, so late, is nimble in approach,
That, like a post, comes on in full career :
How swift the shuttle flies, that weaves thy shroud !
Where is the fable of thy former years ?
Thrown down the gulf of time ; as far from thee
As they had ne'er been thine ; the day in hand,
Like a bird struggling to get loose, is going ;
Scarce now possess'd, so suddenly 'tis gone ;
And each swift moment fled, is death advanc'd
By strides as swift : eternity is all ;
And whose eternity ? Who triumphs there ?
Bathing for ever in the font of bliss !
For ever basking in the Deity !
Lorenzo ! who ?—Thy conscience shall reply.
    O give it leave to speak ; 'twill speak ere long.

Thy leave unaskt : Lorenzo ! hear it now,
While useful its advice, its accent mild.
By the great edict, the divine decree,
Truth is deposited with man's last hour ;
An honest hour, and faithful to her trust ;
Truth, eldest daughter of the Deity ;
Truth, of his council, when he made the worlds ;
Nor less, when he shall judge the worlds he made ;
Tho' silent long, and sleeping ne'er so sound,
Smother'd with errors, and oppress'd with toys,
That heaven-commission'd hour no sooner calls,
But from her cavern in the soul's abyss,
Like him they fable under Ætna whelm'd,
The goddess bursts in thunder, and in flame ;
Loudly convinces, and severely pains.
Dark demons I discharge, and hydra-stings ;
The keen vibration of bright truth—is hell :
Just definition ! tho' by schools untaught.
Ye deaf to truth ! peruse this parson'd page,
And trust, for once, a prophet, and a priest ;
" Men may live fools, but fools they cannot die."

NIGHT V.

THE RELAPSE.

TO THE RIGHT HONOURABLE THE EARL OF LICHFIELD.

Lorenzo ! to recriminate is just.
Fondness for fame is avarice of air.
I grant the man is vain who writes for praise.
Praise no man e'er deserv'd, who sought no more.
    As just thy second charge.   I grant the muse

Has often blusht at her degen'rate sons,
Retain'd by sense to plead her filthy cause;
To raise the low, to magnify the mean,
And subtilize the gross into refin'd:
As if to magic numbers' powerful charm
'Twas given, to make a civet of their song
Obscene, and sweeten ordure to perfume.
Wit, a true pagan, deifies the brute,
And lifts our swine-enjoyments from the mire.
    The fact notorious, nor obscure the cause.
We wear the chains of pleasure and of pride.
These share the man; and these distract him too;
Draw diff'rent ways, and clash in their commands
Pride, like an eagle, builds among the stars;
But pleasure, lark-like, nests upon the ground.
Joys shar'd by brute-creation, pride resents;
Pleasure embraces: man would both enjoy,
And both at once: a point so hard how gain!
But, what can't wit, when stung by strong desire?
    Wit dares attempt this arduous enterprise.
Since joys of sense can't rise to reason's taste;
In subtle sophistry's laborious forge,
Wit hammers out a reason new, that stoops
To sordid scenes, and meets them with applause.
Wit calls the graces the chaste zone to loose;
Nor less than a plump god to fill the bowl:
A thousand phantoms, and a thousand spells,
A thousand opiates scatters, to delude,
To fascinate, inebriate, lay asleep,
And the fool'd mind delightfully confound.
Thus that which shock'd the judgment, shocks no
        more;
That which gave pride offence, no more offends.
Pleasure and pride, by nature mortal foes,

At war eternal, which in man shall reign,
By wit's address, patch up a fatal peace,
And hand in hand lead on the rank bebauch,
From rank refin'd to delicate and gay.
Art, cursed art! wipes off th' indebted blush
From nature's cheek, and bronzes ev'ry shame.
Man smiles in ruin, glories in his guilt,
And infamy stands candidate for praise.

All writ by man in favour of the soul,
These sensual ethics far, in bulk, transcend.
The flowers of eloquence, profusely pour'd
O'er spotted vice, fill half the letter'd world.
Can pow'rs of genius exorcise their page,
And consecrate enormities with song?

But let not these inexpiable strains
Condemn the muse that knows her dignity;
Nor meanly stops at time, but holds the world
As 'tis, in nature's ample field, a point,
A point in her esteem; from whence to start,
And run the round of universal space,
To visit being universal there,
And being's source, that utmost flight of mind!
Yet, spite of this so vast circumference,
Well knows, but what is moral, nought is great:
Sing syrens only? Do not angels sing?
There is in poesy a decent pride,
Which well becomes her when she speaks to prose,
Her younger sister; haply, not more wise.

Think'st thou, Lorenzo! to find pastimes here?
No guilty passion blown into a flame,
No foible flatter'd, dignity disgrac'd,
No fairy field of fiction, all on flow'r,
No rainbow colours, heré, or silken tale:
But solemn counsels, images of awe,

Truths, which eternity lets fall on man
With double weight, thro' these revolving spheres,
This death-deep silence, and incumbent shade :
Thoughts, such as shall revisit your last hour ;
Visit uncall'd, and live when life expires ;
And thy dark pencil, midnight ! darker still
In melancholy dipt, embrowns the whole.

    Yet this, ev'n this, my laughter-loving friends !
Lorenzo ! and thy brothers of the smile !
If, what imports you most, can most engage,
Shall steal your ear, and chain you to my song.
Or if you fail me, know, the wise shall taste
The truths I sing ; the truths I sing shall feel ;
And, feeling, give assent ; and their assent
Is ample recompense ; is more than praise.
But chiefly thine, O Lichfield ! nor mistake ;
Think not unintroduc'd I force my way ;
Narcissa, not unknown, not unallied,
By virtue, or by blood, illustrious youth !
To thee, from blooming amaranthine bow'rs,
Where all the language harmony, descends
Uncall'd, and asks admittance for the muse :
A muse that will not pain thee with thy praise ;
Thy praise she drops, by nobler still inspir'd.

    O thou ! blest spirit ! whether the supreme,
Great antemundane father ! in whose breast
Embryo creation, unborn being, dwelt,
And all its various revolutions roll'd
Present, tho' future ; prior to themselves ;
Whose breath can blow it into nought again ;
Or, from his throne some delegated pow'r,
Who, studious of our peace, dost turn the thought
From vain and vile, to solid and sublime !
Unseen thou lead'st me to delicious draughts

Of inspiration, from a purer stream,
And fuller of the god, than that which burst
From fam'd Castalia: nor is yet allay'd
My sacred thirst; tho' long my soul has rang'd
Thro' pleasing paths of moral, and divine,
By thee sustain'd, and lighted by the stars.

By them best lighted are the paths of thought:
Nights are their days, their most illumin'd hours.
By day, the soul, o'erborne by life's career,
Stunn'd by the din, and giddy with the glare,
Reels far from reason, jostled by the throng.
By day the soul is passive, all her thoughts
Impos'd, precarious, broken ere mature.
By night, from objects free, from passion cool,
Thoughts uncontrol'd, and unimpress'd, the births
Of pure election, arbitrary range,
Not to the limits of one world confin'd;
But from ethereal travels light on earth,
As voyagers drop anchor, for repose.

Let Indians, and the gay, like Indians, fond
Of feather'd fopperies, the sun adore:
Darkness has more divinity for me;
It strikes thought inward; it drives back the soul
To settle on herself, our point supreme!
There lies our theatre! there sits our judge.
Darkness the curtain drops o'er life's dull scene;
'Tis the kind hand of providence stretcht out
'Twixt man and vanity; 'tis reason's reign,
And virtue's too; these tutelary shades
Are man's asylum from the tainted throng.
Night is the good man's friend, and guardian too;
It no less rescues virtue, than inspires.

Virtue, for ever frail, as fair, below,
Her tender nature suffers in the crowd,

Nor touches on the world, without a stain:
The world's infectious; few bring back at eve,
Immaculate, the manners of the morn.
Something we thought, is blotted; we resolv'd,
Is shaken; we renounc'd, returns again.
Each salutation may slide in a sin
Unthought before, or fix a former flaw.
Nor is it strange: light, motion, concourse, noise,
All, scatter us abroad; thought outward-bound,
Neglectful of our home affairs, flies off
In fume and dissipation, quits her charge,
And leaves the breast unguarded to the foe.

  Present example gets within our guard,
And acts with double force, by few repell'd.
Ambition fires ambition; love of gain
Strikes, like a pestilence, from breast to breast;
Riot, pride, perfidy, blue vapours breathe;
And inhumanity is caught from man,
From smiling man. A slight, a single glance,
And shot at random, often has brought home
A sudden fever, to the throbbing heart,
Of envy, rancour, or impure desire.
We see, we hear, with peril; safety dwells
Remote from multitude; the world's a school
Of wrong, and what proficients swarm around !
We must, or imitate, or disapprove;
Must list as their accomplices, or foes;
That stains our innocence; this wounds our peace.
From nature's birth, hence, wisdom has been smit
With sweet recess, and languisht for the shade.

  This sacred shade, and solitude, what is it?
'Tis the felt presence of the deity.
Few are the faults we flatter when alone.
Vice sinks in her allurements, is ungilt,

And looks, like other objects, black by night.
By night an atheist half-believes a God.
   Night is fair virtue's immemorial friend ;
The conscious moon, through ev'ry distant age,
Has held a lamp to wisdom, and let fall,
On contemplation's eye, her purging ray.
The fam'd Athenian, he who woo'd from heaven
Philosophy the fair, to dwell with men,
And form their manners, not inflame their pride,
While o'er his head, as fearful to molest
His lab'ring mind, the stars in silence slide,
And seem all gazing on their future guest,
See him soliciting his ardent suit
In private audience : all the live-long night,
Rigid in thought, and motionless, he stands ;
Nor quits his theme, or posture, till the sun
(Rude drunkard rising rosy from the main !)
Disturbs his nobler intellectual beam,
And gives him to the tumult of the world.
Hail, precious moments ! stol'n from the black
                waste
Of murder'd time ! Auspicious midnight ! hail !
The world excluded, ev'ry passion hush'd,
And open'd a calm intercourse with heaven,
Here the soul sits in council ; ponders past,
Predestines future action ; sees, not feels,
Tumultuous life, and reasons with the storm ;
All her lies answers, and thinks down her charms.
   What awful joy ! what mental liberty !
I am not pent in darkness ; rather say
(If not too bold) in darkness I'm embower'd.
Delightful gloom ! the clust'ring thoughts around
Spontaneous rise, and blossom in the shade ;
But droop by day, and sicken in the sun

Thought borrows light elsewhere ; from that first
Fountain of animation ! whence descends   [fire,
Urania, my celestial guest ! who deigns
Nightly to visit me, so mean ; and now
Conscious how needful discipline to man,
From pleasing dalliance with the charms of night
My wand'ring thought recalls, to what excites
Far other beat of heart ! Narcissa's tomb !
Or is it feeble nature calls me back,
And breaks my spirit into grief again ?
Is it a Stygian vapour in my blood ?
A cold, slow puddle, creeping thro' my veins ?
Or is it thus with all men ?—Thus with all.
What are we ? How unequal ! Now we soar,
And now we sink ; to be the same, transcends
Our present prowess.   Dearly pays the soul
For lodging ill ; too dearly rents her clay.
Reason, a baffled counsellor ! but adds
The blush of weakness to the bane of woe.
The noblest spirit fighting her hard fate,
In this damp, dusky region, charg'd with storms,
But feebly flutters, yet untaught to fly ;
Or, flying, short her flight, and sure her fall.
Our utmost strength, when down, to rise again ;
And not to yield, tho' beaten, all our praise.

    'Tis vain to seek in men for more than man.
Tho' proud in promise, big in previous thought,
Experience damps our triumph.   I, who late,
Emerging from the shadows of the grave,
Where grief detain'd me prisoner, mounting high,
Threw wide the gates of everlasting day,
And call'd mankind to glory, shook off pain,
Mortality shook off, in ether pure,
And struck the stars ; now feel my spirits fail ;

They drop me from the zenith; down I rush,
Like him whom fable fledg'd with waxen wings,
In sorrow drown'd—but not in sorrow lost.
How wretched is the man who never mourn'd!
I dive for precious pearl in sorrow's stream:
Not so the thoughtless man that only grieves;
Takes all the torment, and rejects the gain;
(Inestimable gain!) and gives heaven leave
To make him but more wretched, not more wise.

 If wisdom is our lesson (and what else
Ennobles man? What else have angels learnt?)
Grief! more proficients in thy school are made,
Than genius, or proud learning, e'er could boast.
Voracious learning, often over-fed,
Digests not into sense her motley meal.
This book-case, which dark booty almost burst,
This forager on others' wisdom leaves
Her native farm, her reason, quite untill'd.
With mixt manure she surfeits the rank soil,
Dung'd, but not drest; and rich to beggary.
A pomp untameable of weeds prevails.
Her servant's wealth, incumber'd wisdom mourns.

 And what says genius? " Let the dull be wise."
Genius, too hard for right, can prove it wrong;
And loves to boast, where blush men less inspir'd.
It pleads exemption from the laws of sense;
Considers reason as a leveller;
And scorns to share a blessing with the crowd.
That wise it could be, thinks an ample claim
To glory, and to pleasure gives the rest.
Crassus but sleeps, Ardelio is undone.
Wisdom less shudders at a fool, than wit.

 But wisdom smiles, when humbled mortals weep.
When sorrow wounds the breast, as ploughs the
   glebe,

And hearts obdurate feel her soft'ning shower;
Her seed celestial, then, glad wisdom sows;
Her golden harvest triumphs in the soil.
If so, Narcissa! welcome my relapse;
I'll raise a tax on my calamity,
And reap rich compensation from my pain.
I'll range the plenteous intellectual field;
And gather every thought of sov'reign power
To chase the moral maladies of man;   [skies,
Thoughts, which may bear transplanting to the
Tho' natives of this coarse penurious soil;
Nor wholly wither there, where seraphs sing,
Refin'd, exalted, not annull'd, in heaven.
Reason, the sun that gives them birth, the same
In either clime, tho' more illustrious there.
These choicely cull'd, and elegantly rang'd,
Shall form a garland for Narcissa's tomb;
And, peradventure, of no fading flowers.

 Say on what themes shall puzzled choice descend?
" Th' importance of contemplating the tomb;
Why men decline it; suicide's foul birth;
The various kind of grief; the faults of age;
And death's dread character—invite my song."

 And, first th' importance of our end survey'd.
Friends counsel quick dismission of our grief:
Mistaken kindness! our hearts heal too soon.
Are they more kind than he, who struck the blow?
Who bid it do his errand in our hearts,
And banish peace, till nobler guests arrive,
And bring it back, a true, and endless peace?
Calamities are friends: as glaring day
Of these unnumber'd lustres robs our sight;
Prosperity puts out unnumber'd thoughts
Of import high, and light divine, to man.

The man how blest, who, sick of gaudy scenes,
(Scenes apt to thrust between us and ourselves!)
Is led by choice to take his fav'rite walk,
Beneath death's gloomy, silent, cypress shades,
Unpierc'd by vanity's fantastic ray;
To read his monuments, to weigh his dust,
Visit his vaults and dwell among the tombs!
Lorenzo! read with me Narcissa's stone;
(Narcissa was my fav'rite) let us read
Her moral stone; few doctors preach so well;
Few orators so tenderly can touch
The feeling heart.   What pathos in the date!
Apt words can strike: and yet in them we see
Faint images of what we, here, enjoy.
What cause have we to build on length of life?
Temptations seize, when fear is laid asleep;
And ill foreboded is our strongest guard.

See from her tomb, as from an humble shrine
Truth, radiant goddess! sallies on my soul,
And puts delusion's dusky train to flight;
Dispels the mists our sultry passions raise,
From objects low, terrestrial, and obscene;
And shows the real estimate of things;
Which no man, unafflicted, ever saw;
Pulls off the veil from virtue's rising charms;
Detects temptation in a thousand lies.
Truth bids me look on men, as autumn leaves,
And all they bleed for, as the summer's dust,
Driven by the whirlwind: lighted by her beams,
I widen my horizon, gain new powers,
See things invisible, feel things remote,
Am present with futurities; think nought
To man so foreign, as the joys possest;
Nought so much his, as those beyond the grave.

No folly keeps its colour in her sight;
Pale worldly wisdom loses all her charms;
In pompous promise, from her schemes profound,
If future fate she plans, 'tis all in leaves,
Like sibyl, unsubstantial, fleeting bliss!
At the first blast it vanishes in air.
Not so, celestial: Wouldst thou know, Lorenzo!
How differ worldly wisdom, and divine?
Just as the waning, and the waxing moon.
More empty worldly wisdom ev'ry day;
And ev'ry day more fair her rival shines.
When later, there's less time to play the fool.
Soon our whole term for wisdom is expir'd
(Thou know'st she calls no council in the grave):
And everlasting fool is writ in fire,
Or real wisdom wafts us to the skies.

As worldly schemes resemble sibyl's leaves,
The good man's days to sibyl's books compare,
(In ancient story read, thou know'st the tale)
In price still rising, as in number less,
Inestimable quite his final hour.
For that who thrones can offer, offer thrones;
Insolvent worlds the purchase cannot pay.
" O let me die his death!" all nature cries.
" Then live his life."—All nature falters there.
Our great physician daily to consult,
To commune with the grave, our only cure.

What grave prescribes the best?—A friend's;
              and yet,
From a friend's grave, how soon we disengage?
Ev'n to the dearest, as his marble, cold.
Why are friends ravisht from us? 'Tis to bind,
By soft affection's ties, on human hearts,
The thought of death, which reason, too supine,

Or misemploy'd, so rarely fastens there.
Nor reason, nor affection, no, nor both
Combin'd, can break the witchcrafts of the world.
Behold, th' inexorable hour at hand !
Behold, th' inexorable hour forgot !
And to forget it, the chief aim of life,
Tho' well to ponder it, is life's chief end.

    Is death, that ever threat'ning, ne'er remote,
That all-important, and that only sure,
(Come when he will) an unexpected guest ?
Nay, tho' invited by the loudest calls
Of blind imprudence, unexpected still ?
Tho' numerous messengers are sent before,
To warn his great arrival. What the cause,
The wondrous cause, of this mysterious ill ?
All heaven looks down astonish'd at the sight.

    Is it, that life has sown her joys so thick,
We can't thrust in a single care between ?
Is it, that life has such a swarm of cares,
The thought of death can't enter for the throng ?
Is it, that time steals on with downy feet,
Nor wakes indulgence from her golden dream ?
To-day is so like yesterday, it cheats ;
We take the lying sister for the same.
Life glides away, Lorenzo ! like a brook ;
For ever changing, unperceived the change.
In the same brook none ever bath'd him twice :
To the same life none ever twice awoke.
We call the brook the same ; the same we think
Our life, tho' still more rapid in its flow ;
Nor mark the much, irrevocably laps'd,
And mingled with the sea. Or shall we say
(Retaining still the brook to bear us on)
That life is like a vessel on the stream ?

In life embark'd, we smoothly down the tide
Of time descend, but not on time intent;
Amus'd, unconscious of the gliding wave;
Till on a sudden we perceive a shock;
We start, awake, look out; what see we there?
Our brittle bark is burst on Charon's shore.
　　Is this the cause death flies all human thought?
Or is it judgment, by the will struck blind,
That domineering mistress of the soul!
Like him so strong, by Dalilah the fair?
Or is it fear turns startled reason back,
From looking down a precipice so steep?
'Tis dreadful; and the dread is wisely plac'd
By nature, conscious of the make of man.
A dreadful friend it is, a terror kind,
A flaming sword to guard the tree of life.
By that unaw'd, in life's most smiling hour,
The good man would repine; would suffer joys,
And burn impatient for his promis'd skies.
The bad, on each punctilious pique of pride,
Or gloom of humour, would give rage the rein;
Bound o'er the barrier, rush into the dark,
And mar the schemes of providence below.
　　What groan was that, Lorenzo?—Furies! rise;
And drown in your less execrable yell,
Britannia's shame. There took her gloomy flight,
On wing impetuous, a black sullen soul,
Blasted from hell, with horrid lust of death.
Thy friend, the brave, the gallant Altamont,
So call'd, so thought—And then he fled the field.
Less base the fear of death, than fear of life.
O Britain, infamous for suicide!
An island in thy manners! far disjoin'd
From the whole world of rationals beside!

In ambient waves plunge thy polluted head,
Wash the dire stain, nor shock the continent.

But thou be shock'd, while I detect the cause
Of self-assault, expose the monster's birth,
And bid abhorrence hiss it round the world.
Blame not thy clime, nor chide the distant sun;
The sun is innocent, thy clime absolv'd:
Immoral climes kind nature never made.
The cause I sing, in Eden might prevail,
And proves, it is thy folly, not thy fate.

The soul of man (let man in homage bow,
Who names his soul), a native of the skies!
High-born, and free, her freedom should maintain,
Unsold, unmortgag'd for earth's little bribes.
Th' illustrious stranger, in this foreign land,
Like strangers, jealous of her dignity,
Studious of home, and ardent to return,
Of earth suspicious, earth's inchanted cup
With cool reserve light touching, should indulge,
On immortality, her godlike taste;
There take large draughts; make her chief ban-
        quet there.

But some reject this sustenance divine;
To beggarly vile appetites descend;   [ven!
Ask alms of earth, for guests that came from hea-
Sink into slaves; and sell, for present hire,
Their rich reversion, and (what shares its fate)
Their native freedom, to the prince who sways
This nether world.   And when his payments fail
When his foul basket gorges them no more,
Or their pall'd palates loath the basket full;
Are instantly, with wild demoniac rage,
For breaking all the chains of providence,
And bursting their confinement; tho' fast barr'd

By laws divine and human ; guarded strong
With horrors doubled to defend the pass,
The blackest, nature, or dire guilt can raise ;
And moated round with fathomless destruction,
Sure to receive, and whelm them in their fall.

Such, Britons ! is the cause, to you unknown,
Or worse, o'erlook'd ; o'erlook'd by magistrates,
Thus criminals themselves. I grant the deed
Is madness ; but the madness of the heart.
And what is that ? Our utmost bound of guilt.
A sensual, unreflecting life, is big
With monstrous births, and suicide, to crown
The black infernal brood. The bold to break
Heaven's law supreme, and desperately rush
Thro' sacred nature's murder, on their own,
Because they never think of death, they die.
'Tis equally man's duty, glory, gain,
At once to shun, and meditate, his end.
When by the bed of languishment we sit,
(The seat of wisdom ! if our choice, not fate)
Or, o'er our dying friends, in anguish hang,
Wipe the cold dew, or stay the sinking head,
Number their moments, and, in ev'ry clock,
Start at the voice of an eternity ;
See the dim lamp of life just feebly lift
An agonizing beam, at us to gaze,
Then sink again, and quiver into death,
That most pathetic herald of our own ;
How read we such sad scenes ? As sent to man
In perfect vengeance ? No ; in pity sent,
To melt him down, like wax, and then impress,
Indelible, death's image on his heart ;
Bleeding for others, trembling for himself.
We bleed, we tremble, we forget, we smile.

The mind turns fool, before the cheek is dry.
Our quick-returning folly cancels all ;
As the tide rushing rases what is writ
In yielding sands, and smooths the letter'd shore.
     Lorenzo ! hast thou ever weigh'd a sigh ?
Or studied the philosophy of tears ?
(A science, yet unlectur'd in our schools !)
Hast thou descended deep into the breast,
And seen their source ? If not, descend with me,
And trace these briny riv'lets to their springs.
     Our funeral tears, from diff'rent causes, rise.
As if from sep'rate cisterns in the soul,
Of various kinds, they flow. From tender hearts,
By soft contagion call'd, some burst at once,
And stream obsequious to the leading eye.
Some ask more time, by curious art distill'd.
Some hearts, in secret hard, unapt to melt,
Struck by the magic of the public eye,
Like Moses' smitten rock, gush out amain.
Some weep to share the fame of the deceas'd,
So high in merit, and to them so dear.
They dwell on praises, which they think they share ;
And thus, without a blush, commend themselves.
Some mourn, in proof, that something they could
          love :
They weep not to relieve their grief, but show.
Some weep in perfect justice to the dead,
As conscious all their love is in arrear.
Some mischievously weep, not unappris'd
Tears, sometimes, aid the conquest of an eye.
With what address the soft Ephesians draw
Their sable net-work o'er entangled hearts !
As seen thro' crystal, how their roses glow,
While liquid pearl runs trickling down their cheek ?

Of hers not prouder Egypt's wanton queen,
Carousing gems, herself dissolv'd in love.
Some weep at death, abstracted from the dead,
And celebrate, like Charles, their own decease.
By kind construction some are deem'd to weep,
Because a decent veil conceals their joy.

Some weep in earnest, and yet weep in vain;
As deep in indiscretion, as in woe.
Passion, blind passion! impotently pours
Tears, that deserve more tears; while reason sleeps;
Or gazes like an idiot, unconcern'd;
Nor comprehends the meaning of the storm;
Knows not it speaks to her, and her alone.
Irrationals all sorrow are beneath,
That noble gift! that privilege of man!
From sorrow's pang, the birth of endless joy.
But these are barren of that birth divine:
They weep impetuous, as the summer storm,
And full as short! The cruel grief soon tam'd,
They make a pastime of the stingless tale;
Far as the deep resounding knell, they spread
The dreadful news, and hardly feel it more.
No grain of wisdom pays them for their woe.

Half-round the globe, the tears pumpt up by
death
Are spent in wat'ring vanities of life;
In making folly flourish still more fair.
When the sick soul, her wonted stay withdrawn,
Reclines on earth, and sorrows in the dust;
Instead of learning, there, her true support,
Tho' there thrown down her true support to learn,
Without heaven's aid, impatient to be blest,
She crawls to the next shrub, or bramble vile,
Tho' from the stately cedar's arms she fell;

With stale, forsworn embraces, clings anew,
The stranger weds, and blossoms, as before,
In all the fruitless fopperies of life :
Presents her weed, well-fancied, at the ball,
And raffles for the death's-head on the ring.

So wept Aurelia, till the destin'd youth
Stept in, with his receipt for making smiles,
And blanching sables into bridal bloom.
So wept Lorenzo fair Clarissa's fate ;
Who gave that angel boy, on whom he dotes ;
And died to give him, orphan'd in his birth !
Not such, Narcissa, my distress for thee.
I'll make an altar of thy sacred tomb,
To sacrifice to wisdom.—What wast thou ?
" Young, gay, and fortunate !" Each yields a theme.
I'll dwell on each, to shun thought more severe ;
(Heaven knows I labour with severer still !)
I'll dwell on each, and quite exhaust thy death.
A soul without reflection, like a pile
Without inhabitant, to ruin runs.

And, first, thy youth. What says it to gray hairs !
Narcissa, I'm become thy pupil now—
Early, bright, transient, chaste, as morning dew,
She sparkled, was exhal'd, and went to heaven.
Time on this head has snow'd ; yet still 'tis borne
Aloft ; nor thinks but on another's grave.
Cover'd with shame I speak it, age severe
Old worn-out vice sets down for virtue fair ;
With graceless gravity, chastising youth,
That youth chastis'd surpassing in a fault,
Father of all, forgetfulness of death :
As if, like objects pressing on the sight,
Death had advanc'd too near us to be seen :
Or that life's loan time ripen'd into right ;

And men might plead prescription from the grave;
Deathless, from repetition of reprieve.
Deathless? far from it! such are dead already;
Their hearts are buried, and the world their grave.
   Tell me, some god! my guardian angel! tell,
What thus infatuates? what inchantment plants
The phantom of an age 'twixt us, and death
Already at the door? He knocks, we hear him,
And yet we will not hear. What mail defends
Our untouch'd hearts? What miracle turns off
The pointed thought, which from a thousand quivers
Is daily darted, and is daily shunn'd?
We stand, as in a battle, throngs on throngs
Around us falling; wounded oft ourselves;
Tho' bleeding with our wounds, immortal still!
We see time's furrows on another's brow,
And death intrench'd, preparing his assault;
How few themselves, in that just mirror, see.!
Or, seeing, draw their inference as strong!
There death is certain; doubtful here: he must,
And soon; we may, within an age, expire.
Tho' gray our heads, our thoughts and aims are
     green;
Like damag'd clocks, whose hand and bell dissent;
Folly sings six, while nature points at twelve.
   Absurd longevity! More, more, it cries:
More life, more wealth, more trash of ev'ry kind.
And wherefore mad for more, when relish fails?
Object, and appetite, must club for joy;·
Shall folly labour hard to mend the bow,
Baubles, I mean, that strike us from without,
While nature is relaxing ev'ry string?
Ask thought for joy; grow rich, and hoard within.
Think you the soul, when this life's rattles cease,

Has nothing of more manly to succeed?
Contract the taste immortal; learn ev'n now
To relish what alone subsists hereafter.
Divine, or none, henceforth your joys for ever.
Of age the glory is, to wish to die.
That wish is praise, and promise; it applauds
Past life, and promises our future bliss.
What weakness see not children in their sires?
Grand-climacterical absurdities!
Gray-hair'd authority, to faults of youth,
How shocking: it makes folly thrice a fool;
And our first childhood might our last despise.
Peace and esteem is all that age can hope.
Nothing but wisdom gives the first; the last,
Nothing but the repute of being wise.
Folly bars both; our age is quite undone.

    What folly can be ranker? Like our shadows,
Our wishes lengthen, as our sun declines.
No wish should loiter, then, this side the grave.
Our hearts should leave the world, before the knell
Calls for our carcasses to mend the soil.
Enough to live in tempest, die in port;
Age should fly concourse, cover in retreat
Defects of judgment; and the will's subdue;
Walk thoughtful on the silent, solemn shore
Of that vast ocean it must sail so soon;
And put good-works on board; and wait the wind
That shortly blows us into worlds unknown;
If unconsider'd too, a dreadful scene!

    All should be prophets to themselves; foresee
Their future fate; their future fate foretaste;
This art would waste the bitterness of death.
The thought of death alone, the fear destroys.
A disaffection to that precious thought

Is more than midnight darkness on the soul,
Which sleeps beneath it, on a precipice,
Puff'd off by the first blast, and lost for ever.

Dost ask, Lorenzo, why so warmly prest,
By repetition hammer'd on thine ear,
The thought of death? That thought is the machine,
The grand machine! that heaves us from the dust,
And rears us into men. That thought, plied home,
Will soon reduce the ghastly precipice
O'er-hanging hell, will soften the descent,
And gently slope our passage to the grave;
How warmly to be wisht! What heart of flesh
Would trifle with tremendous? dare extremes?
Yawn o'er the fate of infinite? What hand,
Beyond the blackest brand of censure bold,
(To speak a language too well known to thee)
Would at a moment give its all to chance,
And stamp the die for an eternity?

Aid me, Narcissa! aid me to keep pace
With destiny; and ere her scissars cut
My thread of life, to break this tougher thread
Of moral death, that ties me to the world.
Sting thou my slumb'ring reason to send forth
A thought of observation on the foe;
To sally; and survey the rapid march
Of his ten thousand messengers to man;
Who, Jehu-like, behind him turns them all.
All accident apart, by nature sign'd,
My warrant is gone out, tho' dormant yet;
Perhaps behind one moment lurks my fate.

Must I then forward only look for death?
Backward I turn mine eye, and find him there.
Man is a self-survivor ev'ry year.
Man, like a stream, is in perpetual flow.

Death's a destroyer of quotidian prey.
My youth, my noon-tide, his ; my yesterday ;
The bold invader shares the present hour.
Each moment on the former shuts the grave.
While man is growing, life is in decrease ;
And cradles rock us nearer to the tomb.
Our birth is nothing but our death begun ;
As tapers waste, that instant they take fire.

   Shall we then fear, lest that should come to pass,
Which comes to pass each moment of our lives ?
If fear we must, let that death turn us pale,
Which murders strength and ardour ; what remains
Should rather call on death, than dread his call.
Ye partners of my fault, and my decline !
Thoughtless of death, but when your neighbour's
      knell
(Rude visitant !) knocks hard at your dull sense,
And with its thunder scarce obtains your ear !
Be death your theme, in ev'ry place and hour ;
Nor longer want, ye monumental sires !
A brother tomb to tell you you shall die.
That death you dread (so great is nature's skill !)
Know, you shall court before you shall enjoy.

   But you are learn'd ; in volumes, deep you sit ;
In wisdom, shallow : Pompous ignorance !
Would you be still more learned than the learn'd ?
Learn well to know how much need not be known,
And what that knowledge, which impairs your sense.
Our needful knowledge, like our needful food,
Unhedg'd, lies open in life's common field ;
And bids all welcome to the vital feast.
You scorn what lies before you in the page
Of nature, and experience, moral truth ;
Of indispensable, eternal fruit ;

Fruit, on which mortals feeding, turn to gods:
And dive in science for distinguisht names,
Dishonest fomentation of your pride;
Sinking in virtue, as you rise in fame.
Your learning, like the lunar beam, affords
Light, but not heat; it leaves you undevout,
Frozen at heart, while speculation shines.
Awake, ye curious indagators! fond
Of knowing all, but what avails you known.
If you would learn death's character, attend.
All casts of conduct, all degrees of health,
All dies of fortune, and all dates of age,
Together shook in his impartial urn,
Come forth at random: or, if choice is made,
The choice is quite sarcastic, and insults
All bold conjecture, and fond hopes of man.
What countless multitudes not only leave,
But deeply disappoint us, by their deaths!
Tho' great our sorrow, greater our surprise.

Like other tyrants, death delights to smite,
What, smitten, most proclaims the pride of power,
And arbitrary nod. His joy supreme,
To bid the wretch survive the fortunate;
The feeble wrap th' athletic in his shroud;
And weeping fathers build their children's tomb:
Me thine, Narcissa!—What tho' short thy date?
Virtue, not rolling suns, the mind matures.
That life is long, which answers life's great end.
The time that bears no fruit, deserves no name;
The man of wisdom is the man of years.
In hoary youth Methusalems may die;
O how misdated on their flatt'ring tombs!

Narcissa's youth has lectur'd me thus far
And can her gaiety give counsel too?

That, like the Jews' fam'd oracle of gems,
Sparkles instruction; such as throws new light,
And opens more the character of death;
Ill known to thee, Lorenzo! This thy vaunt:
" Give death his due, the wretched, and the old;
Ev'n let him sweep his rubbish to the grave;
Let him not violate kind nature's laws,
But own man born to live as well as die."
Wretched and old thou giv'st him; young and gay
He takes; and plunder is a tyrant's joy.
What if I prove, " The farthest from the fear,
Are often nearest to the stroke of Fate?"
　　All, more than common, menaces an end.
A blaze betokens brevity of life:
As if bright embers should emit a flame,
Glad spirits sparkled from Narcissa's eye,
And made youth younger, and taught life to live,
As nature's opposites wage endless war,
For this offence, as treason to the deep
Inviolable stupor of his reign,
Where lust, and turbulent ambition, sleep,
Death took swift vengeance. As he life detests
More life is still more odious; and, reduc'd
By conquest, aggrandizes more his power.
But wherefore aggrandiz'd? By heaven's decree,
To plant the soul on her eternal guard,
In awful expectation of our end.　　　　[so,
Thus runs death's dread commission: " Strike, but
As most alarms the living by the dead."
Hence stratagem delights him, and surprise,
And cruel sport with man's securities.
Not simple conquest, triumph is his aim;　[most.
And, where least fear'd, there conquest triumphs
This proves my bold assertion not too bold.

What are his arts to lay our fears asleep?
Tiberian arts his purposes wrap up
In deep dissimulation's darkest night.
Like princes unconfest in foreign courts,
Who travel under cover, death assumes
The name and look of life, and dwells among us.
He takes all shapes that serve his black designs:
Tho' master of a wider empire far
Than that, o'er which the Roman eagle flew.
Like Nero, he's a fiddler, charioteer,
Or drives his phaeton, in female guise;
Quite unsuspected, till, the wheel beneath,
His disarray'd oblation he devours.
    He most affects the forms least like himself,
His slender self.   Hence burly corpulence
Is his familiar wear, and sleek disguise.
Behind the rosy bloom he loves to lurk,
Or ambush in a smile; or wanton dive
In dimples deep; love's eddies, which draw in
Unwary hearts, and sink them in despair.
Such, on Narcissa's couch he loiter'd long
Unknown; and, when detected, still was seen
To smile; such peace has innocence in death!
Most happy they! whom least his arts deceive.
One eye on death, and one full fix'd on heaven,
Becomes a mortal, and immortal man.
Long on his wiles a piqu'd and jealous spy,
I've seen, or dreamt I saw, the tyrant dress;
Lay by his horrors, and put on his smiles.
Say, muse, for thou remember'st, call it back,
And show Lorenzo the surprising scene;
If 'twas a dream, his genius can explain.
    'Twas in a circle of the gay I stood.
Death would have enter'd; Nature pusht him back;

Supported by a doctor of renown,
His point he gain'd.   Then artfully dismist
The sage; for death design'd to be conceal'd.
He gave an old vivacious usurer
His meagre aspect, and his naked bones;
In gratitude for plumping up his prey,
A pamper'd spendthrift; whose fantastic air,
Well-fashion'd figure, and cockaded brow,
He took in change, and underneath the pride
Of costly linen, tuck'd his filthy shroud.
His crooked bow he straighten'd to a cane;
And hid his deadly shafts in Myra's eye.
   The dreadful masquerader, thus equipt,
Out-sallies on adventures. Ask you where?
Where is he not? For his peculiar haunts,
Let this suffice; sure as night follows day,
Death treads in pleasure's footsteps round the world,
When pleasure treads the paths, which reason shuns.
When, against reason, riot shuts the door,
And gaiety supplies the place of sense,
Then, foremost at the banquet, and the ball,
Death leads the dance, or stamps the deadly die;
Nor ever fails the midnight bowl to crown.
Gaily carousing to his gay compeers,
Inly he laughs, to see them laugh at him,
As absent far: And when the revel burns,
When fear is banisht, and triumphant thought,
Calling for all the joys beneath the moon,
Against him turns the key; and bids him sup
With their progenitors—He drops his mask;
Frowns out at full; they start, despair, expire.
   Scarce with more sudden terror and surprise,
From his black masque of nitre, touch'd by fire,
He bursts, expands, roars, blazes, and devours.

And is not this triumphant treachery,
And more than simple conquest, in the fiend?
    And now, Lorenzo, dost thou wrap thy soul
In soft security, because unknown
Which moment is commission'd to destroy?
In death's uncertainty thy danger lies.
Is death uncertain? Therefore thou be fixt;
Fixt as a centinel, all eye, all ear,
All expectation of the coming foe.
Rouse, stand in arms, nor lean against thy spear;
Lest slumber steal one moment o'er thy soul,
And fate surprise thee nodding. Watch, be strong;
Thus give each day the merit, and renown,
Of dying well; tho' doom'd but once to die.
Nor let life's period hidden (as from most)
Hide too from thee the precious use of life.
    Early, not sudden, was Narcissa's fate.
Soon, not surprising, death his visit paid.
Her thought went forth to meet him on his way,
Nor gaiety forgot it was to die:
Tho' fortune too (our third and final theme),
As an accomplice, play'd her gaudy plumes,
And ev'ry glitt'ring gewgaw, on her sight,
To dazzle, and debauch it from its mark.
Death's dreadful advent is the mark of man;
And ev'ry thought that misses it, is blind.
Fortune, with youth and gaiety, conspir'd
To weave a triple wreath of happiness
(If happiness on earth) to crown her brow.
And could death charge thro' such a shining shield?
    That shining shield invites the tyrant's spear,
As if to damp our elevated aims,
And strongly preach humility to man.
O how portentous is prosperity!

How, comet-like, it threatens, while it shines !
Few years but yield us proof of death's ambition,
To cull his victims from the fairest fold,
And sheath his shafts in all the pride of life.
When flooded with abundance, purpled o'er
With recent honours, bloom'd with ev'ry bliss,
Set up in ostentation, made the gaze,
The gaudy centre, of the public eye,
When fortune thus has toss'd her child in air.
Snatcht from the covert of an humble state,
How often have I seen him dropt at once,
Our morning's envy ! and our evening's sigh !
As if her bounties were the signal giv'n,
The flow'ry wreath to mark the sacrifice,
And call death's arrows on the destin'd prey.

   High fortune seems in cruel league with fate
Ask you for what ? To give his war on man
The deeper dread, and more illustrious spoil ;
Thus to keep daring mortals more in awe.
And burns Lorenzo still for the sublime
Of life ? to hang his airy nest on high,
On the slight timber of the topmost bough,
Rockt at each breeze, and menacing a fall ?
Granting grim death at equal distance there ;
Yet peace begins just where ambition ends.
What makes man wretched ? Happiness denied ?
Lorenzo ! no : 'Tis happiness disdain'd.
She comes too meanly drest to win our smile ;
And calls herself Content, a homely name !
Our flame is transport, and content our scorn.
Ambition turns, and shuts the door against her,
And weds a toil, a tempest, in her stead ;
A tempest to warm transport near of kin.
Unknowing what our mortal state admits,

Life's modest joys we ruin, while we raise;
And all our ecstasies are wounds to peace;
Peace, the full portion of mankind below.

   And since thy peace is dear, ambitious youth!
Of fortune fond! as thoughtless of thy fate!
As late I drew death's picture, to stir up
Thy wholesome fears; now, drawn in contrast, see
Gay fortune's, thy vain hopes to reprimand.
See, high in air, the sportive goddess hangs,
Unlocks her casket, spreads her glittering ware,
And calls the giddy winds to puff abroad
Her random bounties o'er the gaping throng.
All rush rapacious; friends o'er trodden friends;
Sons o'er their fathers, subjects o'er their kings,
Priests o'er their gods, and lovers o'er the fair,
(Still more ador'd) to snatch the golden show'r.

   Gold glitters most, where virtue shines no more;
As stars from absent suns have leave to shine.
O what a precious pack of votaries
Unkennell'd from the prisons, and the stews,
Pour in, all op'ning in their idol's praise;
All, ardent, eye each wafture of her hand,
And, wide-expanding their voracious jaws,
Morsel on morsel swallow down unchew'd,
Untasted, thro' mad appetite for more;
Gorg'd to the throat, yet lean and rav'nous still.
Sagacious all, to trace the smallest game,
And bold to seize the greatest. If (blest chance!)
Court-zephyrs sweetly breathe, they launch, they fly,
O'er just, o'er sacred, all-forbidden ground,
Drunk with the burning scent of place or pow'r,
Staunch to the foot of lucre, till they die.

   Or, if for men you take them, as I mark
Their manners, thou their various fates survey.

With aim mis-measur'd, and impetuous speed,
Some darting, strike their ardent wish far off,
Thro' fury to possess it : Some succeed,
But stumble, and let fall the taken prize.
From some, by sudden blasts, 'tis whirl'd away,
And lodg'd in bosoms that ne'er dreamt of gain.
To some it sticks so close, that, when torn off,
Torn is the man, and mortal is the wound.
Some, o'er-enamour'd of their bags, run mad,
Groan under gold, yet weep for want of bread.
Together some (unhappy rivals !) seize,
And rend abundance into poverty ;
Loud croaks the raven of the law, and smiles :
Smiles too the goddess ; but smiles most at those,
(Just victims of exorbitant desire !)
Who perish at their own request, and, whelm'd
Beneath her load of lavish grants, expire.
Fortune is famous for her numbers slain,
The number small, which happiness can bear.
Tho' various for a while their fates ; at last
One curse involves them all : At death's approach,
All read their riches backward into loss,
And mourn, in just proportion to their store.

And death's approach (if orthodox my song)
Is hasten'd by the lure of fortune's smiles.
And art thou still a glutton of bright gold?
And art thou still rapacious of thy ruin?
Death loves a shining mark, a signal blow ;
A blow, which, while it executes, alarms ;
And startles thousands with a single fall.
As when some stately growth of oak, or pine,
Which nods aloft, and proudly spreads her shade,
The sun's defiance, and the flock's defence ;
By the strong strokes of lab'ring hinds subdu'd,

Loud groans her last, and, rushing from her height,
In cumbrous ruin, thunders to the ground:
The conscious forest trembles at the shock,
And hill, and stream, and distant dale, resound.
    These high-aim'd darts of death, and these alone,
Should I collect, my quiver would be full.
A quiver, which, suspended in mid-air,
Or near heaven's archer, in the zodiac, hung,
(So could it be) should draw the public eye,
The gaze and contemplation of mankind!
A constellation awful, yet benign,
To guide the gay through life's tempestuous wave;
Nor suffer them to strike the common rock,
" From greater danger to grow more secure,
And, wrapt in happiness, forget their fate."
    Lysander, happy past the common lot,
Was warn'd of danger, but too gay to fear.
He woo'd the fair Aspasia: she was kind:
In youth, form, fortune, fame, they both were blest:
All who knew, envied; yet in envy lov'd:
Can fancy form more finish'd happiness?
Fix'd was the nuptial hour. Her stately dome
Rose on the sounding beach. The glittering spires
Float in the wave, and break against the shore:
So break those glitt'ring shadows, human joys.
The faithless morning smil'd: he takes his leave,
To re-embrace, in ecstasies, at eve.
The rising storm forbids. The news arrives:
Untold, she saw it in her servant's eye.
She felt it seen (her heart was apt to feel);
And, drown'd, without the furious ocean's aid
In suffocating sorrows, shares his tomb.
Now, round the sumptuous, bridal monument,
The guilty billows innocently roar;

And the rough sailor passing, drops a tear.
A tear?—Can tears suffice?—But not for me.
How vain our efforts! and our arts, how vain!
The distant train of thought I took, to shun,
Has thrown me on my fate—These died together;
Happy in ruin! undivorc'd by death!
Or ne'er to meet, or ne'er to part, is peace—
Narcissa! Pity bleeds at thought of thee.
Yet thou wast only near me; not myself.
Survive myself?—That cures all other woe.
Narcissa lives; Philander is forgot.
O the soft commerce! O the tender ties,
Close-twisted with the fibres of the heart!
Which, broken, break them; and drain off the soul
Of human joy; and make it pain to live—
And is it then to live? When such friends part,
'Tis the survivor dies—My heart, no more.

NIGHT VI.

THE INFIDEL RECLAIMED.

CONTAINING THE NATURE, PROOF, AND IMPORTANCE OF IMMORTALITY.

PART I.—WHERE, AMONG OTHER THINGS, GLORY AND RICHES
ARE PARTICULARLY CONSIDERED.

TO THE RIGHT HONOURABLE HENRY PELHAM, FIRST LORD COM-
MISSIONER OF THE TREASURY, AND CHANCELLOR
OF THE EXCHEQUER.

PREFACE.

FEW ages have been deeper in dispute about religion, than
this. The dispute about religion, and the practice of it,
seldom go together. The shorter, therefore, the dispute,
the better. I think it may be reduced to this single ques-

tion, Is man immortal, or is he not? If he is not, all our
disputes are mere amusements, or trials of skill. In this
case, truth, reason, religion, which give our discourses
such pomp and solemnity, are (as will be shown) mere
empty sounds, without any meaning in them. But if man
is immortal, it will behove him to be very serious about
eternal consequences ; or, in other words, to be truly religious. And this great fundamental truth, unestablished,
or unawakened in the minds of men, is, I conceive, the
real source and support of all our infidelity; how remote
soever the particular objections advanced may seem to be
from it.

Sensible appearances affect most men much more than
abstract reasonings ; and we daily see bodies drop around
us, but the soul is invisible. The power which inclination has over the judgment, is greater than can be well
conceived by those that have not had an experience of it ;
and of what numbers is it the sad interest that souls should
not survive! The heathen world confessed, that they
rather hoped, than firmly believed immortality! And how
many heathens have we still amongst us! The sacred
page assures us, that life and immortality is brought to
light by the Gospel: but by how many is the Gospel re-
jected, or overlooked! From these considerations, and
from my being, accidentally, privy to the sentiments of
some particular persons, I have been long persuaded that
most, if not all, our infidels (whatever name they take, and
whatever scheme, for argument's sake, and to keep themselves in countenance, they patronize,) are supported in
their deplorable error, by some doubt of their immortality,
at the bottom. And I am satisfied, that men once tho-
roughly convinced of their immortality, are not far from
being Christians. For it is hard to conceive, that a man
fully conscious eternal pain or happiness will certainly be
his lot, should not earnestly, and impartially, inquire after
the surest means of escaping one, and securing the other.
And of such an earnest and impartial inquiry, I well know
the consequence.

Here, therefore, in proof of this most fundamental truth,
some plain arguments are offered ; arguments derived from
principles which infidels admit in common with believers ;

arguments, which appear to me altogether irresistible; and such as, I am satisfied, will have great weight with all, who give themselves the small trouble of looking seriously into their own bosoms, and of observing, with any tolerable degree of attention, what daily passes round about them in the world. If some arguments shall, here, occur, which others have declined, they are submitted, with all deference, to better judgments in this, of all points the most important. For, as to the being of a God, that is no longer disputed; but it is undisputed for this reason only; viz. because, where the least pretence to reason is admitted, it must for ever be indisputable. And of consequence no man can be betrayed into a dispute of that nature by vanity; which has a principal share in animating our modern combatants against other articles of our belief.

SHE[1] (for I know not yet her name in heaven)
Not early, like Narcissa, left the scene;
Nor sudden, like Philander.   What avail?
This seeming mitigation but inflames;
This fancied med'cine heightens the disease.
The longer known, the closer still she grew;
And gradual parting is a gradual death.
'Tis the grim tyrant's engine, which extorts,
By tardy pressure's still-increasing weight,
From hardest hearts, confession of distress.

O the long, dark approach through years of pain,
Death's gallery! (might I dare to call it so)
With dismal doubt, and sable terror, hung;
Sick hope's pale lamp its only glimm'ring ray:
There, fate my melancholy walk ordain'd,
Forbid self-love itself to flatter, there.
How oft I gaz'd, prophetically sad!
How oft I saw her dead, while yet in smiles!
In smiles she sunk her grief to lessen mine.

[1] Referring to Night V.

She spoke me comfort, and increas'd my pain.
Like powerful armies trenching at a town,
By slow, and silent, but resistless sap,
In his pale progress gently gaining ground,
Death urg'd his deadly siege ; in spite of art,
Of all the balmy blessings nature lends
To succour frail humanity.   Ye stars !
(Not now first made familiar to my sight)
And thou, O moon ! bear witness ; many a night
He tore the pillow from beneath my head,
Tied down my sore attention to the shock,
By ceaseless depredations on a life
Dearer than that he left me.   Dreadful post
Of observation ! darker ev'ry hour !
Less dread the day that drove me to the brink,
And pointed at eternity below ;
When my soul shudder'd at futurity ;
When, on a moment's point, th' important die
Of life and death spun doubtful, ere it fell,
And turn'd up life ; my title to more woe.

 But why more woe ? More comfort let it be.
Nothing is dead, but that which wish'd to die ;
Nothing is dead, but wretchedness and pain ;
Nothing is dead, but what incumber'd, gall'd,
Block'd up the pass, and barr'd from real life.
Where dwells that wish most ardent of the wise ?
Too dark the sun to see it ; highest stars
Too low to reach it ; death, great death alone,
O'er stars and sun, triumphant, lands us there.

 Nor dreadful our transition ; tho' the mind,
An artist at creating self-alarms,
Rich in expedients for inquietude,
Is prone to paint it dreadful.   Who can take
Death's portrait true ? The tyrant never sat.

Our sketch all random strokes, conjecture all;
Close shuts the grave, nor tells one single tale.
Death, and his image rising in the brain,
Bear faint resemblance; never are alike;
Fear shakes the pencil; fancy loves excess;
Dark ignorance is lavish of her shades:
And these the formidable picture draw.
   But grant the worst; 'tis past; new prospects rise;
And drop a veil eternal o'er her tomb.
Far other views our contemplation claim,
Views that o'erpay the rigours of our life;
Views that suspend our agonies in death.
Wrapt in the thought of immortality,
Wrapt in the single, the triumphant thought!
Long life might lapse, age unperceiv'd come on;
And find the soul unsated with her theme.
Its nature, proof, importance, fire my song.
O that my song could emulate my soul!
Like her, immortal. No!—the soul disdains
A mark so mean; far nobler hope inflames;
If endless ages can outweigh an hour,
Let not the laurel, but the palm, inspire.
   Thy nature, immortality! who knows?
And yet who knows it not? It is but life
In stronger thread of brighter colour spun,
And spun for ever; dipt by cruel fate
In Stygian dye, how black, how brittle here!
How short our correspondence with the sun!
And while it lasts, inglorious! Our best deeds,
How wanting in their weight! Our highest joys
Small cordials to support us in our pain,
And give us strength to suffer. But how great
To mingle interests, converse, amities,
With all the sons of reason, scatter'd wide

Thro' habitable space, wherever born,
Howe'er endow'd ! To live free citizens
Of universal nature ! To lay hold
By more than feeble faith on the Supreme !
To call heaven's rich unfathomable mines
(Mines, which support archangels in their state)
Our own ! To rise in science, as in bliss,
Initiate in the secrets of the skies !
To read creation ; read its mighty plan
In the bare bosom of the Deity !
The plan, and execution, to collate !
To see, before each glance of piercing thought,
All cloud, all shadow, blown remote ; and leave
No mystery—but that of love divine,
Which lifts us on the seraph's flaming wing,
From earth's aceldama, this field of blood,
Of inward anguish, and of outward ill,
From darkness, and from dust, to such a scene !
Love's element ! true joy's illustrious home !
From earth's sad contrast (now deplor'd) more fair !
What exquisite vicissitude of fate !
Blest absolution of our blackest hour !
  Lorenzo, these are thoughts that make man man,
The wise illumine, aggrandize the great.
How great (while yet we tread the kindred clod,
And ev'ry moment fear to sink beneath
The clod we tread ; soon trodden by our sons)
How great, in the wild whirl of time's pursuits,
To stop, and pause, involv'd in high presage,
Thro' the long visto of a thousand years,
To stand contemplating our distant selves,
As in a magnifying mirror seen,
Enlarg'd, ennobled, elevate, divine !
To prophesy our own futurities ;

To gaze in thought on what all thought transcends!
To talk, with fellow-candidates, of joys
As far beyond conception as desert,
Ourselves th' astonish'd talkers, and the tale!
 Lorenzo, swells thy bosom at the thought?
The swell becomes thee: 'tis an honest pride.
Revere thyself;—and yet thyself despise.
His nature no man can o'er-rate; and none
Can underrate his merit. Take good heed,
Nor there be modest, where thou shouldst be proud;
That almost universal error shun.
How just our pride, when we behold those heights!
Not those ambition paints in air, but those
Reason points out, and ardent virtue gains;
And angels emulate; our pride how just! [quit
When mount we? When these shackles cast? When
This cell of the creation? This small nest,
Stuck in a corner of the universe,
Wrapt up in fleecy cloud, and fine-spun air?
Fine-spun to sense; but gross and feculent
To souls celestial; souls ordain'd to breathe
Ambrosial gales, and drink a purer sky;
Greatly triumphant on time's farther shore,
Where virtue reigns, enrich'd with full arrears;
While pomp imperial begs an alms of peace.
 In empire high or in proud science deep,
Ye born of earth! on what can you confer,
With half the dignity, with half the gain,
The gust, the glow of rational delight,
As on this theme, which angels praise and share?
Man's fates and favours are a theme in heaven.
 What wretched repetition cloys us here!
What periodic potions for the sick!
Distemper'd bodies! and distemper'd minds!

In an eternity, what scenes shall strike!
Adventures thicken! novelties surprise!
What webs of wonder shall unravel, there!
What full day pour on all the paths of heaven,
And light th' Almighty's footsteps in the deep!
How shall the blessed day of our discharge
Unwind, at once, the labyrinths of fate,
And straighten its inextricable maze!
　　If inextinguishable thirst in man
To know; how rich, how full, our banquet there!
There, not the moral world alone unfolds;
The world material, lately seen in shades,
And, in those shades, by fragments only seen,
And seen those fragments by the lab'ring eye,
Unbroken, then, illustrious, and entire,
Its ample sphere, its universal frame,
In full dimensions, swells to the survey;
And enters, at one glance, the ravish'd sight.
From some superior point (where, who can tell?
Suffice it, 'tis a point where gods reside)
How shall the stranger man's illumin'd eye,
In the vast ocean of unbounded space,
Behold an infinite of floating worlds
Divide the crystal waves of ether pure,
In endless voyage, without port? the least
Of these disseminated orbs, how great!
Great as they are, what numbers these surpass,
Huge, as Leviathan, to that small race,
Those twinkling multitudes of little life,
He swallows unperceiv'd! stupendous these!
Yet what are these stupendous to the whole?
As particles, as atoms ill-perceiv'd;
As circulating globules in our veins;
So vast the plan.　Fecundity divine!

Exub'rant source ! perhaps, I wrong thee still.
     If admiration is a source of joy,
What transport hence ! yet this the least in heaven.
What this to that illustrious robe he wears,
Who tost this mass of wonders from his hand,
A specimen, an earnest of his power ?
'Tis to that glory, whence all glory flows,
As the mead's meanest flow'ret to the sun,
Which gave it birth. But what, this sun of heaven ?
This bliss supreme of the supremely blest ?
Death, only death, the question can resolve.
By death, cheap-bought th' ideas of our joy ;
The bare ideas ! solid happiness
So distant from its shadow chas'd below.
     And chase we still the phantom thro' the fire,
O'er bog, and brake, and precipice, till death ?
And toil we still for sublunary pay ?
Defy the dangers of the field and flood,
Or, spider-like, spin out our precious all,
Our more than vitals spin (if no regard
To great futurity) in curious webs
Of subtle thought, and exquisite design ;
(Fine net-work of the brain !) to catch a fly !
The momentary buzz of vain renown !
A name ! a mortal immortality !
     Or (meaner still !) instead of grasping air,
For sordid lucre plunge we in the mire ;
Drudge, sweat, thro' ev'ry shame, for ev'ry gain,
For vile contaminating trash ; throw up
Our hope in heaven, our dignity with man ?
And deify the dirt, matur'd to gold ?
Ambition, avarice ; the two demons these,
Which goad thro' every slough our human herd,
Hard-travell'd from the cradle to the grave.

How low the wretches stoop! how steep they climb!
These demons burn mankind; but most possess
Lorenzo's bosom, and turn out the skies.
    Is it in time to hide eternity?
And why not in an atom on the shore
To cover ocean? or a mote, the sun?
Glory and wealth! have they this blinding power?
What if to them I prove Lorenzo blind?
Would it surprise thee? be thou then surpris'd;
Thou neither know'st: their nature learn from me.
    Mark well, as foreign as these subjects seem,
What close connection ties them to my theme.
First, what is true ambition? the pursuit
Of glory, nothing less than man can share.
Were they as vain, as gaudy-minded man,
As flatulent with fumes of self-applause,
Their arts and conquests animals might boast,
And claim their laurel crowns, as well as we;
But not celestial. Here we stand alone;
As in our form, distinct, pre-eminent;
If prone in thought, our stature is our shame;
And man should blush, his forehead meets the skies.
The visible and present are for brutes,
A slender portion! and a narrow bound!
These reason, with an energy divine,
O'erleaps; and claims the future and unseen;
The vast unseen! the future fathomless!
When the great soul buoys up to this high point,
Leaving gross nature's sediments below,
Then, and then only, Adam's offspring quits
The sage and hero of the fields and woods,
Asserts his rank, and rises into man.
This is ambition: this is human fire.
    Can parts or place (two bold pretenders!) make

Lorenzo great, and pluck him from the throng?
    Genius and art, ambition's boasted wings,
Our boast but ill deserve.   A feeble aid !
Dedalian engin'ry ! if these alone
Assist our flight, fame's flight is glory's fall.
Heart merit wanting, mount we ne'er so high,
Our height is but the gibbet of our name.
A celebrated wretch, when I behold,
When I behold a genius bright, and base,
Of tow'ring talents, and terrestrial aims ;
Methinks I see, as thrown from her high sphere,
The glorious fragments of a soul immortal,
With rubbish mixt, and glittering in the dust.
Struck at the splendid, melancholy sight,
At once compassion soft, and envy, rise—
But wherefore envy ? talents angel-bright,
If wanting worth, are shining instruments
In false ambition's hand, to finish faults
Illustrious, and give infamy renown.
    Great ill is an achievement of great powers.
Plain sense but rarely leads us far astray.
Reason the means, affections choose our end ;
Means have no merit, if our end amiss.
If wrong our hearts, our heads are right in vain ;
What is a Pelham's head, to Pelham's heart?
Hearts are proprietors of all applause.
Right ends, and means, make wisdom: worldly-wise
Is but half-witted, at its highest praise.
    Let genius then despair to make thee great ;
Nor flatter station : what is station high ?
'Tis a proud mendicant ; it boasts, and begs ;
It begs an alms of homage from the throng,
And oft the throng denies its charity.
Monarchs and ministers, are awful names ;

Whoever wear them, challenge our devoir.
Religion, public order, both exact
External homage, and a supple knee,
To beings pompously set up, to serve
The meanest slave ; all more is merit's due,
Her sacred and inviolable right ;
Nor ever paid the monarch, but the man.
Our hearts ne'er bow but to superior worth ;
Nor ever fail of their allegiance there.
Fools, indeed, drop the man in their account,
And vote the mantle into majesty.
Let the small savage boast his silver fur ;
His royal robe unborrow'd, and unbought,
His own, descending fairly from his sires.
Shall man be proud to wear his livery,
And souls in ermine scorn a soul without ?
Can place or lessen us, or aggrandize ?
Pygmies are pygmies still, tho' percht on alps ;
And pyramids are pyramids in vales.
Each man makes his own stature, builds himself :
Virtue alone outbuilds the pyramids :
Her monuments shall last, when Egypt's fall.
    Of these sure truths dost thou demand the cause ?
The cause is lodg'd in immortality.
Hear, and assent.   Thy bosom burns for power ;
What station charms thee ? I'll install thee there ;
'Tis thine.   And art thou greater than before ?
Then thou before wast something less than man.
Has thy new post betray'd thee into pride ?
That treach'rous pride betrays thy dignity ;
That pride defames humanity, and calls
The being mean, which staffs or strings can raise.
That pride, like hooded hawks, in darkness soars,
From blindness bold, and tow'ring to the skies.

'Tis born of ignorance, which knows not man:
An angel's second; nor his second, long.
A Nero quitting his imperial throne,
And courting glory from the tinkling string,
But faintly shadows an immortal soul,
With empire's self, to pride, or rapture, fir'd.
If nobler motives minister no cure,
Even vanity forbids thee to be vain.

　　High worth is elevated place: 'tis more;
It makes the post stand candidate for thee;
Makes more than monarchs, makes an honest man;
Tho' no exchequer it commands, 'tis wealth;
And tho' it wears no riband, 'tis renown;
Renown, that would not quit thee, tho' disgrac'd,
Nor leave thee pendent on a master's smile.
Other ambition nature interdicts;
Nature proclaims it most absurd in man,
By pointing at his origin, and end;
Milk, and a swathe, at first, his whole demand;
His whole domain, at last, a turf, or stone;
To whom, between, a world may seem too small.

　　Souls truly great dart forward on the wing
Of just ambition, to the grand result,
The curtain's fall; there, see the buskin'd chief
Unshod behind this momentary scene;
Reduc'd to his own stature, low or high,
As vice, or virtue, sinks him, or sublimes;
And laugh at this fantastic mummery,
This antic prelude of grotesque events,
Where dwarfs are often stilted, and betray
A littleness of soul by worlds o'er-run,
And nations laid in blood.　　Dread sacrifice
To Christian pride! which had with horror shockt
The darkest pagans, offer'd to their gods.

O thou most Christian enemy to peace!
Again in arms? Again provoking fate?
That prince, and that alone, is truly great,
Who draws the sword reluctant, gladly sheathes;
On empire builds what empire far outweighs,
And makes his throne a scaffold to the skies.

Why this so rare? because forgot of all
The day of death; that venerable day,   [nounce
Which sits as judge; that day, which shall pro-
On all our days, absolve them, or condemn.
Lorenzo, never shut thy thought against it;
Be levees ne'er so full, afford it room,
And give it audience in the cabinet.
That friend consulted, flatteries apart,
Will tell thee fair, if thou art great, or mean.

To dote on aught may leave us, or be left,
Is that ambition? then let flames descend,
Point to the centre their inverted spires,
And learn humiliation from a soul,
Which boasts her lineage from celestial fire.
Yet these are they, the world pronounces wise;
The world, which cancels nature's right and wrong
And casts new wisdom: ev'n the grave man lends
His solemn face, to countenance the coin.
Wisdom for parts is madness for the whole.
This stamps the paradox, and gives us leave
To call the wisest weak, the richest poor,
The most ambitious, unambitious, mean;
In triumph, mean; and abject, on a throne.
Nothing can make it less than mad in man,
To put forth all his ardour, all his art,
And give his soul her full unbounded flight,
But reaching him, who gave her wings to fly.
When blind ambition quite mistakes her road,

And downward pores, for that which shines above,
Substantial happiness, and true renown;
Then, like an idiot, gazing on the brook,
We leap at stars, and fasten in the mud;
At glory grasp, and sink in infamy.

    Ambition! powerful source of good and ill!
Thy strength in man, like length of wing in birds,
When disengag'd from earth, with greater ease
And swifter flight transports us to the skies;
By toys entangled, or in guilt bemir'd,
It turns a curse; it is our chain, and scourge,
In this dark dungeon, where confin'd we lie,
Close grated by the sordid bars of sense;
All prospect of eternity shut out;
And, but for execution, ne'er set free.

    With error in ambition justly charg'd,
Find we Lorenzo wiser in his wealth?
What if thy rental I reform? and draw
An inventory new to set thee right?
Where, thy true treasure? Gold says, "Not in me:"
And, "Not in me," the diamond. Gold is poor;
India's insolvent: Seek it in thyself,
Seek in thy naked self, and find it there;
In being so descended, form'd, endow'd;
Sky-born, sky-guided, sky-returning race!
Erect, immortal, rational, divine!
In senses, which inherit earth, and heavens;
Enjoy the various riches nature yields;
Far nobler! give the riches they enjoy;
Give taste to fruits; and harmony to groves;
Their radiant beams to gold, and gold's bright fire;
Take in, at once, the landscape of the world,
At a small inlet, which a grain might close,
And half create the wondrous world they see.

Our senses, as our reason, are divine.
But for the magic organ's powerful charm,
Earth were a rude, uncolour'd chaos still.
Objects are but th' occasion; ours th' exploit;
Ours is the cloth, the pencil, and the paint,
Which nature's admirable picture draws;
And beautifies creation's ample dome.
Like Milton's Eve, when gazing on the lake,
Man makes the matchless image, man admires,
Say then, shall man, his thoughts all sent abroad,
Superior wonders in himself forgot,
His admiration waste on objects round,
When heaven makes him the soul of all he sees?
Absurd; not rare! so great, so mean, is man.

What wealth in senses such as these! What
In fancy, fir'd to form a fairer scene   [wealth
Than sense surveys! In mem'ry's firm record,
Which, should it perish, could this world recall
From the dark shadows of o'erwhelming years!
In colours fresh, originally bright,
Preserve its portrait, and report its fate!
What wealth in intellect, that sov'reign power!
Which sense and fancy summons to the bar;
Interrogates, approves, or reprehends;
And from the mass those underlings import,
From their materials sifted, and refin'd,
And in truth's balance accurately weigh'd,
Forms art, and science, government, and law;
The solid basis, and the beauteous frame,
The vitals, and the grace of civil life!
And manners (sad exception!) set aside,
Strikes out, with master hand, a copy fair
Of His idea, whose indulgent thought
Long, long, ere chaos teem'd, plann'd human bliss.

What wealth in souls that soar, dive, range around,
Disdaining limit, or from place, or time;
And hear at once, in thought extensive, hear
Th' almighty fiat, and the trumpet's sound!
Bold, on creation's outside walk, and view
What was, and is, and more than e'er shall be;
Commanding, with omnipotence of thought,
Creations new in fancy's field to rise!
Souls, that can grasp whate'er th' Almighty made,
And wander wild thro' things impossible!
What wealth, in faculties of endless growth,
In quenchless passions violent to crave,
In liberty to choose, in power to reach,
And in duration (how thy riches rise!)
Duration to perpetuate——boundless bliss!

   Ask you, what power resides in feeble man
That bliss to gain? Is virtue's, then, unknown?
Virtue, our present peace, our future prize.
Man's unprecarious, natural estate,
Improveable at will, in virtue lies;
Its tenure sure; its income is divine.

   High-built abundance, heap on heap! for what?
To breed new wants, and beggar us the more;
Then, make a richer scramble for the throng?
Soon as this feeble pulse, which leaps so long
Almost by miracle, is tired with play,
Like rubbish from disploding engines thrown,
Our magazines of hoarded trifles fly;
Fly diverse; fly to foreigners, to foes;
New masters court, and call the former fool
(How justly!) for dependence on their stay.
Wide scatter, first, our play-things; then, our dust.

   Dost court abundance for the sake of peace?
Learn and lament thy self-defeated scheme:

Riches enable to be richer still ;
And, richer still, what mortal can resist ?
Thus wealth (a cruel task-master !) enjoins
New toils, succeeding toils, an endless train !
And murders peace, which taught it first to shine.
The poor are half as wretched as the rich ;
Whose proud and painful privilege it is,
At once, to bear a double load of woe ;
To feel the stings of envy, and of want,
Outrageous want ! both Indies cannot cure.
  A competence is vital to content.
Much wealth is corpulence, if not disease ;
Sick, or incumber'd, is our happiness,
A competence is all we can enjoy.
O be content, where heaven can give no more !
More, like a flash of water from a lock,
Quickens our spirits' movement for an hour ;
But soon its force is spent, nor rise our joys
Above our native temper's common stream.
Hence disappointment lurks in ev'ry prize,
As bees in flowers ; and stings us with success.
  The rich man, who denies it, proudly feigns ;
Nor knows the wise are privy to the lie.
Much learning shows how little mortals know ;
Much wealth, how little worldlings can enjoy :
At best, it babies us with endless toys,
And keeps us children till we drop to dust.
As monkeys at a mirror stand amaz'd,
They fail to find what they so plainly see ;
Thus men, in shining riches, see the face
Of happiness, nor know it is a shade ;
But gaze, and touch, and peep, and peep again,
And wish, and wonder it is absent still.
  How few can rescue opulence from want !

Who lives to nature, rarely can be poor;
Who lives to fancy, never can be rich.
Poor is the man in debt; the man of gold,
In debt to fortune, trembles at her power.
The man of reason smiles at her, and death.
O what a patrimony this! a being
Of such inherent strength and majesty,
Not worlds possest can raise it; worlds destroy'd
Can't injure; which holds on its glorious course,
When thine, O Nature! ends; too blest to mourn
Creation's obsequies.   What treasure, this!
The monarch is a beggar to the man.

   Immortal! ages past, yet nothing gone!
Morn without eve! a race without a goal!
Unshorten'd by progression infinite!
Futurity for ever future! Life
Beginning still where computation ends!
'Tis the description of a Deity!
'Tis the description of the meanest slave:
The meanest slave dares then Lorenzo scorn?
The meanest slave thy sov'reign glory shares.
Proud youth! fastidious of the lower world!
Man's lawful pride includes humility;
Stoops to the lowest; is too great to find
Inferiors; all immortal! brothers all!
Proprietors eternal of thy love.

   Immortal! what can strike the sense so strong,
As this the soul? it thunders to the thought;
Reason amazes; gratitude o'erwhelms;
No more we slumber on the brink of fate;
Rous'd at the sound, th' exulting soul ascends,
And breathes her native air; an air that feeds
Ambitions high, and fans ethereal fires;
Quick kindles all that is divine within us;

Nor leaves one loit'ring thought beneath the stars.
  Has not Lorenzo's bosom caught the flame?
Immortal! were but one immortal, how
Would others envy! how would thrones adore!
Because 'tis common, is the blessing lost?
How this ties up the bounteous hand of heaven!
O vain, vain, vain, all else! eternity!
A glorious, and a needful refuge, that,
From vile imprisonment, in abject views.
'Tis immortality, 'tis that alone,
Amid life's pains, abasements, emptiness,
The soul can comfort, elevate, and fill.
That only, and that amply, this performs;
Lifts us above life's pains, her joys above;
Their terror those, and these their lustre lose;
Eternity depending covers all;
Eternity depending all achieves;
Sets earth at distance; casts her into shades;
Blends her distinctions; abrogates her powers;
The low, the lofty, joyous, and severe,
Fortune's dread frowns, and fascinating smiles,
Make one promiscuous and neglected heap,
The man beneath; if I may call him man,
Whom immortality's full force inspires.
Nothing terrestrial touches his high thought;
Suns shine unseen, and thunders roll unheard,
By minds quite conscious of their high descent,
Their present province, and their future prize;
Divinely darting upward every wish,
Warm on the wing, in glorious absence lost!
  Doubt you this truth? why labours your belief?
If earth's whole orb by some due distanc'd eye
Were seen at once, her tow'ring Alps would sink,
And levell'd Atlas leave an even sphere.

Thus earth, and all that earthly minds admire,
Is swallow'd in eternity's vast round.
To that stupendous view, when souls awake,
So large of late, so mountainous to man,
Time's toys subside; and equal all below.
    Enthusiastic, this? then all are weak,
But rank enthusiasts.   To this godlike height
Some souls have soar'd; or martyrs ne'er had bled,
And all may do, what has by man been done.
Who, beaten by these sublunary storms,
Boundless, interminable joys can weigh,
Unraptur'd, unexalted, uninflam'd?
What slave unblest, who from to-morrow's dawn
Expects an empire? he forgets his chain,
And, thron'd in thought, his absent sceptre waves.
    And what a sceptre waits us! what a throne!
Her own immense appointments to compute,
Or comprehend her high prerogatives,
In this her dark minority, how toils,
How vainly pants, the human soul divine!
Too great the bounty seems for earthly joy;
What heart but trembles at so strange a bliss?
    In spite of all the truths the muse has sung,
Ne'er to be prized enough! enough revolv'd!
Are there who wrap the world so close about them,
They see no farther than the clouds; and dance
On heedless vanity's fantastic toe,
Till, stumbling at a straw, in their career,
Headlong they plunge, where end both dance and
Are there, Lorenzo? Is it possible?   [song?
Are there on earth (let me not call them men)
Who lodge a soul immortal in their breasts;
Unconscious as the mountain of its ore;
Or rock, of its inestimable gem?

When rocks shall melt, and mountains vanish, these
Shall know their treasure; treasure, then, no more.
    Are there (still more amazing!) who resist
The rising thought? who smother, in its birth,
The glorious truth? who struggle to be brutes?
Who thro' this bosom-barrier burst their way,
And, with reverst ambition, strive to sink?
Who labour downwards thro' th' opposing powers
Of instinct, reason, and the world against them,
To dismal hopes, and shelter in the shock
Of endless night; night darker than the grave's?
Who fight the proofs of immortality?
With horrid zeal, and execrable arts,
Work all their engines, level their black fires,
To blot from man this attribute divine,
(Than vital blood far dearer to the wise)
Blasphemers, and rank atheists to themselves?
    To contradict them, see all nature rise!
What object, what event, the moon beneath,
But argues, or endears, an after-scene?
To reason proves, or weds it to desire?
All things proclaim it needful; some advance
One precious step beyond, and prove it sure.
A thousand arguments swarm round my pen,
From heaven, and earth, and man. Indulge a few,
By nature, as her common habit, worn;
So pressing Providence a truth to teach,
Which truth untaught, all other truths were vain.
    Thou! whose all-providential eye surveys,
Whose hand directs, whose spirit fills and warms
Creation, and holds empire far beyond!
Eternity's inhabitant august!
Of two eternities amazing Lord!
One past, ere man's, or angel's had begun;

Aid! while I rescue from the foe's assault
Thy glorious immortality in man:
A theme for ever, and for all, of weight,
Of moment infinite! but relish'd most
By those who love thee most, who most adore.

Nature, thy daughter, ever changing birth
Of thee the Great Immutable, to man
Speaks wisdom; is his oracle supreme;
And he who most consults her, is most wise.
Lorenzo, to this heavenly Delphos haste;
And come back all-immortal; all divine:
Look nature through, 'tis revolution all;
All change; no death. Day follows night; and night
The dying day; stars rise, and set, and rise;
Earth takes th' example. See, the summer gay,
With her green chaplet, and ambrosial flowers,
Droops into pallid autumn: winter gray,
Horrid with frost, and turbulent with storm,
Blows autumn, and his golden fruits away:
Then melts into the spring: soft spring, with breath
Favonian, from warm chambers of the south,
Recalls the first. All, to re-flourish, fades;
As in a wheel, all sinks, to re-ascend.
Emblems of man, who passes, not expires.

With this minute distinction, emblems just,
Nature revolves, but man advances; both
Eternal, that a circle, this a line.
That gravitates, this soars. Th' aspiring soul,
Ardent, and tremulous, like flame, ascends,
Zeal and humility her wings, to heaven.
The world of matter, with its various forms,
All dies into new life. Life born from death
Rolls the vast mass, and shall for ever roll.
No single atom, once in being, lost,

With change of counsel charges the Most High.
  What hence infers Lorenzo? Can it be?
Matter immortal? And shall spirit die?
Above the nobler, shall less noble rise?
Shall man alone, for whom all else revives,
No resurrection know? shall man alone,
Imperial man! be sown in barren ground,
Less privileg'd than grain, on which he feeds?
Is man, in whom alone is power to prize
The bliss of being, or with previous pain
Deplore its period, by the spleen of fate,
Severely doom'd death's single unredeem'd?
  If nature's revolution speaks aloud,
In her gradation, hear her louder still.
Look nature thro', 'tis neat gradation all.
By what minute degrees her scale ascends!
Each middle nature join'd at each extreme,
To that above it join'd, to that beneath.
Parts, into parts reciprocally shot,
Abhor divorce: what love of union reigns!
Here, dormant matter waits a call to life;
Half-life, half-death, join there; here, life and sense;
There, sense from reason steals a glimm'ring ray;
Reason shines out in man. But how preserv'd
The chain unbroken upward, to the realms
Of incorporeal life? those realms of bliss,
Where death hath no dominion? Grant a make
Half-mortal, half-immortal; earthy, part,
And part ethereal; grant the soul of man
Eternal; or in man the series ends.
Wide yawns the gap; connexion is no more;
Check'd reason halts; her next step wants support;
Striving to climb, she tumbles from her scheme;
A scheme, analogy pronounc'd so true;

Analogy, man's surest guide below.
  Thus far, all nature calls on thy belief.
And will Lorenzo, careless of the call,
False attestation on all nature charge,
Rather than violate his league with death?
Renounce his reason, rather than renounce
The dust belov'd, and run the risk of heaven?
O what indignity to deathless souls!
What treason to the majesty of man!
Of man immortal! Hear the lofty style:
" If so decreed, th' Almighty will be done.
Let earth dissolve, yon pond'rous orbs descend,
And grind us into dust. The soul is safe;
The man emerges; mounts above the wreck,
As tow'ring flame from nature's funeral pyre;
O'er devastation, as a gainer, smiles;
His charter, his inviolable rights,
Well pleas'd to learn from thunder's impotence,
Death's pointless darts, and hell's defeated storms."
  But these chimeras touch not thee, Lorenzo!
The glories of the world thy sevenfold shield.
Other ambition than of crowns in air,
And superlunary felicities,
Thy bosom warm. I'll cool it, if I can;
And turn those glories that enchant, against thee.
What ties thee to this life, proclaims the next.
If wise, the cause that wounds thee is thy cure.
  Come, my ambitious! let us mount together
(To mount, Lorenzo never can refuse);
And from the clouds, where pride delights to dwell,
Look down on earth.—What seest thou? Wondrous
        things!
Terrestrial wonders, that eclipse the skies.
What lengths of labour'd lands! what loaded seas!

Loaded by man, for pleasure, wealth, or war!
Seas, winds, and planets, into service brought,
His art acknowledge, and promote his ends.
Nor can th' eternal rocks his will withstand;
What levell'd mountains! and what lifted vales!
O'er vales and mountains sumptuous cities swell,
And gild our landscape with their glitt'ring spires.
Some mid the wond'ring waves majestic rise;
And Neptune holds a mirror to their charms.
Far greater still! (what cannot mortal might?)
See, wide dominions ravish'd from the deep!
The narrow deep with indignation foams.
Or southward turn; to delicate and grand,
The finer arts there ripen in the sun.
How the tall temples, as to meet their gods,
Ascend the skies! the proud triumphal arch
Shows us half heaven beneath its ample bend.
High thro' mid-air, here, streams are taught to flow;
Whole rivers, there, laid by in basins, sleep.
Here, plains turn oceans; there, vast oceans join
Thro' kingdoms channel'd deep from shore to shore;
And chang'd creation takes its face from man.
Beats thy brave breast for formidable scenes,
Where fame and empire wait upon the sword?
See fields in blood; hear naval thunders rise;
Britannia's voice! that awes the world to peace.
How yon enormous mole projecting breaks
The mid-sea, furious waves! their roar amidst,
Out-speaks the Deity, and says, "O main!
Thus far, nor farther; new restraints obey."
Earth's disembowel'd! measur'd are the skies!
Stars are detected in their deep recess!
Creation widens! vanquish'd nature yields!
Her secrets are extorted! art prevails!

What monument of genius, spirit, power!
And now, Lorenzo! raptur'd at this scene,
Whose glories render heaven superfluous! say,
Whose footsteps these?—Immortals have been here.
Could less than souls immortal this have done?
Earth's cover'd o'er with proofs of souls immortal;
And proofs of immortality forgot.
To flatter thy grand foible, I confess,
These are ambition's works: and these are great:
But this, the least immortal souls can do;
Transcend them all—but what can these transcend?
Dost ask me what?—One sigh for the distrest.
What then for infidels? A deeper sigh.
'Tis moral grandeur makes the mighty man:
How little they, who think aught great below?
All our ambitions death defeats, but one;
And that it crowns.—Here cease we: but, ere long,
More powerful proof shall take the field against thee,
Stronger than death, and smiling at the tomb.

NIGHT VII.

BEING THE SECOND PART OF THE INFIDEL RECLAIMED

CONTAINING THE NATURE, PROOF, AND IMPORTANCE OF IMMORTALITY.

PREFACE.

As we are at war with the power, it were well if we were
at war with the manners, of France. A land of levity is a
land of guilt. A serious mind is the native soil of every
virtue; and the single character that does true honour to

mankind. The soul's immortality has been the favourite theme with the serious of all ages. Nor is it strange; it is a subject by far the most interesting, and important, that can enter the mind of man. Of highest moment this subject always was, and always will be. Yet this its highest moment seems to admit of increase, at this day ; a sort of occasional importance is superadded to the natural weight of it; if that opinion which is advanced in the preface to the preceding night, be just. It is there supposed, that all our infidels, whatever scheme, for argument's sake, and to keep themselves in countenance, they patronize, are betrayed into their deplorable error, by some doubts of their immortality, at the bottom. And the more I consider this point, the more I am persuaded of the truth of that opinion. Though the distrust of a futurity is a strange error; yet it is an error into which bad men may naturally be distressed. For it is impossible to bid defiance to final ruin, without some refuge in imagination, some presumption of escape. And what presumption is there ? There are but two in nature; but two, within the compass of human thought. And these are,—That either God will not or can not punish. Considering the divine attributes, the first is too gross to be digested by our strongest wishes. And since omnipotence is as much a divine attribute as holiness, that God cannot punish, is as absurd a supposition as the former. God certainly can punish as long as wicked men exist. In non-existence, therefore, is their only refuge; and consequently, non-existence is their strongest wish. And strong wishes have a strange influence on our opinions ; they bias the judgment in a manner almost incredible. And since on this member of their alternative, there are some very small appearances in their favour, and none at all on the other, they catch at this reed, they lay hold on this chimera, to save themselves from the shock and horror of an immediate and absolute despair.

On reviewing my subject, by the light which this argument, and others of like tendency, threw upon it, I was more inclined than ever to pursue it, as it appeared to me to strike directly at the main root of all our infidelity. In the following pages it is, accordingly, pursued at large ; and some arguments for immortality, new at least to me.

are ventured on in them. There also the writer has made an attempt to set the gross absurdities and horrors of annihilation in a fuller and more affecting view, than is (I think) to be met with elsewhere.

The gentlemen, for whose sake this attempt was chiefly made, profess great admiration for the wisdom of heathen antiquity: what pity 'tis they are not sincere! If they were sincere, how would it mortify them to consider, with what contempt, and abhorrence, their notions would have been received by those whom they so much admire? What degree of contempt and abhorrence would fall to their share, may be conjectured by the following matter of fact (in my opinion) extremely memorable. Of all their heathen worthies, Socrates, (it is well known) was the most guarded, dispassionate, and composed: yet this great master of temper was angry; and angry at his last hour; and angry with his friend; and angry for what deserved acknowledgment; angry for a right and tender instance of true friendship towards him. Is not this surprising? What could be the cause? The cause was for his honour; it was a truly noble, though, perhaps, a too punctilious regard, for immortality: for his friend asking him, with such an affectionate concern as became a friend, " Where he should deposit his remains?" It was resented by Socrates, as implying a dishonourable supposition, that he could be so mean, as to have a regard for any thing, even in himself, that was not immortal.

This fact well considered, would make our infidels withdraw their admiration from Socrates; or make them endeavour, by their imitation of this illustrious example, to share his glory: and, consequently, it would incline them to peruse the following pages with candour and impartiality: which is all I desire; and that, for their sakes: for I am persuaded, that an unprejudiced infidel must, necessarily, receive some advantageous impressions from them.

July 7, 1744.

HEAVEN gives the needful, but neglected, call.
What day, what hour, but knocks at human hearts,
To wake the soul to sense of future scenes?
Deaths stand, like Mercuries, in ev'ry way,
And kindly point us to our journey's end.
Pope, who couldst make immortals! art thou dead?
I give thee joy: nor will I take my leave;
So soon to follow.   Man but dives in death;
Dives from the sun, in fairer day to rise;
The grave, his subterranean road to bliss.
Yes, infinite indulgence plann'd it so;
Thro' various parts our glorious story runs;
Time gives the preface, endless age unrolls
The volume (ne'er unroll'd!) of human fate.

This earth and skies[1] already have proclaim'd.
The world's a prophecy of worlds to come;
And who, what God foretels (who speaks in things,
Still louder than in words) shall dare deny?
If nature's arguments appear too weak,
Turn a new leaf, and stronger read in man.
If man sleeps on, untaught by what he sees,
Can he prove infidel to what he feels?
He, whose blind thought futurity denies,
Unconscious bears, Bellerophon! like thee,
His own indictment; he condemns himself;
Who reads his bosom, reads immortal life;
Or, nature, there, imposing on her sons,
Has written fables; man was made a lie.

Why discontent for ever harbour'd there?
Incurable consumption of our peace!
Resolve me, why, the cottager, and king,

_____
[1] Night VI.

He, whom sea-sever'd realms obey, and he
Who steals his whole dominion from the waste,
Repelling winter blasts with mud and straw,
Disquieted alike, draw sigh for sigh,
In fate so distant, in complaint so near?

 Is it, that things terrestrial can't content?
Deep in rich pasture will thy flocks complain?
Not so; but to their master is denied
To share their sweet serene. Man, ill at ease
In this, not his own place, this foreign field,
Where nature fodders him with other food,
Than was ordain'd his cravings to suffice,
Poor in abundance, famish'd at a feast,
Sighs on for something more, when most enjoy'd.

 Is heaven then kinder to thy flocks than thee?
Not so; thy pasture richer, but remote;
In part remote; for that remoter part
Man bleats from instinct, tho' perhaps, debauch'd
By sense, his reason sleeps, nor dreams the cause.
The cause how obvious, when his reason wakes!
His grief is but his grandeur in disguise;
And discontent is immortality.

 Shall sons of ether, shall the blood of heaven,
Set up their hopes on earth, and stable here,
With brutal acquiescence in the mire?
Lorenzo! no! they shall be nobly pain'd;
The glorious foreigners, distrest, shall sigh
On thrones; and thou congratulate the sigh:
Man's misery declares him born for bliss;
His anxious heart asserts the truth I sing,
And gives the sceptic in his head the lie. [ers,
 Our heads, our hearts, our passions, and our pow-
Speak the same language; call us to the skies:
Unripen'd these in this inclement clime,

Scarce rise above conjecture, and mistake;
And for this land of trifles those too strong
Tumultuous rise, and tempest human life:
What prize on earth can pay us for the storm?
Meet objects for our passions heaven ordain'd,
Objects that challenge all their fire, and leave
No fault, but in defect: blest Heaven! avert
A bounded ardour for unbounded bliss!
O for a bliss unbounded! far beneath
A soul immortal, is a mortal joy.
Nor are our powers to perish immature;
But, after feeble effort here, beneath
A brighter sun, and in a nobler soil,
Transplanted from this sublunary bed,
Shall flourish fair, and put forth all their bloom.
    Reason progressive, instinct is complete;
Swift instinct leaps; slow reason feebly climbs.
Brutes soon their zenith reach; their little all
Flows in at once; in ages they no more
Could know, or do, or covet, or enjoy.
Were man to live coeval with the sun,
The patriarch-pupil would be learning still;
Yet, dying, leave his lesson half unlearnt.
Men perish in advance, as if the sun
Should set ere noon, in eastern oceans drown'd;
If fit, with dim, illustrious to compare,
The sun's meridian with the soul of man.
To man, why, stepdame nature! so severe?
Why thrown aside thy master-piece half-wrought,
While meaner efforts thy last hand enjoy?
Or, if abortively, poor man must die,
Nor reach, what reach he might, why die in dread?
Why curst with foresight? wise to misery?
Why of his proud prerogative the prey?.

Why less pre-eminent in rank, than pain?
His immortality alone can tell;
Full ample fund to balance all amiss,
And turn the scale in favour of the just!
   His immortality alone can solve
The darkest of enigmas, human hope;
Of all the darkest, if at death we die.
Hope, eager hope, th' assassin of our joy,
All present blessings treading under foot,
Is scarce a milder tyrant than despair.
With no past toils content, still planting new,
Hope turns us o'er to death alone for ease.
Possession, why more tasteless than pursuit?
Why is a wish far dearer than a crown?
That wish accomplish'd, why, the grave of bliss?
Because, in the great future buried deep,
Beyond our plans of empire, and renown,
Lies all that man with ardour should pursue;
And he who made him, bent him to the right.
   Man's heart th' Almighty to the future sets,
By secret and inviolable springs;
And makes his hope his sublunary joy.
Man's heart eats all things, and is hungry still;
" More, more!" the glutton cries: for something
So rages appetite, if man can't mount,   [new
He will descend.   He starves on the possest.
Hence, the world's master, from ambition's spire,
In Caprea plung'd; and div'd beneath the brute
In that rank sty why wallow'd empire's son
Supreme? because he could no higher fly;
His riot was ambition in despair.
   Old Rome consulted birds; Lorenzo! thou
With more success, the flight of hope survey;
Of restless hope, for ever on the wing.

High-perch'd o'er ev'ry thought that falcon sits,
To fly at all that rises in her sight;
And never stooping, but to mount again
Next moment, she betrays her aim's mistake,
And owns her quarry lodg'd beyond the grave.

 There should it fail us (it must fail us there,
If being fails) more mournful riddles rise,
And virtue vies with hope in mystery.
Why virtue? where its praise, its being, fled?
Virtue is true self-interest pursu'd:
What true self-interest of quite-mortal man?
To close with all that makes him happy here.
If vice (as sometimes) is our friend on earth,
Then vice is virtue; 'tis our sov'reign good.
In self-applause is virtue's golden prize;
No self-applause attends it on thy scheme:
Whence self-applause? from conscience of the
   right.
And what is right, but means of happiness?
No means of happiness when virtue yields;
That basis failing, falls the building too,
And lays in ruin ev'ry virtuous joy.

 The rigid guardian of a blameless heart,
So long rever'd, so long reputed wise,
Is weak; with rank knight-errantries o'errun.
Why beats thy bosom with illustrious dreams
Of self-exposure, laudable, and great?
Of gallant enterprise, and glorious death?
Die for thy country!—Thou romantic fool!
Seize, seize the plank thyself, and let her sink:
Thy country! what to thee?—The Godhead, what?
(I speak with awe!) tho' he should bid thee bleed?
If, with thy blood, thy final hope is spilt,
Nor can Omnipotence reward the blow,

Be deaf; preserve thy being; disobey.
　Nor is it disobedience: know, Lorenzo!
Whate'er th' Almighty's subsequent command
His first command is this:—" Man, love thyself."
In this alone, free-agents are not free.
Existence is the basis, bliss the prize;
If virtue costs existence, 'tis a crime;
Bold violation of our law supreme,
Black suicide; tho' nations, which consult
Their gain, at thy expense, resound applause.
　Since virtue's recompense is doubtful, here,
If man dies wholly, well may we demand,
Why is man suffer'd to be good in vain?
Why to be good in vain, is man enjoin'd?
Why to be good in vain, is man betray'd?
Betray'd by traitors lodg'd in his own breast,
By sweet complacencies from virtue felt?
Why whispers nature lies on virtue's part?
Or if blind instinct (which assumes the name
Of sacred conscience) plays the fool in man,
Why reason made accomplice in the cheat?
Why are the wisest loudest in her praise?
Can man by reason's beam be led astray?
Or, at his peril, imitate his God?
Since virtue sometimes ruins us on earth,
Or both are true; or, man survives the grave.
　Or man survives the grave, or own, Lorenzo,
Thy boast supreme, a wild absurdity.
Dauntless thy spirit; cowards are thy scorn.
Grant man immortal, and thy scorn is just.
The man immortal, rationally brave,
Dares rush on death—because he cannot die.
But if man loses all, when life is lost,
He lives a coward, or a fool expires.

A daring infidel (and such there are,
From pride, example, lucre, rage, revenge,
Or pure heroical defect of thought),
Of all earth's madmen, most deserves a chain.
   When to the grave we follow the renown'd
For valour, virtue, science, all we love,
And all we praise; for worth, whose noon-tide beam,
Enabling us to think in higher style,
Mends our ideas of ethereal powers;
Dream we, that lustre of the moral world
Goes out in stench, and rottenness the close?
Why was he wise to know, and warm to praise,
And strenuous to transcribe, in human life,
The mind Almighty? Could it be, that fate,
Just when the lineaments began to shine,
And dawn the Deity, should snatch the draught,
With night eternal blot it out, and give
The skies alarm, lest angels too might die?
   If human souls, why not angelic too
Extinguish'd? and a solitary God,
O'er ghastly ruin, frowning from his throne?
Shall we this moment gaze on God in man?
The next, lose man for ever in the dust?
From dust we disengage, or man mistakes;
And there, where least his judgment fears a flaw.
Wisdom and worth, how boldly he commends!
Wisdom and worth, are sacred names; rever'd,
Where not embrac'd; applauded! deified!
Why not compassion'd too? If spirits die,
Both are calamities, inflicted both,
To make us but more wretched: Wisdom's eye
Acute, for what? to spy more miseries;
And worth, so recompens'd, new points their stings
Or man surmounts the grave, or gain is loss,

And worth exalted humbles us the more.
Thou wilt not patronize a scheme that makes
Weakness, and vice, the refuge of mankind.
    " Has virtue, then, no joys ?"—Yes, joys dear-
        bought.
Talk ne'er so long, in this imperfect state,
Virtue and vice are at eternal war,
Virtue's a combat; and who fights for nought ?
Or for precarious, or for small reward ?
Who virtue's self-reward so loud resound,
Would take degrees angelic·here below,
And virtue, while they compliment, betray,
By feeble motives, and unfaithful guards.
The crown, th' unfading crown, her soul inspires :
'Tis that, and that alone, can countervail
The body's treacheries, and the world's assaults :
On earth's poor pay our famisht virtue dies.
Truth incontestable ! in spite of all
A Bayle has preach'd, or a Voltaire believ'd.

    In man the more we dive, the more we see
Heaven's signet stamping an immortal make.
Dive to the bottom of his soul, the base
Sustaining all ; what find we ? knowledge, love.
As light and heat, essential to the sun,
These to the soul.   And why, if souls expire ?
How little lovely here ? how little known ?
Small knowledge we dig up with endless toil ;
And love unfeign'd may purchase perfect hate.
Why starv'd, on earth, our angel appetites ;
While brutal are indulg'd their fulsome fill ?
Were then capacities divine conferr'd,
As a mock-diadem, in savage sport,
Rank insult of our pompous poverty,
Which reaps but pain, from seeming claims so fair ?

In future age lies no redress? And shuts
Eternity the door on our complaint?
If so, for what strange ends were mortals made!
The worst to wallow, and the best to weep;
The man who merits most, must most complain:
Can we conceive a disregard in heaven,
What the worst perpetrate, or best endure?

　　This cannot be.　To love, and know, in man
Is boundless appetite, and boundless power;
And these demonstrate boundless objects too.
Objects, powers, appetites, heaven suits in all;
Nor, nature thro', e'er violates this sweet,
Eternal concord, on her tuneful string.
Is man the sole exception from her laws?
Eternity struck off from human hope,
(I speak with truth, but veneration too)
Man is a monster, the reproach of heaven,
A stain, a dark impenetrable cloud
On nature's beauteous aspect; and deforms,
(Amazing blot!) deforms her with her lord.
If such is man's allotment, what is heaven?
Or own the soul immortal, or blaspheme.

　　Or own the soul immortal, or invert
All order.　Go, mock-majesty! go, man!
And bow to thy superiors of the stall;
Thro' every scene of sense superior far:
They graze the turf untill'd; they drink the stream
Unbrew'd, and ever full, and unembitter'd
With doubts, fears, fruitless hopes, regrets, des-
　　　　pairs;
Mankind's peculiar! reason's precious dower!
No foreign clime they ransack for their robes;
Nor brothers cite to the litigious bar;
Their good is good entire, unmixt, unmarr'd;

They find a paradise in every field,
On boughs forbidden where no curses hang:
Their ill no more than strikes the sense; unstretcht
By previous dread, or murmur in the rear:
When the worst comes, it comes unfear'd; one
   stroke
 egins, and ends, their woe: they die but once;
Blest, incommunicable privilege! for which
Proud man, who rules the globe, and reads the stars,
Philosopher, or hero, sighs in vain.
 Account for this prerogative in brutes.
No day, no glimpse of day to solve the knot,
But what beams on it from eternity.
O sole, and sweet solution! that unties
The difficult, and softens the severe;
The cloud on nature's beauteous face dispels;
Restores bright order; casts the brute beneath;
And re-inthrones us in supremacy
Of joy, ev'n here: admit immortal life,
And virtue is knight-errantry no more;
Each virtue brings in hand a golden dower,
Far richer in reversion: hope exults;
And tho' much bitter in our cup is thrown,
Predominates, and gives the taste of heaven.
O wherefore is the Deity so kind?
Astonishing beyond astonishment!
Heaven our reward—for heaven enjoy'd below.
 Still unsubdu'd thy stubborn heart?—For there
The traitor lurks who doubts the truth I sing.
Reason is guiltless; will alone rebels.
What, in that stubborn heart, if I should find
New, unexpected witnesses against thee?
Ambition, pleasure, and the love of gain!
Canst thou suspect, that these, which make the soul

The slave of earth, should own her heir of heaven?
Canst thou suspect what makes us disbelieve
Our immortality, should prove it sure?

First, then, ambition, summon to the bar.
Ambition's shame, extravagance, disgust,
And inextinguishable nature, speak.
Each much deposes; hear them in their turn.

Thy soul, how passionately fond of fame!
How anxious, that fond passion to conceal!
We blush, detected in designs on praise,
Tho' for best deeds, and from the best of men:
And why? Because immortal.   Art divine
Has made the body tutor to the soul;
Heaven kindly gives our blood a moral flow;
Bids it ascend the glowing cheek, and there
Upbraid that little heart's inglorious aim,
Which stoops to court a character from man;
While o'er us, in tremendous judgment sit
Far more than man, with endless praise, and blame.

Ambition's boundless appetite outspeaks
The verdict of its shame.   When souls take fire
At high presumptions of their own desert,
One age is poor applause; the mighty shout,
The thunder by the living few begun,
Late time must echo; worlds unborn, resound.
We wish our names eternally to live: [thought.
Wild dream, which ne'er had haunted human
Had not our natures been eternal too.
Instinct points out an int'rest in hereafter;
But our blind reason sees not where it lies;
Or, seeing, gives the substance for the shade.

Fame is the shade of immortality,
And in itself a shadow.   Soon as caught,
Contemn'd · it shrinks to nothing in the grasp.

Consult th' ambitious, 'tis ambition's cure.
" And is this all ?" cried Cæsar at his height,
Disgusted. This third proof ambition brings
Of immortality. The first in fame,
Observe him near, your envy will abate:
Sham'd at the disproportion vast, between
The passion and the purchase, he will sigh
At such success, and blush at his renown.
And why ? Because far richer prize invites
His heart ; far more illustrious glory calls ;
It calls in whispers, yet the deafest hear.
    And can ambition a fourth proof supply ?
It can, and stronger than the former three ;
Yet quite o'erlook'd by some reputed wise.
Tho' disappointments in ambition pain,
And tho' success disgusts ; yet still, Lorenzo !
In vain we strive to pluck it from our hearts ;
By nature planted for the noblest ends.
Absurd the fam'd advice to Pyrrhus given,
More prais'd, than ponder'd ; specious, but unsound ;
Sooner that hero's sword the world had quell'd,
Than reason, his ambition. Man must soar.
An obstinate activity within,
An insuppressive spring, will toss him up
In spite of fortune's load. Not kings alone,
Each villager has his ambition too ;
No sultan prouder than his fetter'd slave :
Slaves build their little Babylons of straw,
Echo the proud Assyrian, in their hearts,
And cry,—" Behold the wonders of my might !"
And why ? because immortal as their lord ;
And souls immortal must for ever heave
At something great ; the glitter, or the gold ;
The praise of mortals, or the praise of heaven.

Nor absolutely vain is human praise,
When human is supported by divine.
I'll introduce Lorenzo to himself;
Pleasure and pride (bad masters!) share our hearts.
As love of pleasure is ordain'd to guard
And feed our bodies, and extend our race ;
The love of praise is planted to protect,
And propagate the glories of the mind.
What is it, but the love of praise, inspires,
Matures, refines, embellishes, exalts,
Earth's happiness ? From that, the delicate,
The grand, the marvellous, of civil life,
Want and convenience, under-workers, lay
The basis, on which love of glory builds.
Nor is thy life, O virtue ! less in debt
To praise, thy secret stimulating friend.
Were men not proud, what merit should we miss!
Pride made the virtues of the pagan world.
Praise is the salt that seasons right to man,
And whets his appetite for moral good.
Thirst of applause is virtue's second guard ;
Reason, her first ; but reason wants an aid ;
Our private reason is a flatterer ;
Thirst of applause calls public judgment in,
To poise our own, to keep an even scale,
And give endanger'd virtue fairer play.
　　Here a fifth proof arises, stronger still :
Why this so nice construction of our hearts?
These delicate moralities of sense ;
This constitutional reserve of aid
To succour virtue, when our reason fails ;
If virtue, kept alive by care and toil,
And oft, the mark of injuries on earth,
When labour'd to maturity (its bill

Of disciplines, and pains, unpaid) must die ?
Why freighted-rich, to dash against a rock ?
Were man to perish when most fit to live,
O how misspent were all these stratagems,
By skill divine inwoven in our frame !
Where are heaven's holiness and mercy fled ?
Laughs heaven, at once, at virtue, and at man ?
If not, why that discourag'd, this destroy'd ?

    Thus far ambition. What says avarice ?
This her chief maxim, which has long been thine:
" The wise and wealthy are the same,"—I grant it.
To store up treasure, with incessant toil,
This is man's province, this his highest praise.
To this great end keen instinct stings him on.
To guide that instinct, reason ! is thy charge ;
'Tis thine to tell us where true treasure lies :
But, reason failing to discharge her trust,
Or to the deaf discharging it in vain,
A blunder follows ; and blind industry,
Gall'd by the spur, but stranger to the course,
(The course where stakes of more than gold are won)
O'er-loading, with the cares of distant age,
The jaded spirits of the present hour,
Provides for an eternity below.

    " Thou shalt not covet," is a wise command ;
But bounded to the wealth the sun surveys :
Look farther, the command stands quite revers'd,
And av'rice is a virtue most divine.
Is faith a refuge for our happiness ?
Most sure : and is it not for reason too ?
Nothing this world unriddles, but the next.
Whence inextinguishable thirst of gain ?
From inextinguishable life in man :
Man, if not meant, by worth, to reach the skies,

Had wanted wing to fly so far in guilt.
Sour grapes, I grant, ambition, avarice,
Yet still their root is immortality .
These its wild growths so bitter, and so base,
(Pain and reproach !) religion can reclaim,
Refine, exalt, throw down their pois'nous lee,
And make them sparkle in the bowl of bliss.

    See, the third witness laughs at bliss remote,
And falsely promises an Eden here :
Truth she shall speak for once, tho' prone to lie,
A common cheat, and pleasure is her name.
To pleasure never was Lorenzo deaf;
Then hear her now, now first thy real friend.

    Since nature made us not more fond than proud
Of happiness (whence hypocrites in joy !
Makers of mirth ! artificers of smiles !)
Why should the joy most poignant sense affords,
Burn us with blushes, and rebuke our pride?—
Those heaven-born blushes tell us man descends.
Ev'n in the zenith of his earthly bliss :
Should reason take her infidel repose,
This honest instinct speaks our lineage high ;
This instinct calls on darkness to conceal
Our rapturous relation to the stalls.
Our glory covers us with noble shame,
And he that's unconfounded, is unmann'd.
The man that blushes, is not quite a brute.
Thus far with thee, Lorenzo ! will I close,
Pleasure is good, and man for pleasure made ;
But pleasure full of glory, as of joy ;
Pleasure which neither blushes, nor expires.

    The witnesses are heard ; the cause is o'er ;
Let conscience file the sentence in her court,
Dearer than deeds that half a realm convey ;

Thus seal'd by truth, th' authentic record runs.

　" Know all; know, infidels,—unapt to know!
'Tis immortality your nature solves;
'Tis immortality deciphers man,
And opens all the myst'ries of his make.
Without it, half his instincts are a riddle;
Without it, all his virtues are a dream.
His very crimes attest his dignity;
His sateless thirst of pleasure, gold, and fame,
Declares him born for blessings infinite:
What less than infinite makes unabsurd
Passions, which all on earth but more inflames?
Fierce passions, so mismeasur'd to this scene,
Stretch'd out, like eagles' wings, beyond our nest,
Far, far beyond the worth of all below,
For earth too large, presage a nobler flight,
And evidence our title to the skies."

　Ye gentle theologues, of calmer kind!
Whose constitution dictates to your pen,
Who, cold yourselves, think ardour comes from hell!
Think not our passions from corruption sprung,
Tho' to corruption now they lend their wings;
That is their mistress, not their mother.　All
(And justly) reason deem divine: I see,
I feel a grandeur in the passions too,
Which speaks their high descent, and glorious end;
Which speaks them rays of an eternal fire.
In Paradise itself they burnt as strong,
Ere Adam fell; tho' wiser in their aim.
Like the proud eastern, struck by providence,
What tho' our passions are run mad, and stoop
With low, terrestrial appetite, to graze
On trash, on toys, dethron'd from high desire?
Yet still, thro' their disgrace, no feeble ray

Of greatness shines, and tells us whence they fell:
But these (like that fall'n monarch when reclaim'd),
When reason moderates the rein aright,
Shall reascend, remount their former sphere,
Where once they soar'd illustrious; ere seduc'd
By wanton Eve's debauch, to stroll on earth,
And set the sublunary world on fire.

But grant their frenzy lasts; their frenzy fails
To disappoint one providential end,
For which heaven blew up ardour in our hearts:
Were reason silent, boundless passion speaks
A future scene of boundless objects too,
And brings glad tidings of eternal day.
Eternal day! 'tis that enlightens all;
And all, by that enlighten'd, proves it sure.
Consider man as an immortal being,
Intelligible all; and all is great;
A crystalline transparency prevails,
And strikes full lustre thro' the human sphere:
Consider man as mortal, all is dark,
And wretched; reason weeps at the survey.

The learn'd Lorenzo cries, " And let her weep,
Weak, modern reason: ancient times were wise.
Authority, that venerable guide,
Stands on my part; the fam'd Athenian porch
(And who for wisdom so renown'd as they?)
Denied this immortality to man."
I grant it; but affirm, they prov'd it too.
A riddle this!—Have patience; I'll explain.

What noble vanities, what moral flights,
Glitt'ring thro' their romantic wisdom's page,
Make us, at once, despise them, and admire?
Fable is flat to these high season'd sires;
They leave th' extravagance of song below.

" Flesh shall not feel ; or, feeling, shall enjoy
The dagger, or the rack ; to them, alike
A bed of roses, or the burning bull."
In men exploding all beyond the grave,
Strange doctrine, this ! As doctrine, it was strange ;
But not as prophecy ; for such it prov'd,
And, to their own amazement, was fulfill'd :
They feign'd a firmness christians need not feign.
The christian truly triumph'd in the flame :
The stoic saw, in double wonder lost,
Wonder at them, and wonder at himself,
To find the bold adventures of his thought
Not bold, and that he strove to lie in vain.

   Whence, then, those thoughts ? those tow'ring
         thoughts, that flew
Such monstrous heights ?—From instinct and from
The glorious instinct of a deathless soul,   [pride.
Confus'dly conscious of her dignity,
Suggested truths they could not understand.
In lust's dominion, and in passion's storm,
Truth's system broken, scatter'd fragments lay,
As light in chaos, glimm'ring thro' the gloom :
Smit with the pomp of lofty sentiments,
Pleas'd pride proclaim'd, what reason disbeliev'd.
Pride, like the Delphic priestess, with a swell,
Rav'd nonsense, destin'd to be future sense,
When life immortal, in full day, shall shine ;
And death's dark shadows fly the gospel sun.
They spoke, what nothing but immortal souls
Could speak ; and thus the truth they question'd
         prov'd.

   Can then absurdities, as well as crimes,
Speak man immortal ? All things speak him so.
Much has been urg'd ; and dost thou call for more ?

Call; and with endless questions be distrest,
All unresolvable, if earth is all.

    " Why life, a moment; infinite, desire?
Our wish, eternity? Our home, the grave?
Heaven's promise dormant lies in human hope;
Who wishes life immortal, proves it too.
Why happiness pursued, tho' never found?
Man's thirst of happiness declares it is,
(For nature never gravitates to nought);
That thirst unquencht declares it is not here.
My Lucia, thy Clarissa, call to thought;
Why cordial friendship riveted so deep,
As hearts to pierce at first, at parting, rend,
If friend, and friendship, vanish in an hour?
Is not this torment in the mask of joy?
Why by reflection marr'd the joys of sense?
Why past, and future, preying on our hearts,
And putting all our present joys to death?
Why labours reason? instinct were as well;
Instinct far better; what can choose, can err:
O how infallible the thoughtless brute!
'Twere well his holiness were half as sure.
Reason with inclination, why at war?
Why sense of guilt? why conscience up in arms?"

    Conscience of guilt, is prophecy of pain,
And bosom-council to decline the blow.
Reason with inclination ne'er had jarr'd,
If nothing future paid forbearance here:
Thus on—these, and a thousand pleas uncall'd,
All promise, some ensure, a second scene;
Which, were it doubtful, would be dearer far
Than all things else most certain: were it false,
What truth on earth so precious as the lie?
This world it gives us let what will ensue;

This world it gives in that high cordial, hope :
The future of the present is the soul :
How this life groans, when sever'd from the next !
Poor mutilated wretch, that disbelieves !
By dark distrust his being cut in two,
In both parts perishes ; life void of joy,
Sad prelude of eternity in pain !
    Couldst thou persuade me, the next life could fail
Our ardent wishes ; how should I pour out
My bleeding heart in anguish, new, as deep !
Oh ! with what thoughts, thy hope, and my despair,
Abhorr'd annihilation ! blasts the soul,
And wide extends the bounds of human woe !
Could I believe Lorenzo's system true,
In this black channel would my ravings run.
" Grief from the future borrow'd peace, ere while.
The future vanisht ! and the present pain'd !
Strange import of unprecedented ill !
Fall, how profound ! like Lucifer's, the fall !
Unequal fate ! his fall, without his guilt !
From where fond hope built her pavilion high,
The gods among, hurl'd headlong, hurl'd at once
To night ! to nothing ! darker still than night.
If 'twas a dream, why wake me, my worst foe,
Lorenzo ! boastful of the name of friend !
O for delusion ! O for error still !
Could vengeance strike much stronger than to plant
A thinking being in a world like this,
Not over rich before, now beggar'd quite ;
More curst than at the fall ?—The sun goes out !
The thorns shoot up ! What thorns in ev'ry thought !
Why sense of better ? It imbitters worse.
Why sense ? why life ? If but to sigh, then sink
To what I was ! twice nothing ! and much woe !

Woe, from heaven's bounties! woe from what was
To flatter most, high intellectual pow'rs.   [wont
Thought, virtue, knowledge! blessings, by thy
   scheme,
All poison'd into pains.   First, knowledge, once
My soul's ambition, now her greatest dread.
To know myself, true wisdom?—No, to shun
That shocking science, parent of despair!
Avert thy mirror: if I see, I die.
 " Know my Creator! climb his blest abode
By painful speculation, pierce the veil,
Dive in his nature, read his attributes,
And gaze in admiration—on a foe,
Obtruding life, withholding happiness!
From the full rivers that surround his throne,
Not letting fall one drop of joy on man ;
Man gasping for one drop, that he might cease
To curse his birth, nor envy reptiles more!
Ye sable clouds! ye darkest shades of night!
Hide him, for ever hide him, from my thought,
Once all my comfort; source, and soul of joy!
Now leagu'd with furies, and with thee,[1] against me.
 " Know his achievements? study his renown?
Contemplate this amazing universe,
Dropt from his hand, with miracles replete!
For what?   Mid miracles of nobler name,
To find one miracle of misery?
To find the being, which alone can know
And praise his works, a blemish on his praise?
Thro' nature's ample range, in thought, to stroll,
And start at man, the single mourner there,
Breathing high hope! chain'd down to pangs, and
   death?

    [1] Lorenzo.

Knowing is suff'ring : and shall virtue share
The sigh of knowledge ?—Virtue shares the sigh.
By straining up the steep of excellent,
By battles fought, and, from temptation, won,
What gains she, but the pang of seeing worth,
Angelic worth, soon shuffled in the dark
With ev'ry vice, and swept to brutal dust ?
Merit is madness ; virtue is a crime ;
A crime to reason, if it costs us pain
Unpaid : what pain, amidst a thousand more,
To think the most abandon'd, after days
Of triumph o'er their betters, find in death
As soft a pillow, nor make fouler clay !
　　" Duty ! religion !——These, our duty done,
Imply reward.　Religion is mistake.
Duty !—There's none, but to repel the cheat.
Ye cheats ! away ! ye daughters of my pride !
Who feign yourselves the fav'rites of the skies :
Ye tow'ring hopes ! abortive energies !
That toss, and struggle, in my lying breast,
To scale the skies, and build presumptions there,
As I were heir of an eternity.
Vain, vain ambitions ! trouble me no more.
Why travel far in quest of sure defeat ?
As bounded as my being, be my wish.
All is inverted, wisdom is a fool.
Sense ! take the rein ; blind passion ! drive us on ;
And, ignorance ! befriend us on our way ;
Ye new, but truest patrons of our peace !
Yes ; give the pulse full empire ; live the brute,
Since, as the brute, we die. The sum of man,
Of Godlike man ! to revel, and to rot.
　　" But not on equal terms with other brutes :
Their revels a more poignant relish yield,

And safer too ; they never poisons choose.
Instinct, than reason, makes more wholesome meals,
And sends all-marring murmur far away.
For sensual life they best philosophize ;
Theirs, that serene, the sages sought in vain :
'Tis man alone expostulates with heaven ;
His, all the power, and all the cause, to mourn.
Shall human eyes alone dissolve in tears ?
And bleed, in anguish, none but human hearts ?
The wide-stretch'd realm of intellectual woe,
Surpassing sensual far, is all our own.
In life so fatally distinguish'd, why
Cast in one lot, confounded, lump'd, in death ?
   " Ere yet in being, was mankind in guilt ?
Why thunder'd this peculiar clause against us,
All-mortal, and all-wretched !—Have the skies
Reasons of state, their subjects may not scan,
Nor humbly reason, when they sorely sigh ?
All-mortal, and all-wretched !—'Tis too much :
Unparallel'd in nature : 'Tis too much
On being unrequested at Thy hands,
Omnipotent ! for I see nought but power.
   " And why see that ? why thought ? To toil, and
       eat,
Then make our bed in darkness, needs no thought.
What superfluities are reas'ning souls !
Oh give eternity ! or thought destroy.
But without thought our curse were half unfelt ;
Its blunted edge would spare the throbbing heart ;
And, therefore, 'tis bestow'd, I thank thee, reason !
For aiding life's too small calamities,
And giving being to the dread of death.
Such are thy bounties !—Was it then too much
For me, to trespass on the brutal rights ?

Too much for heaven to make one emmet more ?
Too much for chaos to permit my mass
A longer stay with essences unwrought,
Unfashion'd, untormented into man ?
Wretched preferment to this round of pains !
Wretched capacity of phrensy, thought !
Wretched capacity of dying, life !
Life, thought, worth, wisdom, all (O foul revolt !)
Once friends to peace, gone over to the foe.

  " Death, then, has chang'd his nature too : O death,
Come to my bosom, thou best gift of heaven !
Best friend of man ! since man is man no more.
Why in this thorny wilderness so long,
Since there's no promis'd land's ambrosial bower,
To pay me with its honey for my stings ?
If needful to the selfish schemes of heaven
To sting us sore, why mock'd our misery ?
Why this so sumptuous insult o'er our heads ?
Why this illustrious canopy display'd ?
Why so magnificently lodg'd despair ?
At stated periods, sure-returning, roll
These glorious orbs, that mortals may compute
Their length of labours, and of pains ; nor lose
Their misery's full measure ?—Smiles with flowers,
And fruits, promiscuous, ever-teeming earth,
That man may languish in luxurious scenes,
And in an Eden mourn his wither'd joys ?
Claim earth and skies man's admiration, due
For such delights ! Blest animals ! too wise
To wonder ; and too happy to complain !

  " Our doom decreed demands a mournful scene :
Why not a dungeon dark, for the condemn'd ?
Why not the dragon's subterranean den,
For man to howl in ? Why not his abode

Of the same dismal colour with his fate ?
A Thebes, a Babylon, at vast expense
Of time, toil, treasure, art, for owls and adders,
As congruous, as, for man, this lofty dome,
Which prompts proud thought, and kindles high de-
If, from her humble chamber in the dust,   [sire;
While proud thought swells, and high desire in-
      flames,
The poor worm calls us for her inmates there ;
And, round us, death's inexorable hand
Draws the dark curtain close ; undrawn no more.
  " Undrawn no more !—Behind the cloud of death,
Once, I beheld a sun ; a sun which gilt
That sable cloud, and turn'd it all to gold :
How the grave's altered ! fathomless as hell !
A real hell to those who dreamt of heaven.
Annihilation ! How it yawns before me !
Next moment I may drop from thought, from sense
The privilege of angels, and of worms,
An outcast from existence ! And this spirit,
This all-pervading, this all-conscious soul,
This particle of energy divine,
Which travels nature, flies from star to star,
And visits gods, and emulates their powers,
For ever is extinguisht, horror ! death !
Death of that death I fearless once survey'd !--
When horror universal shall descend,
And heaven's dark concave urn all human race
On that enormous, unrefunding tomb,
How just this verse ! this monumental sigh !"

    Beneath the lumber of demolisht worlds,
    Deep in the rubbish of the gen'ral wreck,
    Swept ignominious to the common mass

Of matter, never dignified with life,
Here lie proud rationals; the sons of heaven!
The lords of earth! the property of worms!
Beings of yesterday, and no to-morrow!
Who liv'd in terror, and in pangs expir'd!
All gone to rot in chaos; or to make
Their happy transit into blocks or brutes,
Nor longer sully their Creator's name.

Lorenzo! hear, pause, ponder, and pronounce.
Just is this history? If such is man,
Mankind's historian, tho' divine, might weep.
And dares Lorenzo smile!—I know thee proud;
For once let pride befriend thee; pride looks pale
At such a scene, and sighs for something more.
Amid thy boasts, presumptions, and displays,
And art thou then a shadow? less than shade?
A nothing? less than nothing? to have been,
And not to be, is lower than unborn.
Art thou ambitious? Why then make the worm
Thine equal? Runs thy taste of pleasure high?
Why patronize sure death of every joy?
Charm riches? Why choose beggary in the grave,
Of every hope a bankrupt! and for ever?
Ambition, pleasure, avarice, persuade thee
To make that world of glory, rapture, wealth,
They[1] lately prov'd, the soul's supreme desire.

    What art thou made of? rather, how unmade?
Great nature's master-appetite destroy'd!
Is endless life, and happiness, despis'd?
Or both wish't, here, where neither can be found?
Such man's perverse, eternal war with heaven!
Dar'st thou persist? And is there nought on earth,
But a long train of transitory forms,

[1] In the Sixth Night.

Rising, and breaking, millions in an hour?
Bubbles of a fantastic deity, blown up
In sport, and then in cruelty destroy'd?
Oh! for what crime, unmerciful Lorenzo!
Destroys thy scheme the whole of human race?
Kind is fell Lucifer, compar'd to thee:
Oh! spare this waste of being half-divine;
And vindicate th' economy of heaven.

    Heaven is all love; all joy in giving joy:
It never had created but to bless:
And shall it, then, strike off the list of life,
A being blest, or worthy so to be?
Heaven starts at an annihilating God.

    Is that, all nature starts at, thy desire?
Art such a clod to wish thyself all clay?
What is that dreadful wish?—The dying groan
Of nature, murder'd by the blackest guilt.
What deadly poison has thy nature drank?
To nature undebaucht no shock so great;
Nature's first wish is endless happiness;
Annihilation is an after-thought,
A monstrous wish, unborn till virtue dies.
And, oh! what depth of horror lies inclos'd!
For non-existence no man ever wisht,
But, first, he wisht the Deity destroy'd.

    If so; what words are dark enough to draw
Thy picture true? The darkest are too fair.
Beneath what baleful planet, in what hour
Of desperation, by what fury's aid,
In what infernal posture of the soul,
All hell invited, and all hell in joy
At such a birth, a birth so near of kin,
Did thy foul fancy whelp so black a scheme
Of hopes abortive, faculties half-blown,

And deities begun, reduc'd to dust?

 There's nought (thou say'st) but one eternal flux
Of feeble essences, tumultuous driven
Thro' time's rough billows into night's abyss.
Say, in this rapid tide of human ruin,
Is there no rock, on which man's tossing thought
Can rest from terror, dare his fate survey,
And boldly think it something to be born?
Amid such hourly wrecks of being fair,
Is there no central, all-sustaining base,
All-realizing, all-connecting power,
Which, as it call'd forth all things, can recall,
And force destruction to refund her spoil?
Command the grave restore her taken prey?
Bid death's dark vale its human harvest yield,
And earth, and ocean, pay their debt of man,
True to the grand deposit trusted there?
Is there no potentate, whose outstretcht arm,
When rip'ning time calls forth th' appointed hour,
Pluckt from foul devastation's famisht maw,
Binds present, past, and future, to his throne?
His throne, how glorious, thus divinely grac'd,
By germinating beings clust'ring round!
A garland worthy the divinity!
A throne, by heaven's omnipotence in smiles,
Built (like a pharos tow'ring in the waves)
Amidst immense effusions of his love!
An ocean of communicated bliss!
 An all-prolific, all-preserving God!
This were a God indeed.—And such is man,
As here presum'd: he rises from his fall.
Think'st thou Omnipotence a naked root,
Each blossom fair of Deity destroy'd?
Nothing is dead; nay, nothing sleeps; each soul,

That ever animated human clay,
Now wakes; is on the wing: and where, O where
Will the swarm settle?—When the trumpet's call,
As sounding brass, collects us, round heaven's
Conglob'd, we bask in everlasting day,   [throne
(Paternal splendour!) and adhere for ever.
Had not the soul this outlet to the skies,
In this vast vessel of the universe,
How should we gasp, as in an empty void!
How in the pangs of famisht hope expire! [thine!

   How bright my prospect shines! how gloomy,
A trembling world! and a devouring god!
Earth, but the shambles of Omnipotence!
Heaven's face all stain'd with causeless massacres
Of countless millions, born to feel the pang
Of being lost.   Lorenzo! can it be?
This bids us shudder at the thoughts of life.
Who would be born to such a phantom world,
Where nought substantial but our misery?
Where joy (if joy) but heightens our distress,
So soon to perish, and revive no more?
The greater such a joy, the more it pains.
A world, so far from great (and yet how great
It shines to thee!) there's nothing real in it;
Being, a shadow; consciousness, a dream?
A dream, how dreadful!   Universal blank
Before it, and behind!   Poor man, a spark
From non-existence struck by wrath divine,
Glitt'ring a moment, nor that moment sure,
'Midst upper, nether, and surrounding night,
His sad, sure, sudden, and eternal tomb!

   Lorenzo! dost thou feel these arguments?
Or is there nought but vengeance can be felt?
How hast thou dar'd the Deity dethrone?

How dar'd indict him of a world like this?
If such the world, creation was a crime;
For what is crime, but cause of misery?
Retract, blasphemer! and unriddle this,
Of endless arguments above, below,
Without us, and within, the short result——
" If man's immortal, there's a God in heaven."
　　But wherefore such redundancy? such waste
Of argument? One sets my soul at rest!
One obvious, and at hand, and, oh!—at heart.
So just the skies, Philander's life so pain'd,
His heart so pure; that, or succeeding scenes
Have palms to give, or ne'er had he been born.
　　" What an old tale is this!" Lorenzo cries.—
I grant this argument is old; but truth
No years impair; and had not this been true
Thou never hadst despis'd it for its age.
Truth is immortal as thy soul; and fable
As fleeting as thy joys: be wise, nor make
Heaven's highest blessing, vengeance; O be wise!
Nor make a curse of immortality.
　　Say, know'st thou what it is, or what thou art?
Know'st thou th' importance of a soul immortal?
Behold this midnight glory: worlds on worlds!
Amazing pomp! redouble this amaze;
Ten thousand add; add twice ten thousand more;
Then weigh the whole; one soul outweighs them all;
And calls th' astonishing magnificence
Of unintelligent creation poor.
　　For this, believe not me; no man believe;
Trust not in words, but deeds; and deeds no less
Than those of the Supreme; nor his, a few;
Consult them all; consulted, all proclaim
Thy soul's importance: tremble at thyself;

For whom Omnipotence has wak'd so long:
Has wak'd, and work'd, for ages; from the birth
Of nature to this unbelieving hour.
 In this small province of his vast domain
(All nature bow, while I pronounce his name!)
What has God done, and not for this sole end,
To rescue souls from death? The soul's high price
Is writ in all the conduct of the skies.
The soul's high price is the creation's key,
Unlocks its mysteries, and naked lays
The genuine cause of every deed divine:
That, is the chain of ages, which maintains
Their obvious correspondence, and unites
Most distant periods in one blest design:
That, is the mighty hinge, on which have turn'd
All revolutions, whether we regard
The natural, civil, or religious, world;
The former two but servants to the third:
To that their duty done, they both expire,
Their mass new-cast, forgot their deeds renown'd;
And angels ask, "Where once they shone so fair?"
 To lift us from this abject, to sublime;
This flux, to permanent; this dark, to day;
This foul, to pure; this turbid, to serene;
This mean, to mighty!—for this glorious end
Th' Almighty, rising, his long sabbath broke!
The world was made; was ruin'd; was restor'd;
Laws from the skies were publish'd; were repeal'd;
On earth kings, kingdoms, rose; kings, kingdoms,
Fam'd sages lighted up the pagan world;   [fell;
Prophets from Sion darted a keen glance
Thro' distant age; saints travell'd; martyrs bled;
By wonders sacred nature stood control'd;
The living were translated; dead were rais'd;

Angels, and more than angels, came from heaven;
And, oh! for this, descended lower still;
Guilt was hell's gloom; astonish'd at his guest,
For one short moment Lucifer ador'd:
Lorenzo! and wilt thou do less?—For this,
That hallow'd page, fools scoff at, was inspir'd,
Of all these truths thrice venerable code!
Deists! perform your quarantine; and then
Fall prostrate, ere you touch it, lest you die.
    Nor less intensely bent infernal powers
To mar, than those of light, this end to gain.
O what a scene is here!—Lorenzo! wake!
Rise to the thought; exert, expand thy soul
To take the vast idea: it denies
All else the name of great. Two warring worlds!
Not Europe against Afric; warring worlds!
Of more than mortal! mounted on the wing!
On ardent wings of energy, and zeal,
High-hov'ring o'er this little brand of strife!
This sublunary ball—but strife, for what?
In their own cause conflicting? No; in thine,
In man's. His single int'rest blows the flame;
His the sole stake; his fate the trumpet sounds,
Which kindles war immortal. How it burns!
Tumultuous swarms of deities in arms!
Force, force opposing, till the waves run high,
And tempest nature's universal sphere.
Such opposites eternal, steadfast, stern,
Such foes implacable, are good, and ill;   [them.
Yet man, vain man, would mediate peace between
    Think not this fiction, "There was war in hea-
      ven."   [hung,
From heaven's high crystal mountain, where it
Th' Almighty's outstretcht arm took down his bow:

And shot his indignation at the deep :
Re-thunder'd hell, and darted all her fires.—
And seems the stake of little moment still ?
And slumbers man, who singly caus'd the storm ?
He sleeps.—And art thou shockt at mysteries ?
The greatest, thou.   How dreadful to reflect,
What ardour, care, and counsel, mortals cause
In breasts divine ! How little in their own !

   Where'er I turn, how new proofs pour upon me !
How happily this wondrous view supports
My former argument ! How strongly strikes
Immortal life's full demonstration, here !
Why this exertion ? Why this strange regard
From heaven's Omnipotent indulg'd to man ?—
Because, in man, the glorious dreadful power,
Extremely to be pain'd, or blest, for ever.
Duration gives importance ; swells the price.
An angel, if a creature of a day,
What would he be ? A trifle of no weight ;
Or stand, or fall ; no matter which ; he's gone.
Because immortal, therefore is indulg'd
This strange regard of deities to dust.   [eyes :
Hence, heaven looks down on earth with all her
Hence, the soul's mighty moment in her sight :
Hence, every soul has partisans above,
And every thought a critic in the skies :
Hence, clay, vile clay ! has angels for its guard,
And every guard a passion for his charge :
Hence, from all age, the cabinet divine
Has held high counsel o'er the fate of man.

   Nor have the clouds those gracious counsels hid,
Angels undrew the curtain of the throne,
And Providence came forth to meet mankind :
In various modes of emphasis and awe,

He spoke his will, and trembling nature heard;
He spoke it loud, in thunder and in storm.
Witness, thou Sinai! whose cloud-cover'd height,
And shaken basis, own'd the present God:
Witness, ye billows! whose returning tide,
Breaking the chain that fasten'd it in air,
Swept Egypt, and her menaces, to hell:
Witness, ye flames! th' Assyrian tyrant blew
To sevenfold rage, as impotent, as strong:
And thou, earth! witness, whose expanding jaws
Clos'd o'er¹ presumption's sacrilegious sons:
Has not each element, in turn, subscrib'd
The soul's high price, and sworn it to the wise?
Has not flame, ocean, ether, earthquake, strove
To strike this truth, thro' adamantine man?
If not all adamant, Lorenzo! hear;
All is delusion; nature is wrapt up,
In tenfold night, from reason's keenest eye;
There's no consistence, meaning, plan, or end,
In all beneath the sun, in all above,
(As far as man can penetrate) or heaven
Is an immense, inestimable prize;
Or all is nothing, or that prize is all.—
And shall each toy be still a match for heaven,
And full equivalent for groans below?
Who would not give a trifle to prevent
What he would give a thousand worlds to cure?

    Lorenzo! thou hast seen (if thine to see)
All nature, and her God (by nature's course,
And nature's course control'd) declare for me:
The skies above proclaim, " immortal man!"
And, " man immortal!" all below resounds.
The world's a system of theology,

Korah, &c.

Read by the greatest strangers to the schools ;
If honest, learn'd ; and sages o'er a plough.
Is not, Lorenzo ! then, impos'd on thee
This hard alternative ; or, to renounce
Thy reason, or thy sense ; or, to believe ?
What then is unbelief ? 'Tis an exploit ;
A strenuous enterprise : to gain it, man
Must burst thro' every bar of common sense,
Of common shame, magnanimously wrong ;
And what rewards the sturdy combatant ?
His prize, repentance ; infamy, his crown

    But wherefore, infamy ?—For want of faith,
Down the steep precipice of wrong he slides ;
There's nothing to support him in the right.
Faith in the future wanting, is, at least
In embryo, every weakness, every guilt ;
And strong temptation ripens it to birth.
If this life's gain invites him to the deed,
Why not his country sold, his father slain ?
'Tis virtue to pursue our good supreme ;
And his supreme, his only good is here.
Ambition, av'rice, by the wise disdain'd,
Is perfect wisdom, while mankind are fools,
And think a turf, or tombstone, covers all :
These find employment, and provide for sense
A richer pasture, and a larger range ;
And sense by right divine ascends the throne,
When virtue's prize and prospect are no more ;
Virtue no more we think the will of heaven.
Would heaven quite beggar virtue, if belov'd ?

    " Has virtue charms ?"—I grant her heavenly
But if unportion'd, all will int'rest wed ;   [fair ;
Tho' that our admiration, this our choice.
The virtues grow on immortality ;

That root destroy'd, they wither and expire.
A Deity believ'd will nought avail;
Rewards and punishments make God ador'd;
And hopes and fears give conscience all her power
  As in the dying parent dies the child,
Virtue, with immortality, expires.
Who tells me he denies his soul immortal,
Whate'er his boast, has told me, he's a knave.
His duty 'tis, to love himself alone;
Nor care tho' mankind perish, if he smiles.
Who thinks ere long the man shall wholly die,
Is dead already; nought but brute survives.

  And are there such?—Such candidates there are
For more than death; for utter loss of being,
Being, the basis of the Deity!
Ask you the cause?—The cause they will not tell:
Nor need they: Oh the sorceries of sense!
They work this transformation on the soul,
Dismount her, like the serpent at the fall,
Dismount her from her native wing (which soar'd
Erewhile ethereal heights), and throw her down,
To lick the dust, and crawl in such a thought.

  Is it in words to paint you? O ye fall'n!
Fall'n from the wings of reason, and of hope!
Erect in stature, prone in appetite!
Patrons of pleasure, posting into pain!
Lovers of argument, averse to sense!
Boasters of liberty, fast bound in chains!
Lords of the wide creation, and the shame!
More senseless than th' irrationals you scorn!
More base than those you rule! than those you pity,
Far more undone! O ye most infamous
Of beings, from superior dignity!
Deepest in woe from means of boundless bliss!

Ye curst by blessings infinite ! Because
Most highly favour'd, most profoundly lost !
Ye motley mass of contradiction strong !
And are you, too, convinc'd your souls fly off
In exhalation soft, and die in air,
From the full flood of evidence against you ?
In the coarse drudgeries, and sinks of sense,
Your souls have quite worn out the make of heaven,
By vice new-cast, and creatures of your own :
But tho' you can deform, you can't destroy ;
To curse, not uncreate, is all your power.

Lorenzo ! this black brotherhood renounce ;
Renounce St. Evremont, and read St. Paul.
Ere rapt by miracle, by reason wing'd,
His mounting mind made long abode in heaven.
This is freethinking, unconfin'd to parts,
To send the soul, on curious travel bent,
Thro' all the provinces of human thought ;
To dart her flight, thro' the whole sphere of man ;
Of this vast universe to make the tour ;
In each recess of space, and time, at home ;
Familiar with their wonders ; 'diving deep ;
And, like a prince of boundless int'rests there,
Still most ambitious of the most remote ;
To look on truth unbroken, and entire ;
Truth in the system, the full orb ; where truths
By truths enlighten'd, and sustain'd, afford
An arch-like, strong foundation, to support
Th' incumbent weight of absolute, complete
Conviction ; here, the more we press, we stand
More firm ; who most examine, most believe.
Parts, like half sentences, confound ; the whole
Conveys the sense, and God is understood ;
Who not in fragments writes to human race :

Read his whole volume, sceptic! then reply.
  This, this, is thinking free, a thought that grasps
Beyond a grain, and looks beyond an hour.
Turn up thine eye, survey this midnight scene;
What are earth's kingdoms, to yon boundless orbs,
Of human souls, one day, the destin'd range?
And what yon boundless orbs, to godlike man?
Those num'rous worlds that throng the firmament,
And ask more space in heaven, can roll at large
In man's capacious thought, and still leave room
For ampler orbs, for new creations, there.
Can such a soul contract itself, to gripe
A point of no dimension, of no weight?
It can; it does: the world is such a point:
And, of that point, how small a part enslaves!
  How small a part—of nothing, shall I say?
Why not?—Friends, our chief treasure! how they
Lucia, Narcissa fair, Philander, gone!   [drop!
The grave, like fabled Cerberus, has op'd
A triple mouth; and, in an awful voice,
Loud calls my soul, and utters all I sing.
How the world falls to pieces round about us,
And leaves us in a ruin of our joy!
What says this transportation of my friends?
It bids me love the place where now they dwell,
And scorn this wretched spot, they leave so poor.
Eternity's vast ocean lies before thee;
There; there, Lorenzo! thy Clarissa sails.
Give thy mind sea-room; keep it wide of earth,
That rock of souls immortal; cut thy cord;
Weigh anchor; spread thy sails; call every wind;
Eye thy great Pole-star; make the land of life.
  Two kinds of life has double natur'd man,
And two of death; the last far more severe.

Life animal is nurtur'd by the sun ;
Thrives on his bounties, triumphs in his beams.
Life rational subsists on higher food,
Triumphant in his beams, who made the day.
When we leave that sun, and are left by this,
(The fate of all who die in stubborn guilt)
'Tis utter darkness; strictly double death.
We sink by no judicial stroke of heaven,
But nature's course; as sure as plummets fall.
Since God, or man, must alter, ere they meet,
(Since light and darkness blend not in one sphere)
'Tis manifest, Lorenzo! who must change.
　　If, then, that double death should prove thy lot,
Blame not the bowels of the Deity ;
Man shall be blest, as far as man permits.
Not man alone, all rationals, heaven arms
With an illustrious, but tremendous, power
To counteract its own most gracious ends ;
And this, of strict necessity, not choice ;
That power denied, men, angels, were no more
But passive engines, void of praise, or blame.
A nature rational implies the power
Of being blest, or wretched, as we please ;
Else idle reason would have nought to do ;
And he that would be barr'd capacity
Of pain, courts incapacity of bliss.
Heaven wills our happiness, allows our doom ;
Invites us ardently, but not compels ;
Heaven but persuades, almighty man decrees ;
Man is the maker of immortal fates.
Man falls by man, if finally he falls ;
And fall he must, who learns from death alone,
The dreadful secret,—that he lives for ever.
　　Why this to thee ?—Thee yet, perhaps, in doubt

Of second life ?   But wherefore doubtful still ?
Eternal life is nature's ardent wish :
What ardently we wish, we soon believe :
Thy tardy faith declares that wish destroy'd :
What has destroy'd it ?—Shall I tell thee what ?
When fear'd the future, 'tis no longer wisht ;
And, when unwisht, we strive to disbelieve.
" Thus infidelity our guilt betrays."
Nor that the sole detection ! Blush, Lorenzo !
Blush for hypocrisy, if not for guilt.
The future fear'd ?—An infidel, and fear ?
Fear what ? a dream ? a fable ?—How thy dread,
Unwilling evidence, and therefore strong,
Affords my cause an undesign'd support !
How disbelief affirms, what it denies !
" It, unawares, asserts immortal life."—
Surprising ! infidelity turns out
A creed, and a confession of our sins :
Apostates, thus, are orthodox divines.

   Lorenzo ! with Lorenzo clash no more ;
Nor longer a transparent vizor wear.
Think'st thou, Religion only has her mask ?
Our infidels are Satan's hypocrites,
Pretend the worst, and, at the bottom, fail.
When visited by thought (thought will intrude),
Like him they serve, they tremble, and believe.
Is there hypocrisy so foul as this ?
So fatal to the welfare of the world ?
What detestation, what contempt, their due !
And, if unpaid, be thank'd for their escape
That Christian candour they strive hard to scorn.
If not for that asylum, they might find
A hell on earth ; nor 'scape a worse below.

   With insolence, and impotence of thought,

Instead of racking fancy, to refute,
Reform thy manners, and the truth enjoy.—
But shall I dare confess the dire result?
Can thy proud reason brook so black a brand?
From purer manners, to sublimer faith,
Is nature's unavoidable ascent;
An honest deist, where the gospel shines,
Matur'd to nobler, in the Christian ends.
When that blest change arrives, e'en cast aside
This song superfluous; life immortal strikes
Conviction, in a flood of light divine.
A Christian dwells, like[1] Uriel, in the sun;
Meridian evidence puts doubt to flight;
And ardent hope anticipates the skies.
Of that bright sun, Lorenzo! scale the sphere;
'Tis easy! it invites thee; it descends   [came;
From heaven to woo, and waft thee whence it
Read and revere the sacred page; a page
Where triumphs immortality; a page
Which not the whole creation could produce;
Which not the conflagration shall destroy;
'Tis printed in the mind of gods for ever,
In nature's ruins not one letter lost.

In proud disdain of what e'en gods adore,
Dost smile?—Poor wretch! thy guardian angel
Angels, and men, assent to what I sing; [weeps.
Wits smile, and thank me for my midnight dream.
How vicious hearts fume phrensy to the brain!
Parts push us on to pride, and pride to shame;
Pert infidelity is wit's cockade,
To grace the brazen brow that braves the skies,
By loss of being, dreadfully secure.
Lorenzo! if thy doctrine wins the day,

[1] Milton.

And drives my dreams, defeated, from the field;
If this is all, if earth a final scene,
Take heed; stand fast; be sure to be a knave;
A knave in grain! ne'er deviate to the right:
Shouldst thou be good—how infinite thy loss!
Guilt only makes annihilation gain.
Blest scheme! which life deprives of comfort, death
Of hope; and which vice only recommends.
If so, where, infidels! your bait thrown out
To catch weak converts? Where your lofty boast
Of zeal for virtue, and of love to man?
Annihilation! I confess, in these.

    What can reclaim you? Dare I hope profound
Philosophers the converts of a song?
Yet know, its[1] title flatters you, not me;
Yours be the praise to make my title good;
Mine, to bless heaven, and triumph in your praise.
But since so pestilential your disease,
Tho' sovereign is the med'cine I prescribe,
As yet, I'll neither triumph, nor despair:
But hope, ere long, my midnight dream will wake
Your hearts, and teach your wisdom—to be wise:
For why should souls immortal, made for bliss,
E'er wish (and wish in vain!) that souls could die?
What ne'er can die, Oh! grant to live; and crown
The wish, and aim, and labour of the skies;
Increase, and enter on the joys of heaven:
Thus shall my title pass a sacred seal,
Receive an imprimatur from above,
While angels shout—an infidel reclaimed!

    To close, Lorenzo! spite of all my pains,
Still seems it strange, that thou shouldst live for
       ever?

[1] The Infidel Reclaimed.

Is it less strange, that thou shouldst live at all ?
This is a miracle ; and that no more.
Who gave beginning, can exclude an end.
Deny thou art : then, doubt if thou shalt be.
A miracle with miracles inclos'd,
Is man ; and starts his faith at what is strange ?
What less than wonders, from the wonderful ;
What less than miracles, from God, can flow ?
Admit a God—that mystery supreme !
That cause uncaus'd ! all other wonders cease ;
Nothing is marvellous for him to do :
Deny him—all is mystery besides ;
Millions of mysteries ? Each darker far,
Than that thy wisdom would, unwisely, shun.
If weak thy faith, why choose the harder side ?
We nothing know, but what is marvellous ;
Yet what is marvellous, we can't believe.
So weak our reason, and so great our God,
What most surprises in the sacred page,
Or full as strange, or stranger, must be true.
Faith is not reason's labour, but repose.

To faith, and virtue, why so backward, man ?
From hence :—the present strongly strikes us all;
The future, faintly : can we, then, be men ?
If men, Lorenzo ! the reverse is right.
Reason is man's peculiar : sense, the brute's.
The present is the scanty realm of sense ;
The future, reason's empire unconfin'd :
On that expending all her godlike power,
She plans, provides, expatiates, triumphs, there ;
There, builds her blessings ! there, expects her
And nothing asks of fortune, or of men. [praise;
And what is reason ? Be she, thus, defin'd ;
Reason is upright stature in the soul.

Oh ! be a man ;—and strive to be a god. [life ?"
  " For what ? (thou say'st) to damp the joys of
No ; to give heart and substance to thy joys.
That tyrant, hope ; mark how she domineers ;
She bids us quit realities, for dreams ;
Safety, and peace, for hazard and alarm ;
That tyrant o'er the tyrants of the soul,
She bids ambition quit its taken prize,
Spurn the luxuriant branch on which it sits,
Tho' bearing crowns, to spring at distant game ;
And plunge in toils and dangers—for repose.
If hope precarious, and of things, when gain'd,
Of little moment, and as little stay,
Can sweeten toils, and dangers into joys ;
What then, that hope, which nothing can defeat,
Our leave unask'd ? Rich hope of boundless bliss !
Bliss, past man's power to paint it ; time's to close !
    This hope is earth's most estimable prize :
This is man's portion, while no more than man :
Hope, of all passions, most befriends us here ;
Passions of prouder name befriend us less.
Joy has her tears ; and transport has her death ;
Hope, like a cordial, innocent, tho' strong,
Man's heart, at once, inspirits, and serenes ;
Nor makes him pay his wisdom for his joys ;
'Tis all, our present state can safely bear,
Health to the frame ! and vigour to the mind !
A joy attemper'd ! a chastis'd delight !
Like the fair summer evening, mild, and sweet '
'Tis man's full cup ; his paradise below !
    A blest hereafter, then, or hop'd, or gain'd
Is all ;—our whole of happiness : full proof,
I chose no trivial or inglorious theme.
And know, ye foes to song ! (well **meaning men,**

Tho' quite forgotten[1] half your Bible's praise !)
Important truths, in spite of verse, may please :
Grave minds you praise ; nor can you praise too
If there is weight in an eternity,   [much :
Let the grave listen ;—and be graver still.

NIGHT VIII.

VIRTUE'S APOLOGY;

OR, THE MAN OF THE WORLD ANSWERED. IN WHICH ARE
CONSIDERED, THE LOVE OF THIS LIFE ;
THE AMBITION AND PLEASURE, WITH THE WIT AND WISDOM
OF THE WORLD.

AND has all nature, then, espous'd my part ?
Have I brib'd heaven, and earth, to plead against
          thee ?
And is thy soul immortal ?—What remains ?
All, all, Lorenzo !—Make immortal, blest.
Unblest immortals !—What can shock us more ?
And yet Lorenzo still affects the world ;
There, stows his treasure ; thence, his title draws,
Man of the world (for such wouldst thou be call'd)
And art thou proud of that inglorious style ?
Proud of reproach ? for a reproach it was,
In ancient days ; and Christian,—in an age,
When men were men, and not asham'd of heaven
Fir'd their ambition, as it crown'd their joy.
Sprinkled with dews from the Castalian font,
Fain would I re-baptize thee, and confer
A purer spirit, and a nobler name.

The poetical parts of it.

Thy fond attachments fatal, and inflam'd,
Point out my path, and dictate to my song:
To thee, the world how fair! How strongly strikes
Ambition! and gay pleasure stronger still!
Thy triple bane! the triple bolt that lays
Thy virtue dead! Be these my triple theme;
Nor shall thy wit, or wisdom, be forgot.

Common the theme; not so the song; if she
My song invokes, Urania, deigns to smile.
The charm that chains us to the world, her foe,
If she dissolves, the man of earth, at once,
Starts from his trance, and sighs for other scenes;
Scenes, where these sparks of night, these stars
          shall shine
Unnumber'd suns (for all things, as they are,
The blest behold); and, in one glory, pour
Their blended blaze on man's astonisht sight;
A blaze—the least illustrious object there.

Lorenzo! since eternal is at hand,
To swallow time's ambitions; as the vast
Leviathan, the bubbles vain, that ride
High on the foaming billow; what avail
High titles, high descent, attainments high,
If unattain'd our highest? O Lorenzo!
What lofty thoughts, these elements above,
What tow'ring hopes, what sallies from the sun
What grand surveys of destiny divine,
And pompous presage of unfathom'd fate,
Should roll in bosoms, where a spirit burns,
Bound for eternity! In bosoms read
By him, who foibles in archangels sees!
On human hearts he bends a jealous eye,
And marks, and in heaven's register enrolls,
The rise, and progress, of each option there;

Sacred to doomsday ! that the page unfolds,
And spreads us to the gaze of gods and men.
     And what an option, O Lorenzo ! thine ?
This world ! and this, unrivall'd by the skies !
A world, where lust of pleasure, grandeur, gold,
Three demons that divide its realms between them,
With strokes alternate buffet to and fro
Man's restless heart, their sport, their flying ball ;
Till, with the giddy circle sick, and tir'd,
It pants for peace, and drops into despair.
Such is the world Lorenzo sets above
That glorious promise angels were esteem'd
Too mean to bring ; a promise, their ador'd
Descended to communicate, and press,
By counsel, miracle, life, death, on man.
Such is the world Lorenzo's wisdom woos,
And on its thorny pillow seeks repose ;
A pillow, which, like opiates ill-prepar'd,
Intoxicates, but not composes ; fills
The visionary mind with gay chimeras,
All the wild trash of sleep, without the rest ;
What unfeign'd travel, and what dreams of joy !
     How frail, men, things ! How momentary, both !
Fantastic chase of shadows hunting shades !
The gay, the busy, equal, tho' unlike ;
Equal in wisdom, differently wise !
Thro' flow'ry meadows, and thro' dreary wastes,
One bustling, and one dancing, into death.
There's not a day, but, to the man of thought,
Betrays some secret, that throws new reproach
On life, and makes him sick of seeing more.
The scenes of bus'ness tell us—" What are men ;"
The scenes of pleasure—" What is all beside ;"
There, others we despise ; and here, ourselves

Amid disgust eternal dwells delight?
'Tis approbation strikes the string of joy.

What wondrous prize has kindled this career,
Stuns with the din, and chokes us with the dust,
On life's gay stage, one inch above the grave?
The proud run up and down in quest of eyes;
The sensual, in pursuit of something worse;
The grave, of gold; the politic, of power;
And all, of other butterflies, as vain!
As eddies draw things frivolous, and light,
How is man's heart by vanity drawn in;
On the swift circle of returning toys,   [gulf'd,
Whirl'd, straw-like, round and round, and then in-
Where gay delusion darkens to despair!

"This is a beaten track."—Is this a track
Should not be beaten? Never beat enough,
Till enough learnt the truths it would inspire.
Shall truth be silent, because folly frowns?
Turn the world's history; what find we there,
But fortune's sports, or nature's cruel claims,
Or woman's artifice, or man's revenge,
And endless inhumanities on man?
Fame's trumpet seldom sounds, but, like the knell,
It brings bad tidings: how it hourly blows
Man's misadventures round the listening world!
Man is the tale of narrative old time;
Sad tale; which high as Paradise begins;
As if, the toil of travel to delude,
From stage to stage, in his eternal round,
The days, his daughters, as they spin our hours
On fortune's wheel, where accident unthought
Oft, in a moment, snaps life's strongest thread.
Each, in her turn, some tragic story tells,
With, now-and-then, a wretched farce between;

And fills his chronicle with human woes.   [us;
   Time's daughters, true as those of men, deceive
Not one, but puts some cheat on all mankind:
While in their father's bosom, not yet ours,
They flatter our fond hopes; and promise much
Of amiable; but hold him not o'erwise,
Who dares to trust them; and laugh round the year
At still-confiding, still-confounded, man,
Confiding, tho' confounded; hoping on,
Untaught by trial, unconvinc'd by proof,
And ever looking for the never-seen.
Life to the last, like harden'd felons, lies;
Nor owns itself a cheat, till it expires.
Its little joys go out by one and one,
And leave poor man, at length, in perfect night;
Night darker, than what, now, involves the pole.
   O thou, who dost permit these ills to fall,
For gracious ends, and wouldst that man should
          mourn!
O thou, whose hands this goodly fabric fram'd,
Who know'st it best, and would'st that man should
          know!
What is this sublunary world? A vapour;
A vapour all it holds; itself, a vapour;
From the damp bed of chaos, by thy beam
Exhal'd, ordain'd to swim its destin'd hour
In ambient air, then melt, and disappear.
Earth's days are number'd nor remote her doom;
As mortal, tho' less transient, than her sons;
Yet they dote on her, as the world and they
Were both eternal, solid; thou, a dream.
   They dote! on what? Immortal views apart,
A region of outsides! a land of shadows!
A fruitful field of flow'ry promises!

A wilderness of joys! perplext with doubts,
And sharp with thorns! a troubled ocean, spread
With bold adventurers, their all on board!
No second hope, if here their fortune frowns;
Frown soon it must.   Of various rates they sail,
Of ensigns various; all alike in this,
All restless, anxious; tost with hopes, and fears,
In calmest skies; obnoxious all to storm;
And stormy the most gen'ral blast of life:
All bound for happiness; yet few provide
The chart of knowledge, pointing where it lies;
Or virtue's helm, to shape the course design'd:
All, more or less, capricious fate lament,
Now lifted by the tide, and now resorb'd,
And farther from their wishes than before:
All, more or less, against each other dash.
To mutual hurt, by gusts of passion driven,
And suff'ring more from folly, than from fate.
    Ocean! thou dreadful and tumultuous home
Of dangers, at eternal war with man!
Death's capital, where most he domineers,
With all his chosen terrors frowning round,
(Tho' lately feasted high at ¹Albion's cost)
Wide-op'ning, and loud-roaring still for more!
Too faithful mirror! how dost thou reflect
The melancholy face of human life!
The strong resemblance tempts me farther still:
And, haply, Britain may be deeper struck
By moral truth, in such a mirror seen,
Which nature holds for ever at her eye.
    Self-flatter'd, unexperienc'd, high in hope,
When young, with sanguine cheer, and streamers
        gay,

¹ Admiral Balchen, &c.

We cut our cable, launch into the world,
And fondly dream each wind and star our friend ;
All in some darling enterprise embarkt :
But where is he can fathom its extent ?
Amid a multitude of artless hands,
Ruin's sure perquisite ! her lawful prize !
Some steer aright ; but the black blast blows hard,
And puffs them wide of hope : with hearts of proof,
Full against wind and tide, some win their way ;
And when strong effort has deserv'd the port,
And tugg'd it into view, 'tis won ! 'tis lost !
Tho' strong their oar, still stronger is their fate :
They strike ; and while they triumph they expire.
In stress of weather, most ; some sink outright ;
O'er them, and o'er their names, the billows close ;
To-morrow knows not they were ever born.
Others a short memorial leave behind,
Like a flag floating, when the bark's ingulf'd ;
It floats a moment, and is seen no more :
One Cæsar lives ; a thousand are forgot.
How few, beneath auspicious planets born,
(Darlings of Providence ! fond fate's elect !)
With swelling sails make good the promis'd port,
With all their wishes freighted ! Yet ev'n these,
Freighted with all their wishes, soon complain ;
Free from misfortune, not from nature free,
They still are men ; and when is man secure ?
As fatal time, as storm ! the rush of years
Beats down their strength ; their numberless escapes
In ruin end : and, now, their proud success
But plants new terrors on the victor's brow :
What pain to quit the world, just made their own,
Their nest so deeply down'd, and built so high !
Too low they build, who build beneath the stars.

Woe then apart (if woe apart can be
From mortal man), and fortune at our nod,
The gay! rich! great! triumphant! and august!
What are they?—the most happy (strange to say!)
Convince me most of human misery;
What are they? Smiling wretches of to-morrow!
More wretched, then, than e'er their slave can be;
Their treach'rous blessings, at the day of need,
Like other faithless friends, unmask, and sting:
Then, what provoking indigence in wealth!
What aggravated impotence in power!
High titles, then, what insult of their pain!
If that sole anchor, equal to the waves,
Immortal hope! defies not the rude storm,
Takes comfort from the foaming billows' rage,
And makes a welcome harbour of the tomb.

Is this a sketch of what thy soul admires?
" But here (thou say'st) the miseries of life
Are huddled in a group.   A more distinct
Survey, perhaps, might bring thee better news."
Look on life's stages: they speak plainer still;
The plainer they, the deeper wilt thou sigh.
Look on thy lovely boy; in him behold
The best that can befall the best on earth;
The boy has virtue by his mother's side:
Yes, on Florello look: a father's heart
Is tender, tho' the man's is made of stone;
The truth, thro' such a medium seen, may make
Impression deep, and fondness prove thy friend.

Florello lately cast on this rude coast
A helpless infant; now a heedless child;
To poor Clarissa's throes, thy care succeeds;
Care full of love, and yet severe as hate!
O'er thy soul's joy how oft thy fondness frowns!

Needful austerities his will restrain ;
As thorns fence in the tender plant from harm
As yet, his reason cannot go alone ;
But asks a sterner nurse to lead it on.
His little heart is often terrified ;
The blush of morning, in his cheek, turns pale ,
Its pearly dewdrop trembles in his eye ;
His harmless eye ! and drowns an angel there.
Ah ! what avails his innocence ? The task
Injoin'd must discipline his early powers ;
He learns to sigh, ere he is known to sin ;
Guiltless, and sad ! A wretch before the fall !
How cruel this ! more cruel to forbear.
Our nature such, with necessary pains,
We purchase prospects of precarious peace :
Tho' not a father, this might steal a sigh.

Suppose him disciplin'd aright (if not,
'Twill sink our poor account to poorer still) ;
Ripe from the tutor, proud of liberty,
He leaps inclosure, bounds into the world !
The world is taken, after ten years' toil,
Like ancient Troy ; and all its joys his own.
Alas ! the world's a tutor more severe ;
Its lessons hard, and ill deserve his pains ;
Unteaching all his virtuous nature taught,
Or books (fair virtue's advocates !) inspir'd.

For who receives him into public life ?
Men of the world, the terræ-filial breed,
Welcome the modest stranger to their sphere,
(Which glitter'd long, at distance, in his sight)
And, in their hospitable arms, inclose :
Men, who think nought so strong of the romance,
So rank knight-errant, as a real friend :
Men, that act up to reason's golden rule,

All weakness of affection quite subdu'd :
Men, that would blush at being thought sincere,
And feign, for glory, the few faults they want;
That love a lie, where truth would pay as well ;
As if to them, vice shone her own reward.

    Lorenzo ! canst thou bear a shocking sight ?
Such, for Florello's sake, 'twill now appear :
See, the steel'd files of season'd veterans,
Train'd to the world, in burnisht falsehood bright;
Deep in the fatal stratagems of peace ;
All soft sensation, in the throng, rubb'd off;
All their keen purpose, in politeness, sheath'd ;
His friends eternal—during interest ;
His foes implacable—when worth their while ;
At war with ev'ry welfare, but their own ;
As wise as Lucifer; and half as good ;
And by whom none, but Lucifer, can gain—
Naked, thro' these (so common fate ordains),
Naked of heart, his cruel course he runs,
Stung out of all, most amiable in life,
Prompt truth, and open thought, and smiles un-
Affection, as his species, wide diffus'd ; [feign'd;
Noble presumptions to mankind's renown ;
Ingenuous trust, and confidence of love.

    These claims to joy (if mortals joy might claim)
Will cost him many a sigh ; till time, and pains,
From the slow mistress of this school, experience,
And her assistant, pausing, pale, distrust,
Purchase a dear-bought clue to lead his youth
Thro' serpentine obliquities of life,
And the dark labyrinth of human hearts.
And happy ! if the clue shall come so cheap :
For, while we learn to fence with public guilt,
Full oft we feel its foul contagion too,

If less than heavenly virtue is our guard.
Thus, a strange kind of curst necessity
Brings down the sterling temper of his soul,
By base alloy, to bear the current stamp,
Below call'd wisdom; sinks him into safety;
And brands him into credit with the world;
Where specious titles dignify disgrace,
And nature's injuries are arts of life;
Where brighter reason prompts to bolder crimes;
And heavenly talents make infernal hearts;
That unsurmountable extreme of guilt!
　　Poor Machiavel! who labour'd hard his plan,
Forgot, that genius need not go to school;
Forgot, that man, without a tutor wise,
His plan had practis'd, long before 'twas writ.
The world's all title-page; there's no contents;
The world's all face; the man who shows his heart,
Is hooted for his nudities, and scorn'd.
A man I knew, who liv'd upon a smile;
And well it fed him; he look'd plump and fair;
While rankest venom foam'd thro' every vein.
Lorenzo! what I tell thee, take not ill!
Living, he fawn'd on ev'ry fool alive;
And, dying, curs'd the friend on whom he liv'd.
To such proficients thou art half a saint.
In foreign realms (for thou hast travell'd far)
How curious to contemplate two state-rooks,
Studious their nests to feather in a trice,
With all the necromantics of their art,
Playing the game of faces on each other,
Making court sweet-meats of their latent gall,
In foolish hope, to steal each other's trust;
Both cheating, both exulting, both deceiv'd;
And, sometimes, both (let earth rejoice) undone!

Their parts we doubt not; but be that their shame;
Shall men of talents, fit to rule mankind,
Stoop to mean wiles, that would disgrace a fool;
And lose the thanks of those few friends they serve?
For who can thank the man he cannot see?

Why so much cover? It defeats itself.
Ye, that know all things! know ye not, men's hearts
Are therefore known, because they are conceal'd
For why conceal'd?—The cause they need not tell?
I give him joy, that's awkward at a lie;
Whose feeble nature truth keeps still in awe;
His incapacity is his renown.
'Tis great, 'tis manly, to disdain disguise;
It shows our spirit, or it proves our strength.
Thou say'st, 'tis needful: is it therefore right?
Howe'er, I grant it some small sign of grace,
To strain at an excuse: and wouldst thou then
Escape that cruel need? thou may'st, with ease;
Think no post needful that demands a knave.
When late our civil helm was shifting hands,
So Pulteney thought: think better, if you can.

But this, how rare! the public path of life
Is dirty:—yet, allow that dirt its due,
It makes the noble mind more noble still:
The world's no neuter; it will wound, or save;
Or virtue quench, or indignation fire.
You say, the world, well known, will make a man:
The world, well known, will give our hearts to
        heaven.
Or make us demons, long before we die.

To show how fair the world, thy mistress, shines
Take either part, sure ills attend the choice;
Sure, tho' not equal, detriment ensues.
Not virtue's self is deified on earth;

Virtue has her relapses, conflicts, foes ;
Foes, that ne'er fail to make her feel their hate.
Virtue has her peculiar set of pains.
True friends to virtue, last, and least, complain ;
But if they sigh, can others hope to smile ?
If wisdom has her miseries to mourn,
How can poor folly lead a happy life ?
And if both suffer, what has earth to boast,
Where he most happy, who the least laments ?
Where much, much patience, the most envied state,
And some forgiveness, needs, the best of friends ?
For friend, or happy life, who looks not higher
Of neither shall he find the shadow here.

   The world's sworn advocate, without a fee,
Lorenzo smartly, with a smile, replies ;
" Thus far thy song is right ; and all must own,
Virtue has her peculiar set of pains.—
And joys peculiar who to vice denies ?
If vice it is, with nature to comply :
If pride, and sense, are so predominant,
To check, not overcome, them, makes a saint,
Can nature in a plainer voice proclaim
Pleasure, and glory, the chief good of man ?"
   Can pride, and sensuality, rejoice ?
From purity of thought, all pleasure springs ;
And, from an humble spirit, all our peace.
Ambition, pleasure ! let us talk of these :
Of these, the porch, and academy, talk'd ;
Of these, each following age had much to say :
Yet, unexhausted, still, the needful theme.
Who talks of these, to mankind all at once
He talks ; for where the saint from either free ?
Are these thy refuge ?—No : these rush upon thee ;
Thy vitals seize, and vulture-like, devour ;

I'll try, if I can pluck thee from thy rock,
Prometheus! from this barren ball of earth;
If reason can unchain thee, thou art free.

   And, first, thy Caucasus, ambition, calls;
Mountain of torments! eminence of woes!
Of courted woes! and courted thro' mistake!
'Tis not ambition charms thee; 'tis a cheat
Will make thee start, as H—— at his moor.
Dost grasp at greatness? First, know what it is:
Think'st thou thy greatness in distinction lies?
Not in the feather, wave it e'er so high,
By fortune stuck, to mark us from the throng,
Is glory lodg'd: 'tis lodg'd in the reverse;
In that which joins, in that which equals, all,
The monarch and his slave;—" A deathless soul,
Unbounded prospect, and immortal kin,
A father God,, and brothers in the skies;"
Elder, indeed, in time; but less remote
In excellence, perhaps, than thought by man;
Why greater what can fall, than what can rise?

   If still delirious, now, Lorenzo! go;
And with thy full-blown brothers of the world,
Throw scorn around thee; cast it on thy slaves;
Thy slaves, and equals: how scorn cast on them
Rebounds on thee! If man is mean, as man,
Art thou a god? If fortune makes him so,
Beware the consequence: a maxim that,
Which draws a monstrous picture of mankind,
Where, in the drapery, the man is lost;
Externals flutt'ring, and the soul forgot.
Thy greatest glory, when dispos'd to boast,
Boast that aloud, in which thy servants share.

   We wisely strip the steed we mean to buy:
Judge we in their caparisons, of men?

It nought avails thee, where, but what, thou art;
All the distinctions of this little life
Are quite cutaneous, foreign to the man,
When, thro' death's streights, earth's subtle ser-
            pents creep,
Which wriggle into wealth, or climb renown.
As crooked Satan the forbidden tree,
They leave their party-colour'd robe behind,
All that now glitters, while they rear aloft
Their brazen crests, and hiss at us below.
Of fortune's fucus strip them, yet alive;
Strip them of body, too; nay, closer still,
Away with all, but moral, in their minds;
And let, what then remains, impose their name,
Pronounce them weak, or worthy; great, or mean.
How mean that snuff of glory fortune lights,
And death puts out! Dost thou demand a test,
A test, at once, infallible, and short,
Of real greatness? That man greatly lives,
Whate'er his fate, or fame, who greatly dies;
High-flush'd with hope, where heroes shall despair.
If this a true criterion, many courts,
Illustrious, might afford but few grandees.

    Th' Almighty, from his throne, on earth surveys
Nought greater, than an honest, humble heart;
An humble heart, his residence! pronounc'd
His second seat; and rival to the skies.
The private path, the secret acts of men,
If noble, far the noblest of our lives!
How far above Lorenzo's glory sits
Th' illustrious master of a name unknown;
Whose worth unrivall'd, and unwitness'd, loves
Life's sacred shades, where gods converse with men;
And peace, beyond the world's conceptions, smiles!

As thou (now dark), before we part, shalt see.
　But thy great soul this skulking glory scorns.
Lorenzo's sick, but when Lorenzo's seen ;
And, when he shrugs at public bus'ness, lies.
Denied the public eye, the public voice,
As if he liv'd on others' breath, he dies.
Fain would he make the world his pedestal ;
Mankind the gazers, the sole figure, he.
Knows he, that mankind praise against their will,
And mix as much detraction as they can?
Knows he, that faithless fame her whisper has,
As well as trumpet ? That his vanity
Is so much tickled from not hearing all?
Knows this all knower, that from itch of praise,
Or, from an itch more sordid, when he shines,
Taking his country by five hundred ears,
Senates at once admire him, and despise,
With modest laughter lining loud applause,
Which makes the smile more mortal to his fame?
His fame, which (like the mighty Cæsar), crown'd
With laurels, in full senate, greatly falls,
By seeming friends, that honour, and destroy.
We rise in glory, as we sink in pride :
Where boasting ends, there dignity begins :
And yet, mistaken beyond all mistake,
The blind Lorenzo's proud—of being proud ;
And dreams himself ascending in his fall.
　An eminence, tho' fancied, turns the brain :
All vice wants hellebore ; but of all vice,
Pride loudest calls, and for the largest bowl ;
Because, unlike all other vice, it flies,
In fact, the point, in fancy most pursu'd.
Who court applause, oblige the world in this ;
They gratify man's passion to refuse.

Superior honour, when assum'd, is lost ;
Ev'n good men turn banditti, and rejoice,
Like Kouli-Kan, in plunder of the proud.
　Tho' somewhat disconcerted, steady still
To the world's cause, with half a face of joy,
Lorenzo cries—" Be, then, ambition cast ;
Ambition's dearer far stands unimpeach'd,
Gay pleasure! proud ambition is her slave ;
For her, he soars at great, and hazards ill ;
For her, he fights, and bleeds, or overcomes ;
And paves his way, with crowns, to reach her smile :
Who can resist her charms ?"—Or, should? Lorenzo !
What mortal shall resist, where angels yield ?
Pleasure's the mistress of ethereal powers ;
For her contend the rival gods above ;
Pleasure's the mistress of the world below ;
And well it was for man, that pleasure charms ;
How would all stagnate, but for pleasure's ray !
How would the frozen stream of action cease !
What is the pulse of this so busy world ?
The love of pleasure : that, thro' ev'ry vein,
Throws motion, warmth ; and shuts out death from
　Tho' various are the tempers of mankind, [life.
Pleasure's gay family hold all in chains :
Some most affect the black ; and some, the fair ;
Some honest pleasure court ; and some, obscene.
Pleasures obscene are various, as the throng
Of passions, that can err in human hearts ;
Mistake their objects, or transgress their bounds.
Think you there's but one whoredom ? Whoredom,
But when our reason licenses delight.   [all,
Dost doubt, Lorenzo ? Thou shalt doubt no more.
Thy father chides thy gallantries ; yet hugs
An ugly, common harlot, in the dark ;

A rank adulterer with others' gold !
And that hag, vengeance, in a corner, charms.
Hatred her brothel has, as well as love,
Where horrid epicures debauch in blood.
Whate'er the motive, pleasure is the mark :
For her, the black assassin draws his sword ;
For her, dark statesmen trim their midnight lamp,
To which no single sacrifice may fall ;
For her, the saint abstains ; the miser starves ;
The stoic proud, for pleasure, pleasure scorn'd ;
For her, affliction's daughters grief indulge,
And find, or hope, a luxury in tears ;
For her, guilt, shame, toil, danger, we defy ;
And, with an aim voluptuous, rush on death.
Thus universal her despotic power !

And as her empire wide, her praise is just.
Patron of pleasure ! doter on delight !
I am thy rival ; pleasure I profess ;
Pleasure the purpose of my gloomy song.
Pleasure is nought but virtue's gayer name ;
I wrong her still, I rate her worth too low ;
Virtue the root, and pleasure is the flower ;
And honest Epicurus' foes were fools.

But this sounds harsh, and gives the wise offence ;
If o'erstrain'd wisdom still retains the name.
How knits austerity her cloudy brow,
And blames, as bold, and hazardous, the praise
Of pleasure, to mankind, unprais'd, too dear !
Ye modern stoics ! hear my soft reply ;
Their senses men will trust : we can't impose ;
Or, if we could, is imposition right ?
Own honey sweet ; but, owning, add this sting ;
" When mixt with poison, it is deadly too."
Truth never was indebted to a lie.

Is nought but virtue to be prais'd, as good?
Why then is health preferr'd before disease?
What nature loves is good, without our leave.
And where no future drawback cries, " Beware;
Pleasure, tho' not from virtue, should prevail.
'Tis balm to life, and gratitude to heaven;
How cold our thanks for bounties unenjoy'd!
The love of pleasure is man's eldest-born,
Born in his cradle, living to his tomb;
Wisdom, her younger sister, tho' more grave,
Was meant to minister, and not to mar,
Imperial pleasure, queen of human hearts.

Lorenzo! thou, her majesty's renown'd,
Tho' uncoift, counsel, learned in the world!
Who think'st thyself a Murray, with disdain
May'st look on me.   Yet, my Demosthenes!
Canst thou plead pleasure's cause as well as I?
Know'st thou her nature, purpose, parentage?
Attend my song, and thou shalt know them all;
And know thyself; and know thyself to be
(Strange truth!) the most abstemious man alive
Tell not Calista; she will laugh thee dead;
Or send thee to her hermitage with L——.
Absurd presumption! thou who never knew'st
A serious thought! shalt thou dare dream of joy?
No man ere found a happy life by chance;
Or yawn'd it into being, with a wish;
Or, with the snout of grov'ling appetite,
E'er smelt it out, and grubb'd it from the dirt.
An art it is, and must be learnt; and learnt
With unremitting effort, or be lost;
And leaves us perfect blockheads, in our bliss.
The clouds may drop down titles and estates;
Wealth may seek us; but wisdom must be sought;

Sought before all ; but (how unlike all else
We seek on earth !) 'tis never sought in vain.
   First, pleasure's birth, rise, strength, and gran-
       deur, see
Brought forth by wisdom, nurst by discipline,
By patience taught, by perseverance crown'd,
She rears her head majestic ; round her throne,
Erected in the bosom of the just,
Each virtue, listed, forms her manly guard.
For what are virtues ? (formidable name !)
What, but the fountain, or defence, of joy ?
Why, then, commanded ? Need mankind commands,
At once to merit, and to make, their bliss ?—
Great legislator ! scarce so great, as kind !
If men are rational, and love delight,
Thy gracious law but flatters human choice ;
In the transgression lies the penalty ;
And they the most indulge, who most obey.
   Of pleasure, next, the final cause explore :
Its mighty purpose, its important end.
Not to turn human brutal, but to build
Divine on human, pleasure came from heaven.
In aid to reason was the goddess sent ;
To call up all its strength by such a charm.
Pleasure, first, succours virtue ; in return,
Virtue gives pleasure an eternal reign.
What, but the pleasure of food, friendship, faith,
Supports life natural, civil, and divine ?
'Tis from the pleasure of repast, we live ;
'Tis from the pleasure of applause, we please ;
'Tis from the pleasure of belief, we pray
(All pray'r would cease, if unbeliev'd the prize) :
It serves ourselves, our species, and our God ;
And to serve more, is past the sphere of man.

Glide, then, for ever, pleasure's sacred stream!
Through Eden, as Euphrates ran, it runs,
And fosters ev'ry growth of happy life;
Makes a new Eden where it flows;—but such
As must be lost, Lorenzo! by thy fall.
   "What mean I by thy fall?"—Thou'lt shortly see,
While pleasure's nature is at large display'd;
Already sung her origin, and ends.
Those glorious ends, by kind, or by degree,
When pleasure violates, 'tis then a vice,
A vengeance too; it hastens into pain.
From due refreshment, life, health, reason, joy;
From wild excess, pain, grief, distraction, death;
Heaven's justice this proclaims, and that her love.
What greater evil can I wish my foe,
Than his full draught of pleasure, from a cask
Unbroach'd by just authority, ungaug'd
By temperance, by reason unrefin'd?
A thousand demons lurk within the lee.
Heaven, others, and ourselves! uninjur'd these,
Drink deep; the deeper, then, the more divine;
Angels are angels, from indulgence there;
'Tis unrepenting pleasure makes a god.
   Dost think thyself a god from other joys?
A victim rather! shortly sure to bleed.   [fail?
The wrong must mourn: can heaven's appointments
Can man outwit Omnipotence? strike out
A self-wrought happiness unmeant by him
Who made us, and the world we would enjoy?
Who forms an instrument, ordains from whence
Its dissonance, or harmony, shall rise.
Heaven bid the soul this mortal frame inspire!
Bid virtue's ray divine inspire the soul
With unprecarious flows of vital joy;

And, without breathing, man as well might hope
For life, as without piety, for peace.
 " Is virtue, then, and piety the same ?"—
No ; piety is more ; 'tis virtue's source ;
Mother of ev'ry worth, as that of joy.
Men of the world this doctrine ill digest ;
They smile at piety ; yet boast aloud
Good will to men ; nor know they strive to part
What nature joins ; and thus confute themselves.
With piety begins all good on earth ;
'Tis the first-born of rationality.
Conscience, her first law broken, wounded lies ;
Enfeebled, lifeless, impotent to good ;
A feign'd affection bounds her utmost power.
Some we can't love, but for th' Almighty's sake ;
A foe to God was ne'er true friend to man ·
Some sinister intent taints all he does ;
And, in his kindest actions, he's unkind.
 On piety, humanity is built ;
And, on humanity, much happiness ;
And yet still more on piety itself.
A soul in commerce with her God, is heaven,
Feels not the tumults and the shocks of life ;
The whirls of passions, and the strokes of heart.
A deity believ'd, is joy begun ;
A deity ador'd, is joy advanc'd ;
A deity belov'd, is joy matur'd.
Each branch of piety delight inspires ;
Faith builds a bridge from this world to the next,
O'er death's dark gulf, and all its horror hides ;
Praise, the sweet exhalation of our joy,
That joy exalts, and makes it sweeter still ;
Prayer ardent opens heaven, lets down a stream
Of glory on the consecrated hour

Of man, in audience with the Deity.
Who worships the great God, that instant joins
The first in heaven, and sets his foot on hell.

   Lorenzo! when wast thou at church before?
Thou think'st the service long: but is it just?
Tho' just, unwelcome: thou hadst rather tread
Unhallow'd ground; the muse, to win thine ear,
Must take an air less solemn.   She complies.
Good conscience! at the sound the world retires;
Verse disaffects it, and Lorenzo smiles;
Yet has she her seraglio full of charms;
And such as age shall heighten, not impair.
Art thou dejected? Is thy mind o'ercast?
Amid her fair ones, thou the fairest choose, [truth;
To chase thy gloom.—" Go, fix some weighty
Chain down some passion; do some gen'rous good;
Teach ignorance to see, or grief to smile;
Correct thy friend; befriend thy greatest foe;
Or with warm heart, and confidence divine,
Spring up, and lay strong hold on him who made
     thee."
Thy gloom is scatter'd, sprightly spirits flow;
Tho' wither'd is thy vine, and harp unstrung.

   Dost call the bowl, the viol, and the dance,
Loud mirth, mad laughter? Wretched comforters!
Physicians! more than half of thy disease.
Laughter, tho' never censur'd yet as sin,
(Pardon a thought that only seems severe)
Is half-immoral: is it much indulg'd?
By venting spleen, or dissipating thought,
It shows a scorner, or it makes a fool;
And sins, as hurting others, or ourselves.
'Tis pride, or emptiness, applies the straw,
That tickles little minds to mirth effuse;

Of grief approaching, the portentous sign!
The house of laughter makes a house of woe.
A man triumphant is a monstrous sight;
A man dejected is a sight as mean.
What cause for triumph, where such ills abound?
What for dejection, where presides a power,
Who call'd us into being to be blest?
So grieve, as conscious, grief may rise to joy;
So joy, as conscious, joy to grief may fall.
Most true, a wise man never will be sad;
But neither will sonorous, bubbling mirth,
A shallow stream of happiness betray:
Too happy to be sportive, he's serene.

    Yet wouldst thou laugh (but at thy own expense)
This counsel strange should I presume to give—
" Retire, and read thy Bible, to be gay."
There truths abound of sov'reign aid to peace;
Ah! do not prize them less, because inspir'd,
As thou, and thine, are apt and proud to do.
If not inspir'd, that pregnant page had stood,
Time's treasure! and the wonder of the wise!
Thou think'st, perhaps, thy soul alone at stake;
Alas!—Should men mistake thee for a fool;—
What man of taste for genius, wisdom, truth,
Tho' tender of thy fame, could interpose?
Believe me, sense, here, acts a double part,
And the true critic is a Christian too.   [joy.—

    But these, thou think'st, are gloomy paths to
True joy in sunshine ne'er was found at first;
They, first, themselves offend, who greatly please;
And travel only gives us sound repose.
Heaven sells all pleasure; effort is the price;
The joys of conquest, are the joys of man;
And glory the victorious laurel spreads

O'er pleasure's pure, perpetual, placid stream.
   There is a time, when toil must be preferr'd,
Or joy, by mistim'd fondness, is undone.
A man of pleasure, is a man of pains.
Thou wilt not take the trouble to be blest.
False joys, indeed, are born from want of thought;
From thoughts full bent, and energy, the true;
And that demands a mind in equal poise,
Remote from gloomy grief, and glaring joy.
Much joy not only speaks small happiness,
But happiness that shortly must expire.
Can joy, unbottom'd in reflection, stand?
And, in a tempest, can reflection live?
Can joy, like thine, secure itself an hour?
Can joy, like thine, meet accident unshock'd?
Or ope the door to honest poverty?
Or talk with threat'ning death, and not turn pale?
In such a world, and such a nature, these
Are needful fundamentals of delight:
These fundamentals give delight indeed;
Delight, pure, delicate, and durable;
Delight, unshaken, masculine, divine;
A constant, and a sound, but serious joy.
   Is joy the daughter of severity?
It is:—yet far my doctrine from severe.
" Rejoice for ever:" it becomes a man;
Exalts, and sets him nearer to the gods.
" Rejoice for ever!" Nature cries, " Rejoice;"
And drinks to man, in her nectareous cup,
Mixt up of delicates for every sense;
To the great founder of the bounteous feast,
Drinks glory, gratitude, eternal praise;
And he that will not pledge her, is a churl.
Ill firmly to support, good fully taste,

Is the whole science of felicity :
Yet sparing pledge : her bowl is not the best
Mankind can boast.—" A rational repast ;
Exertion, vigilance, a mind in arms,
A military discipline of thought,
To foil temptation in the doubtful field ;
And ever-waking ardour for the right."
'Tis these, first, give, then guard, a cheerful heart.
Nought that is right, think little ; well aware,
What reason bids, God bids ; by his command
How aggrandiz'd, the smallest thing we do !
Thus, nothing is insipid to the wise ;
To thee, insipid all, but what is mad ;
Joys season'd high, and tasting strong of guilt.
" Mad ! (thou repliest, with indignation fir'd)
Of ancient sages proud to tread the steps,
I follow nature."—Follow nature still,
But look it be thine own : Is conscience, then,
No part of nature ? Is she not supreme ?
Thou regicide ! O raise her from the dead !
Then, follow nature ; and resemble God.
    When, spite of conscience, pleasure is pursu'd,
Man's nature is unnaturally pleas'd :
And what's unnatural, is painful too
At intervals, and must disgust ev'n thee !
The fact thou know'st; but not, perhaps, the cause.
Virtue's foundations with the world's were laid ;
Heaven mixt her with our make, and twisted close
Her sacred int'rests with the strings of life.
Who breaks her awful mandate, shocks himself,
His better self: and is it greater pain,
Our soul should murmur, or our dust repine ?
And one, in their eternal war, must bleed.
    If one must suffer, which should least be spar'd?

The pains of mind surpass the pains of sense:
Ask, then, the gout, what torment is in guilt.
The joys of sense to mental joys are mean:
Sense on the present only feeds; the soul
On past, and future, forages for joy.
'Tis hers, by retrospect, thro' time to range;
And forward time's great sequel to survey.
Could human courts take vengeance on the mind,
Axes might rust, and racks, and gibbets, fall:
Guard, then, thy mind, and leave the rest to fate.
    Lorenzo! wilt thou never be a man?
The man is dead, who for the body lives
Lur'd, by the beating of his pulse, to list
With ev'ry lust, that wars against his peace;
And sets him quite at variance with himself.
Thyself, first, know; then love: a self there is
Of virtue fond, that kindles at her charms.
A self there is, as fond of every vice,
While every virtue wounds it to the heart:
Humility degrades it, justice robs,
Blest bounty beggars it, fair truth betrays,
And godlike magnanimity destroys.
This self, when rival to the former, scorn;
When not in competition, kindly treat,
Defend it, feed it:—but when virtue bids,
Toss it, or to the fowls, or to the flames.
And why? 'tis love of pleasure bids thee bleed;
Comply, or own self-love extinct, or blind.
    For what is vice? self-love in a mistake:
A poor blind merchant buying joys too dear.
And virtue, what? 'tis self-love in her wits,
Quite skilful in the market of delight.
Self-love's good sense is love of that dread power,
From whom herself, and all she can enjoy.

Other self-love is but disguis'd self-hate ;
More mortal than the malice of our foes ;
A self-hate, now, scarce felt ; then felt full sore,
When being, curst ; extinction, loud implor'd ;
And every thing preferr'd to what we are.

Yet this self-love Lorenzo makes his choice ;
And, in this choice triumphant, boasts of joy.
How is his want of happiness betray'd,
By disaffection to the present hour !
Imagination wanders far a-field :
The future pleases : why ? the present pains.—
' But that's a secret." Yes, which all men know ;
And know from thee, discover'd unawares.
Thy ceaseless agitation, restless roll
From cheat to cheat, impatient of a pause ;
What is it ?—'Tis the cradle of the soul,
From instinct sent, to rock her in disease,
Which her physician, Reason, will not cure.
A poor expedient ! yet thy best ; and while
It mitigates thy pain, it owns it too.

Such are Lorenzo's wretched remedies !
The weak have remedies ; the wise have joys.
Superior wisdom is superior bliss.
And what sure mark distinguishes the wise ?
Consistent wisdom ever wills the same ;
Thy fickle wish is ever on the wing
Sick of herself, is folly's character ;
As wisdom's is, a modest self-applause.
A change of evils is thy good supreme ;
Nor, but in motion, canst thou find thy rest.
Man's greatest strength is shown in standing still.
The first sure symptom of a mind in health,
Is rest of heart, and pleasure felt at home.
False pleasure from abroad her joys imports ;

Rich from within, and self-sustain'd, the true.
The true is fixt, and solid as a rock;
Slipp'ry the false, and tossing, as the wave.
This, a wild wanderer on earth, like Cain;
That, like the fabled, self-enamour'd boy,
Home-contemplation her supreme delight;
She dreads an interruption from without,
Smit with her own condition; and the more
Intense she gazes, still it charms the more.

No man is happy, till he thinks, on earth
There breathes not a more happy than himself:
Then envy dies, and love o'erflows on all;
And love o'erflowing makes an angel here.
Such angels, all, intitled to repose
On him who governs fate: tho' tempest frowns,
Tho' nature shakes, how soft to lean on heaven!
To lean on him, on whom archangels lean!
With inward eyes, and silent as the grave,
They stand collecting every beam of thought,
Till their hearts kindle with divine delight;
For all their thoughts, like angels, seen of old
In Israel's dream, come from, and go to, heaven:
Hence, are they studious of sequester'd scenes;
While noise, and dissipation, comfort thee.

Were all men happy, revellings would cease,
That opiate for inquietude within.
Lorenzo! never man was truly blest,
But it compos'd, and gave him such a cast,
As folly might mistake for want of joy.
A cast, unlike the triumph of the proud;
A modest aspect, and a smile at heart.
O for a joy from thy Philander's spring!
A spring perennial, rising in the breast,
And permanent, as pure! no turbid stream

Of rapturous exultation, swelling high;
Which, like land floods, impetuous pour awhile,
Then sink at once, and leave us in the mire.
What does the man, who transient joy prefers?
What, but prefer the bubbles to the stream?
  Vain are all sudden sallies of delight;
Convulsions of a weak, distemper'd joy.
Joy's a fixt state; a tenure, not a start.
Bliss there is none, but unprecarious bliss:
That is the gem: sell all, and purchase that.
Why go a begging to contingencies,
Not gain'd with ease, nor safely lov'd, if gain'd?
At good fortuitous, draw back, and pause;
Suspect it; what thou canst ensure, enjoy;
And nought but what thou giv'st thyself, is sure.
Reason perpetuates joy that reason gives,
And makes it as immortal as herself:
To mortals, nought immortal, but their worth.
  Worth, conscious worth! should absolutely reign;
And other joys ask leave for their approach;
Nor, unexamin'd, ever leave obtain.
Thou art all anarchy; a mob of joys
Wage war, and perish in intestine broils;
Not the least promise of internal peace!
No bosom-comfort! or unborrow'd bliss!
Thy thoughts are vagabonds; all outward-bound,
Mid sands, and rocks, and storms, to cruise for plea-
        sure;   [gain'd.
If gain'd, dear bought; and better miss'd than
Much pain must expiate, what much pain procur'd
Fancy, and sense, from an infected shore,
Thy cargo bring; and pestilence the prize.
Then, such thy thirst (insatiable thirst!
By fond indulgence but inflam'd the more!)

Fancy still cruises, when poor sense is tir'd.
 Imagination is the Paphian shop,
Where feeble happiness, like Vulcan, lame,
Bids foul ideas, in their dark recess,
And hot as hell (which kindled the black fires),
With wanton art, those fatal arrows form, [fame.
Which murder all thy time, health, wealth, and
Wouldst thou receive them, other thoughts there are,
On angel wing, descending from above,
Which these, with art divine, would counter-work,
And form celestial armour for thy peace.
 In this is seen imagination's guilt;
But who can count her follies? She betrays thee,
To think in grandeur there is something great.
For works of curious art, and ancient fame,
Thy genius hungers, elegantly pain'd;
And foreign climes must cater for thy taste.
Hence, what disaster!—Tho' the price was paid,
That persecuting priest, the Turk of Rome,
Whose foot (ye gods!) tho' cloven, must be kiss'd,
Detain'd thy dinner on the Latian shore;
(Such is the fate of honest Protestants!)
And poor magnificence is starv'd to death.
Hence just resentment, indignation, ire!—
Be pacified, if outward things are great,
'Tis magnanimity great things to scorn;
Pompous expenses, and parades august,
And courts, that insalubrious soil to peace.
True happiness ne'er enter'd at an eye;
True happiness resides in things unseen.
No smiles of fortune ever blest the bad,
Nor can her frowns rob innocence of joys;
That jewel wanting, triple crowns are poor:
So tell his holiness, and be reveng'd.

Pleasure, we both agree, is man's chief good;
Our only contest, what deserves the name.
Give pleasure's name to nought, but what has pass'd
Th' authentic seal of reason (which like Yorke,
Demurs on what it passes), and defies
The tooth of time; when past, a pleasure still;
Dearer on trial, lovelier for its age,
And doubly to be priz'd, as it promotes
Our future, while it forms our present, joy.
Some joys the future overcast; and some
Throw all their beams that way, and gild the tomb.
Some joys endear eternity; some give
Abhorr'd annihilation dreadful charms.
Are rival joys contending for thy choice?
Consult thy whole existence, and be safe;
That oracle will put all doubt to flight.
Short is the lesson, tho' my lecture long,
Be good—and let heaven answer for the rest.

Yet, with a sigh o'er all mankind, I grant
In this our day of proof, our land of hope,
The good man has his clouds that intervene;
Clouds, that obscure his sublunary day,
But never conquer: ev'n the best must own,
Patience, and resignation, are the pillars
Of human peace on earth.   The pillars, these:
But those of Seth not more remote from thee,
Till this heroic lesson thou hast learnt;
To frown at pleasure, and to smile in pain.
Fir'd at the prospect of unclouded bliss,
Heaven in reversion, like the sun, as yet
Beneath th' horizon, cheers us in this world;
It sheds, on souls susceptible of light,
The glorious dawn of our eternal day.

" This (says Lorenzo) is a fair harangue:

But can harangues blow back strong nature's
    stream;
Or stem the tide heaven pushes thro' our veins,
Which sweeps away man's impotent resolves,
And lays his labour level with the world?"
    Themselves men make their comment on man-
    kind;
And think nought is, but what they find at home:
Thus, weakness to chimera turns the truth.
Nothing romantic has the muse prescrib'd.
[1] Above, Lorenzo saw the man of earth,
The mortal man; and wretched was the sight.
To balance that, to comfort, and exalt
Now see the man immortal: him, I mean,
Who lives as such; whose heart, full bent on heaven,
Leans all that way, his bias to the stars.
The world's dark shades, in contrast set, shall raise
His lustre more; tho' bright, without a foil:
Observe his awful portrait, and admire
Nor stop at wonder; imitate, and live.
    Some angel guide my pencil, while I draw,
What nothing less than angel can exceed:
A man on earth devoted to the skies;
Like ships in sea, while in, above the world.
    With aspect mild, and elevated eye,
Behold him seated on a mount serene,
Above the fogs of sense, and passion's storm;
All the black cares, and tumults, of this life,
Like harmless thunders, breaking at his feet,
Excite his pity, not impair his peace.
Earth's genuine sons, the sceptred, and the slave,
A mingled mob! a wand'ring herd! he sees,
Bewilder'd in the vale; in all unlike!

          [1] In a former Night.

His full reverse in all! What higher praise?
What stronger demonstration of the right?
   The present all their care; the future, his.
When public welfare calls, or private want,
They give to fame; his bounty he conceals.
Their virtues varnish nature; his exalt.
Mankind's esteem they court; and he, his own.
Theirs, the wild chase of false felicities;
His, the compos'd possession of the true.
Alike throughout is his consistent peace,
All of one colour, and an even thread;
While party-colour'd shreds of happiness,
With hideous gaps between, patch up for them
A madman's robe; each puff of fortune blows
The tatters by, and shows their nakedness.
   He sees with other eyes than theirs: where they
Behold a sun, he spies a Deity;
What makes them only smile, makes him adore.
Where they see mountains, he but atoms sees;
An empire, in his balance, weighs a grain.
They things terrestrial worship, as divine:
His hopes immortal blow them by, as dust,
That dims his sight, and shortens his survey,
Which longs, in infinite, to lose all bound.
Titles and honours (if they prove his fate)
He lays aside to find his dignity;
No dignity they find in aught besides.
They triumph in externals (which conceal
Man's real glory), proud of an eclipse.
Himself too much he prizes to be proud,
And nothing thinks so great in man, as man.
Too dear he holds his int'rest, to neglect
Another's welfare, or his right invade;
Their int'rest, like a lion, lives on prey.

They kindle at the shadow of a wrong;
Wrong he sustains with temper, looks on heaven,
Nor stoops to think his injurer his foe;　[peace.
Nought, but what wounds his virtue, wounds his
A cover'd heart their character defends;
A cover'd heart denies him half his praise.
With nakedness his innocence agrees;
While their broad foliage testifies their fall:
Their no joys end, where his full feast begins:
His joys create, theirs murder, future bliss.
To triumph in existence, his alone;
And his alone, triumphantly to think
His true existence is not yet begun.
His glorious course was, yesterday, complete;
Death, then, was welcome; yet life still is sweet.

But nothing charms Lorenzo, like the firm,
Undaunted breast—and whose is that high praise?
They yield to pleasure, tho' they danger brave,
And show no fortitude, but in the field;
If there they show it, 'tis for glory shown;
Nor will that cordial always man their hearts.
A cordial his sustains, that cannot fail;
By pleasure unsubdu'd, unbroke by pain,
He shares in that Omnipotence he trusts.
All-bearing, all-attempting, till he falls;
And when he falls, writes Vici on his shield.
From magnanimity, all fear above;
From nobler recompense, above applause;
Which owes to man's short out-look all its charms.

Backward to credit what he never felt,
Lorenzo cries,—" Where shines this miracle?
From what root rises this immortal man?"
A root that grows not in Lorenzo's ground;
The root dissect, nor wonder at the flower.

He follows nature (not like [1]thee) and shows us
An uninverted system of a man.
His appetite wears reason's golden chain,
And finds, in due restraint, its luxury.
His passion, like an eagle well reclaim'd,
Is taught to fly at nought, but infinite.
Patient his hope, unanxious is his care,
His caution fearless, and his grief (if grief
The gods ordain) a stranger to despair.
And why?—Because affection, more than meet,
His wisdom leaves not disengaged from heaven.
Those secondary goods that smile on earth,
He, loving in proportion, loves in peace.
They most the world enjoy, who least admire.
His understanding 'scapes the common cloud
Of fumes, arising from a boiling breast.
His head is clear, because his heart is cool,
By worldly competitions uninflam'd.
The mod'rate movements of his soul admit
Distinct ideas, and matur'd debate,
An eye impartial, and an even scale;
Whence judgment sound, and unrepenting choice.
Thus, in a double sense, the good are wise;
On its own dunghill, wiser than the world.
What then, the world? it must be doubly weak;
Strange truth! as soon would they believe their
    Yet thus it is; nor otherwise can be; [creed.
So far from aught romantic, what I sing.
Bliss has no being, virtue has no strength,
But from the prospect of immortal life.
Who think earth all, or (what weighs just the same)
Who care no farther, must prize what it yields;
Fond of its fancies, proud of its parades.

See page 207, line 15.

Who thinks earth nothing, can't its charms admire;
He can't a foe, tho' most malignant, hate,
Because that hate would prove his greater foe.
'Tis hard for them (yet who so loudly boast
Good-will to men?) to love their dearest friend;
For may not he invade their good supreme,
Where the least jealousy turns love to gall?
All shines to them, that for a season shines.
Each act, each thought, he questions, " What its
         weight,
Its colour what, a thousand ages hence?"——
And what it there appears, he deems it now.
Hence, pure are the recesses of his soul.
The godlike man has nothing to conceal.
His virtue, constitutionally deep,
Has habits firmness, and affection's flame;
Angels, allied, descend to feed the fire;
And death, which others slays, makes him a god.
   And now, Lorenzo! bigot of this world!
Wont to disdain poor bigots caught by heaven!
Stand by thy scorn, and be reduc'd to nought:
For what art thou?—Thou boaster! while thy glare,
Thy gaudy grandeur, and mere worldly worth,
Like a broad mist, at distance, strikes us most;
And, like a mist, is nothing when at hand;
His merit, like a mountain, on approach,
Swells more, and rises nearer to the skies,
By promise now, and, by possession, soon,
(Too soon, too much, it cannot be) his own.
   From this thy just annihilation rise,
Lorenzo! rise to something, by reply.
The world, thy client, listens, and expects;
And longs to crown thee with immortal praise
Canst thou be silent? no; for wit is thine;

And wit talks most, when least she has to say,
And reason interrupts not her career.
She'll say—that mists above the mountains rise;
And, with a thousand pleasantries, amuse;
She'll sparkle, puzzle, flutter, raise a dust,
And fly conviction, in the dust she rais'd.

Wit, how delicious to man's dainty taste!
'Tis precious, as the vehicle of sense;
But, as its substitute, a dire disease.
Pernicious talent! flatter'd by the world,
By the blind world, which thinks the talent rare.
Wisdom is rare, Lorenzo! wit abounds;
Passion can give it; sometimes wine inspires
The lucky flash; and madness rarely fails.
Whatever cause the spirit strongly stirs,
Confers the bays, and rivals thy renown.
For thy renown, 'twere well, was this the worst;
Chance often hits it; and, to pique thee more,
See dulness, blund'ring on vivacities,
Shakes her sage head at the calamity,
Which has expos'd, and let her down to thee.
But wisdom, awful wisdom! which inspects,
Discerns, compares, weighs, separates, infers,
Seizes the right, and holds it to the last;
How rare! In senates, synods, sought in vain;
Or if there found, 'tis sacred to the few;
While a lewd prostitute to multitudes,
Frequent, as fatal, wit: in civil life,
Wit makes an enterpriser; sense, a man.
Wit hates authority; commotion loves,
And thinks herself the lightning of the storm.
In states, 'tis dangerous; in religion, death:
Shall wit turn Christian, when the dull believe?
Sense is our helmet, wit is but the plume;

The plume exposes, 'tis out helmet saves.
Sense is the diamond, weighty, solid, sound;
When cut by wit, it casts a brighter beam;
Yet, wit apart, it is a diamond still.
Wit, widow'd of good sense, is worse than nought;
It hoists more sail to run against a rock.
Thus, a half-Chesterfield is quite a fool;
Whom dull fools scorn, and bless their want of wit.

How ruinous the rock I warn thee shun,
Where sirens sit, to sing thee to thy fate!
A joy, in which our reason bears no part,
Is but a sorrow tickling, ere it stings.
Let not the cooings of the world allure thee;
Which of her lovers ever found her true?
Happy! of this bad world who little know?--
And yet, we much must know her, to be safe,
To know the world, not love her, is thy point;
She gives but little, nor that little, long.
There is, I grant, a triumph of the pulse;
A dance of spirits, a mere froth of joy,
Our thoughtless agitation's idle child,
That mantles high, that sparkles, and expires,
Leaving the soul more vapid than before.
An animal ovation! such as holds
No commerce with our reason, but subsists
On juices, thro' the well ton'd tubes, well strain'd;
A nice machine! scarce ever tun'd aright;
And when it jars—thy sirens sing no more,
Thy dance is done; the demi-god is thrown
(Short apotheosis!) beneath the man,
In coward gloom immers'd, or fell despair.

Art thou yet dull enough despair to dread,
And startle at destruction? If thou art,
Accept a buckler, take it to the field;

(A field of battle is this mortal life !)
When danger threatens, lay it on thy heart;
A single sentence proof against the world.
" Soul, body, fortune ! Every good pertains
To one of these ; but prize not all alike ;
The goods of fortune to thy body's health,
Body to soul, and soul submit to God."
Wouldst thou build lasting happiness ? Do this;
Th' inverted pyramid can never stand.

Is this truth doubtful ? it outshines the sun ;
Nay, the sun shines not, but to show us this,
The single lesson of mankind on earth.
And yet—yet, what ? no news ! Mankind is mad;
Such mighty number's list against the right,
(And what can't numbers, when bewitch'd,
          achieve !)
They talk themselves to something like belief,
That all earth's joys are theirs : as Athen's fool
Grinn'd from the port, on every sail his own.
    They grin ; but wherefore ? and how long the
          laugh ?
Half ignorance, their mirth ; and half, a lie ;
To cheat the world, and cheat themselves, they
          smile.
Hard either task ! the most abandon'd own,
That others, if abandon'd, are undone :
Then, for themselves, the moment reason wakes,
(And Providence denies it long repose)
O how laborious is their gaiety !
They scarce can swallow their ebullient spleen,
Scarce muster patience to support the farce,
And pump sad laughter till the curtain falls.
Scarce, did I say ? some cannot sit it out ;
Oft their own daring hands the curtain draw,

And show us what their joy, by their despair.
   The clotted hair! gor'd breast! blaspheming eye!
Its impious fury still alive in death!
Shut, shut the shocking scene.—But heaven denies
A cover to such guilt; and so should man.
Look round, Lorenzo! see the reeking blade,
Th' invenom'd phial, and the fatal ball;
The strangling cord, and suffocating stream;
The loathsome rottenness, and foul decays
From raging riot (slower suicides!)
And pride in these, more execrable still!
How horrid all to thought!—But horrors, these,
That vouch the truth; and aid my feeble song.
   From vice, sense, fancy, no man can be blest:
Bliss is too great, to lodge within an hour:
When an immortal being aims at bliss,
Duration is essential to the name.
O for a joy from reason! Joy from that,
Which makes man man; and, exercis'd aright,
Will make him more: a bounteous joy! that gives,
And promises; that weaves, with art divine,
The richest prospect into present peace:
A joy ambitious! joy in common held
With thrones ethereal, and their greater far;
A joy high-privileg'd from chance, time, death!
A joy, which death shall double, judgment crown!
Crown'd higher, and still higher, at each stage,
Thro' blest eternity's long day; yet still,
Not more remote from sorrow, than from him,
Whose lavish hand, whose love stupendous, pours
So much of deity on guilty dust.
There, O my Lucia! may I meet thee there,
Where not thy presence can improve my bliss!
   Affects not this the sages of the world?

Can nought affect them, but what fools them too?
Eternity, depending on an hour,   [praise,
Makes serious thought man's wisdom, joy, and
Nor need you blush (tho' sometimes your designs
May shun the light) at your designs on heaven :
Sole point ! where over-bashful is your blame.
Are you not wise ?—You know you are : yet hear
One truth, amid your num'rous schemes, mislaid,
Or overlook'd, or thrown aside, if seen ;
" Our schemes to plan by this world, or the next,
Is the sole difference between wise and fool."
All worthy men will weigh you in this scale ;
What wonder then, if they pronounce you light?
Is their esteem alone not worth your care ?
Accept my simple scheme of common sense :
Thus, save your fame, and make two worlds your
    own.
    The world replies not ;—but the world persists;
And puts the cause off to the longest day,
Planning evasions for the day of doom.
So far, at that re-hearing, from redress,
They then turn witnesses against themselves,
Hear that, Lorenzo ! Nor be wise to-morrow.
Haste, haste ! a man, by nature, is in haste ;
For who shall answer for another hour ?
'Tis highly prudent, to make one sure friend ;
And that thou canst not do, this side the skies.
    Ye sons of earth ! (nor willing to be more !)
Since verse you think from priestcraft somewhat
    free,
Thus, in an age so gay, the muse plain truths
(Truths, which, at church, you might have heard
    in prose)
Has ventur'd into light; well pleas'd the verse

Should be forgot, if you the truths retain;
And crown her with your welfare, not your praise.
But praise she need not fear: I see my fate;
And headlong leap, like Curtius, down the gulf.
Since many an ample volume, mighty tome,
Must die; and die unwept; O thou minute
Devoted page! go forth among thy foes;
Go, nobly proud of martyrdom for truth,
And die a double death: mankind incens'd,
Denies thee long to live: nor shalt thou rest,
When thou art dead; in Stygian shades arraign'd
By Lucifer, as traitor to his throne;
And bold blasphemer of his friend,—the world;
The world, whose legions cost him slender pay,
And volunteers, around his banner swarm;
Prudent, as Prussia, in her zeal for Gaul.

   "Are all, then, fools?" Lorenzo cries.—Yes, all,
But such as hold this doctrine (new to thee);
" The mother of true wisdom is the will;"
The noblest intellect, a fool without it.
World-wisdom much has done, and more may do,
In arts and sciences, in wars, and peace;
But art and science, like thy wealth, will leave thee.
And make thee twice a beggar at thy death.
This is the most indulgence can afford;—
" Thy wisdom all can do, but—make thee wise."
Nor think this censure is severe on thee;
Satan, thy master, I dare call a dunce.

NIGHT IX. AND LAST.

THE CONSOLATION.

CONTAINING, AMONG OTHER THINGS, I. A MORAL SURVEY
OF THE NOCTURNAL HEAVENS.   II. A NIGHT
ADDRESS TO THE DEITY.
HUMBLY INSCRIBED TO HIS GRACE THE DUKE OF NEWCASTLE,
ONE OF HIS MAJESTY'S PRINCIPAL SECRETARIES
OF STATE.

——————— Fatis contraria fata rependens.—VIRG.

As when a traveller, a long day past
In painful search of what he cannot find,
At night's approach, content with the next cot,
There ruminates, a while, his labour lost;
Then cheers his heart with what his fate affords,
And chants his sonnet to deceive the time,
Till the due season calls him to repose:
Thus I, long-travell'd in the ways of men,
And dancing, with the rest, the giddy maze,
Where disappointment smiles at hope's career;
Warn'd by the languor of life's evening ray,
At length have hous'd me in an humble shed
Where, future wand'ring banish'd from my thought,
And waiting, patient, the sweet hour of rest,
I chase the moments with a serious song.
Song soothes our pains; and age has pains to soothe.
　　When age, care, crime, and friends embrac'd at
　　　　　heart,   [shade,
Torn from my bleeding breast, and death's dark
Which hovers o'er me, quench th' ethereal fire;
Canst thou, O night! indulge one labour more?
One labour more indulge! then sleep, my strain!

Till, haply, wak'd by Raphael's golden lyre,
Where night, death, age, care, crime, and sorrow,
To bear a part in everlasting lays;   [cease;
Though far, far higher set, in aim, I trust,
Symphonious to this humble prelude here.

Has not the muse asserted pleasures pure,
Like those above; exploding other joys?
Weigh what was urg'd, Lorenzo! fairly weigh;
And tell me, hast thou cause to triumph still?
I think, thou wilt forbear a boast so bold.
But if, beneath the favour of mistake,
Thy smile's sincere; not more sincere can be
Lorenzo's smile, than my compassion for him.
The sick in body call for aid; the sick
In mind are covetous of more disease;   [well.
And when at worst, they dream themselves quite
To know ourselves diseas'd, is half our cure.
When nature's blush by custom is wip'd off,
And conscience, deaden'd by repeated strokes,
Has into manners naturaliz'd our crimes;
The curse of curses is, our curse to love;
To triumph in the blackness of our guilt
(As Indians glory in the deepest jet),
And throw aside our senses with our peace.

But grant no guilt, no shame, no least alloy;
Grant joy and glory quite unsullied shone;
Yet, still, it ill deserves Lorenzo's heart.
No joy, no glory, glitters in thy sight,
But, through the thin partition of an hour,
I see its sables wove by destiny;
And that in sorrow buried; this, in shame;
While howling furies ring the doleful knell;
And conscience, now so soft thou scarce canst hear
Her whisper, echoes her eternal peal.

Where the prime actors of the last year's scene;
Their port so proud, their buskin, and their plume?
How many sleep, who kept the world awake
With lustre, and with noise! has death proclaim'd
A truce, and hung his sated lance on high?
'Tis brandish'd still; nor shall the present year
Be more tenacious of her human leaf,
Or spread of feeble life a thinner fall.

But needless monuments to wake the thought;
Life's gayest scenes speak man's mortality;
Though in a style more florid, full as plain,
As mausoleums, pyramids, and tombs.
What are our noblest ornaments, but deaths
Turn'd flatterers of life, in paint, or marble,
The well stain'd canvass, or the featur'd stone?
Our fathers grace, or rather haunt, the scene.
Joy peoples her pavilion from the dead.

" Profest diversions! cannot these escape?"—
Far from it: these present us with a shroud;
And talk of death, like garlands o'er a grave.
As some bold plunderers, for buried wealth,
We ransack tombs for pastime; from the dust
Call up the sleeping hero; bid him tread
The scene for our amusement: how like gods
We sit; and, wrapt in immortality,
Shed gen'rous tears on wretches born to die;
Their fate deploring, to forget our own!

What all the pomps and triumphs of our lives,
But legacies in blossom? Our lean soil,
Luxuriant grown, and rank in vanities,
From friends interr'd beneath; a rich manure!
Like other worms, we banquet on the dead;
Like other worms, shall we crawl on, nor know
Our present frailties, or approaching fate?

Lorenzo ! such the glories of the world !
What is the world itself ? Thy world—a grave.
Where is the dust that has not been alive ?
The spade, the plough, disturb our ancestors ;
From human mould we reap our daily bread.
The globe around earth's hollow surface shakes,
And is the ceiling of her sleeping sons.
O'er devastation we blind revels keep ;
Whole buried towns support the dancer's heel.
The moist of human frame the sun exhales ;·
Winds scatter through the mighty void the dry ;
Earth repossesses part of what she gave,
And the freed spirit mounts on wings of fire ;
Each element partakes our scatter'd spoils ;
As nature, wide, our ruins spread : man's death
Inhabits all things, but the thought of man.

Nor man alone ; his breathing bust expires,
His tomb is mortal ; empires die : where, now,
The Roman ? Greek ? They stalk, an empty name !
Yet few regard them in this useful light ;
Though half our learning is their epitaph.
When down thy vale, unlockt by midnight thought,
That loves to wander in thy sunless realms,
O death ! I stretch my view : what visions rise !
What triumphs ! toils imperial ! arts divine !
In wither'd laurels glide before my sight !
What lengths of far-fam'd ages, billow'd high
With human agitation, roll along
In unsubstantial images of air !
The melancholy ghosts of dead renown,
Whisp'ring faint echoes of the world's applause,
With penitential aspect, as they pass,
All point at earth, and hiss at human pride,
The wisdom of the wise, and prancings of the great.

But, O Lorenzo ! far the rest above,
Of ghastly nature, and enormous size,
One form assaults my sight, and chills my blood,
And shakes my frame.   Of one departed world
I see the mighty shadow : oozy wreath
And dismal sea-weed crown her ; o'er her urn
Reclin'd, she weeps her desolated realms,
And bloated sons ; and, weeping, prophesies
Another's dissolution, soon, in flames.
But, like Cassandra, prophesies in vain ;
In vain, to many ; not, I trust, to thee.

For, know'st thou not, or art thou loth to know
The great decree, the counsel of the skies ?
Deluge and conflagration, dreadful powers !
Prime ministers of vengeance ! chain'd in caves
Distinct, apart the giant furies roar ;
Apart ; or, such their horrid rage for ruin,
In mutual conflict would they rise, and wage
Eternal war, till one was quite devour'd.
But not for this, ordain'd their boundless rage ;
When heaven's inferior instruments of wrath,
War, famine, pestilence, are found too weak
To scourge a world for her enormous crimes,
These are let loose, alternate : down they rush,
Swift and tempestuous, from th' eternal throne,
With irresistible commission arm'd,
The world, in vain corrected, to destroy,
And ease creation of the shocking scene.

Seest thou, Lorenzo ! what depends on man ?
The fate of nature ; as for man, her birth.
Earth's actors change earth's transitory scenes
And make creation groan with human guilt.
How must it groan, in a new deluge whelm'd,
But not of waters ! At the destin'd hour,

By the loud trumpet summon'd to the charge,
See, all the formidable sons of fire,
Eruptions, earthquakes, comets, lightnings, play
Their various engines; all at once disgorge
Their blazing magazines; and take, by storm,
This poor terrestrial citadel of man.

    Amazing period! when each mountain-height
Out-burns Vesuvius; rocks eternal pour
Their melted mass, as rivers once they pour'd;
Stars rush; and final ruin fiercely drives
Her ploughshare o'er creation!—while aloft,
More than astonishment! if more can be!
Far other firmament than e'er was seen,
Than e'er was thought by man! far other stars!
Stars animate, that govern these of fire;
Far other sun!—A sun, O how unlike
The Babe at Bethlem! how unlike the man,
That groan'd on Calvary!—Yet he it is;
That man of sorrows! O how chang'd! what pomp!
In grandeur terrible, all heaven descends!
And gods, ambitious, triumph in his train.
A swift archangel, with his golden wing,
As blots and clouds, that darken and disgrace
The scene divine, sweeps stars and suns aside.
And now, all dross remov'd, heaven's own pure day,
Full on the confines of our ether, flames.
While (dreadful contrast!) far, how far beneath!
Hell, bursting, belches forth her blazing seas,
And storms sulphureous; her voracious jaws
Expanding wide, and roaring for her prey.

    Lorenzo! welcome to this scene; the last
In nature's course; the first in wisdom's thought.
This strikes, if aught can strike thee; this awakes
The most supine; this snatches man from death.

Rouse, rouse, Lorenzo, then, and follow me,
Where truth, the most momentous man can hear,
Loud calls my soul, and ardour wings her flight.
I find my inspiration in my theme;
The grandeur of my subject is my muse.

At midnight, when mankind is wrapt in peace,
And worldly fancy feeds on golden dreams;
To give more dread to man's most dreadful hour,
At midnight, 'tis presum'd, this pomp will burst
From tenfold darkness; sudden as the spark
From smitten steel; from nitrous grain, the blaze.
Man, starting from his couch, shall sleep no more!
The day is broke, which never more shall close!
Above, around, beneath, amazement all!
Terror and glory join'd in their extremes!
Our God in grandeur, and our world on fire!
All nature struggling in the pangs of death!
Dost thou not hear her? Dost thou not deplore
Her strong convulsions, and her final groan?
Where are we now? Ah me! the ground is gone,
On which we stood; Lorenzo! while thou may'st,
Provide more firm support, or sink for ever!
Where? how? from whence? vain hope! it is too late!
Where, where, for shelter, shall the guilty fly,
When consternation turns the good man pale?

Great day! for which all other days were made;
For which earth rose from chaos, man from earth;
And an eternity, the date of gods,
Descended on poor earth-created man!
Great day of dread, decision, and despair!
At thought of thee each sublunary wish
Lets go its eager grasp, and drops the world;
And catches at each reed of hope in heaven.
At thought of thee!—and art thou absent then?

Lorenzo! no; 'tis here; it is begun;—
Already is begun the grand assize,
In thee, in all : deputed conscience scales
The dread tribunal, and forestalls our doom ;
Forestalls ; and, by forestalling, proves it sure.
Why on himself should man void judgment pass?
Is idle nature laughing at her sons?
Who conscience sent, her sentence will support,
And God above assert that God in man.

   Thrice happy they! that enter now the court
Heaven opens in their bosoms : but, how rare,
Ah me! that magnanimity, how rare !
What hero, like the man who stands himself ;
Who dares to meet his naked heart alone ;
Who hears, intrepid, the full charge it brings,
Resolv'd to silence future murmurs there ?
The coward flies ; and, flying, is undone.
(Art thou a coward? No:) The coward flies ;
Thinks, but thinks slightly; asks, but fears to know;
Asks, " What is truth;" with Pilate ; and retires;
Dissolves the court, and mingles with the throng;
Asylum sad! from reason, hope, and heaven!

   Shall all, but man, look out with ardent eye,
For that great day, which was ordain'd for man?
O day of consummation! mark supreme
(If men are wise) of human thought ! nor least,
Or in the sight of angels, or their king !
Angels, whose radiant circles, height o'er height,
Order o'er order, rising, blaze o'er blaze,
As in a theatre, surround this scene,
Intent on man, and anxious for his fate.
Angels look out for thee; for thee, their Lord,
To vindicate his glory; and for thee,
Creation universal calls aloud,

To disinvolve the moral world, and give
To nature's renovation brighter charms.
 Shall man alone, whose fate, whose final fate,
Hangs on that hour, exclude it from his thought?
I think of nothing else; I see! I feel it!
All nature, like an earthquake, trembling round!
All deities, like summer's swarms, on wing!
All basking in the full meridian blaze!
I see the judge inthron'd! the flaming guard!
The volume open'd! open'd ev'ry heart!
A sunbeam pointing out each secret thought!
No patron! intercessor none! now past
The sweet, the clement, mediatorial hour!
For guilt no plea! to pain, no pause! no bound!
Inexorable, all! and all, extreme!
 Nor man alone; the foe of God and man,
From his dark den, blaspheming, drags his chain,
And rears his brazen front, with thunder scarr'd:
Receives his sentence, and begins his hell.
All vengeance past, now, seems abundant grace:
Like meteors in a stormy sky, how roll
His baleful eyes! he curses whom he dreads;
And deems it the first moment of his fall.
'Tis present to my thought!—and yet where is it?
Angels can't tell me; angels cannot guess
The period; from created beings lock'd
In darkness. But the process, and the place,
Are less obscure; for these may man enquire.
Say, thou great close of human hopes and fears!
Great key of hearts! great finisher of fates!
Great end! and great beginning! say, where art thou?
Art thou in time, or in eternity?
Nor in eternity, nor time, I find thee.
These, as two monarchs, on their borders meet,

(Monarchs of all elaps'd, or unarriv'd !)
As in debate, how best their pow'rs allied,
May swell the grandeur, or discharge the wrath,
Of him, whom both their monarchies obey.

   Time, this fast fabric for him built (and doom'd
With him to fall) now bursting o'er his head;
His lamp, the sun, extinguish'd; from beneath
The frown of hideous darkness, calls his sons
From their long slumber; from earth's heaving
        womb,
To second birth! contemporary throng!
Rous'd at one call, upstarted from one bed,
Prest in one crowd, appall'd with one amaze,
He turns them o'er, eternity! to thee.
Then (as a king depos'd disdains to live)
He falls on his own scythe; nor falls alone ·
His greatest foe falls with him; time, and he
Who murder'd all time's offspring, death, expire.

   Time was! eternity now reigns alone
Awful eternity! offended queen!
And her resentment to mankind, how just!
With kind intent, soliciting access,
How often has she knock'd at human hearts!
Rich to repay their hospitality,
How often call'd ! and with the voice of God !
Yet bore repulse, excluded as a cheat!
A dream! while foulest foes found welcome there!
A dream, a cheat, now, all things, but her smile.

   For, lo ! her twice ten thousand gates thrown
As thrice from Indus to the frozen pole,   [wide,
With banners streaming as the comet's blaze,
And clarions, louder than the deep in storms,
Sonorous as immortal breath can blow,
Pour forth their myriads, potentates, and powers,

Of light, of darkness; in a middle field,
Wide, as creation! populous, as wide!
A neutral region! there to mark th' event
Of that great drama, whose preceding scenes
Detain'd them close spectators, through a length
Of ages, ripening to this grand result;
Ages, as yet unnumber'd, but by God;
Who now, pronouncing sentence, vindicates
The rights of virtue, and his own renown.

Eternity, the various sentence past,
Assigns the sever'd throng distinct abodes,
Sulphureous, or ambrosial: what ensues?
The deed predominant! the deed of deeds!
Which makes a hell of hell, a heaven of heaven.
The goddess, with determin'd aspect, turns
Her adamantine key's enormous size
Through destiny's inextricable wards,
Deep driving every bolt, on both their fates.
Then, from the crystal battlements of heaven,
Down, down, she hurls it thro' the dark profound,
Ten thousand thousand fathom; there to rust,
And ne'er unlock her resolution more.
The deep resounds, and hell, through all her glooms,
Returns, in groans, the melancholy roar.

O how unlike the chorus of the skies!
O how unlike those shouts of joy, that shake
The whole ethereal! how the concave rings!
Nor strange! when deities their voice exalt;
And louder far, than when creation rose,
To see creation's godlike aim, and end,
So well accomplish'd! so divinely clos'd!
To see the mighty dramatist's last act
(As meet) in glory rising o'er the rest.
No fancied god, a God indeed descends,

To solve all knots ; to strike the moral home;
To throw full day on darkest scenes of time ;
To clear, commend, exalt, and crown the whole.
Hence, in one peal of loud, eternal praise,
The charm'd spectators thunder their applause ;
And the vast void beyond, applause resounds.
    What then am I ?—
                            Amidst applauding worlds,
And worlds celestial, is there found on earth,
A peevish, dissonant, rebellious string,
Which jars in the grand chorus, and complains ?
Censure on thee, Lorenzo! I suspend,
And turn it on myself; how greatly due !
All, all is right; by God ordain'd or done ;
And who, but God, resum'd the friends He gave ?
And have I been complaining, then, so long ?
Complaining of his favours; pain, and death ?
Who, without pain's advice, would e'er be good ?
Who, without death, but would be good in vain ?
Pain is to save from pain ; all punishment,
To make for peacé ; and death to save from death ;
And second death, to guard immortal life ;
To rouse the careless, the presumptuous awe,
And turn the tide of souls another way ;
By the same tenderness divine ordain'd,
That planted Eden, and high-bloom'd for man,
A fairer Eden, endless, in the skies.
    Heaven gives us friends to bless the present
        scene ;
Resumes them, to prepare us for the next.
All evils natural are moral goods ;
All discipline, indulgence, on the whole.
None are unhappy: all have cause to smile,
But such as to themselves that cause deny.

Our faults are at the bottom of our pains;
Error, in acts, or judgment, is the source
Of endless sighs: we sin, or we mistake;
And nature tax, when false opinion stings.
Let impious grief be banish'd, joy indulg'd;
But chiefly then, when grief puts in her claim
Joy from the joyous, frequently betrays,
Oft lives in vanity, and dies in woe.
Joy, amidst ills, corroborates, exalts;
'Tis joy and conquest; joy, and virtue too.
A noble fortitude in ills, delights
Heaven, earth, ourselves; 'tis duty, glory, peace.
Affliction is the good man's shining scene;
Prosperity conceals his brightest ray;
As night to stars, woe lustre gives to man.
Heroes in battle, pilots in the storm,
And virtue in calamities, admire.
The crown of manhood is a winter joy;
An evergreen, that stands the northern blast,
And blossoms in the rigour of our fate
    'Tis a prime part of happiness, to know
How much unhappiness must prove our lot:
A part which few possess! I'll pay life's tax,
Without one rebel murmur, from this hour,
Nor think it misery to be a man;
Who thinks it is, shall never be a God.
Some ills we wish for, when we wish to live.
    What spoke proud passion?—" [1] Wish my being
        lost?"
Presumptuous! blasphemous! absurd! and false!
The triumph of my soul is,—that I am;
And therefore that I may be—what? Lorenzo!

---

[1] Referring to the first night.

Look inward, and look deep ; and deeper still ;
Unfathomably deep our treasure runs
In golden veins, through all eternity !
Ages, and ages, and succeeding still
New ages, where the phantom of an hour,
Which courts each night, dull slumber, for repair,
Shall wake, and wonder, and exult, and praise,
And fly through infinite, and all unlock ;
And (if deserv'd) by heaven's redundant love,
Made half-adorable itself, adore ;
And find, in adoration, endless joy !
Where thou, not master of a moment here,
Frail as the flower, and fleeting as the gale,
May'st boast a whole eternity, enrich'd
With all a kind Omnipotence can pour.
Since Adam fell, no mortal, uninspir'd,
Has ever yet conceiv'd, or ever shall,
How kind is God, how great (if good) is man.
No man too largely from heaven's love can hope,
If what is hop'd he labours to secure.
      Ills ?—there are none : All-gracious ! none from
            thee ;
From man full many ! numerous is the race
Of blackest ills, and those immortal too
Begot by madness on fair liberty ;
Heaven's daughter, hell debauch'd ! her hand alone
Unlocks destruction to the sons of men,
Fast barr'd by thine : high-wall'd with adamant,
Guarded with terrors reaching to this world,
And cover'd with the thunders of thy law ;
Whose threats are mercies, whose injunctions
            guides,
Assisting, not restraining, reason's choice ;
Whose sanctions, unavoidable results

From nature's course, indulgently reveal'd ;
If unreveal'd, more dang'rous, nor less sure.
Thus, an indulgent father warns his sons,
" Do this; fly that"—nor always tells the cause ;
Pleas'd to reward, as duty to his will,
A conduct needful to their own repose.

Great God of wonders ! (if, thy love survey'd,
Aught else the name of wonderful retains)
What rocks are these, on which to build our trust!
Thy ways admit no blemish ; none I find ;
Or this alone—" That none is to be found."
Not one, to soften censure's hardy crime ;
Not one, to palliate peevish grief's complaint,
Who like a demon, murm'ring from the dust,
Dares into judgment call her judge.—Supreme !
For all I bless thee ; most, for the severe ;
[1] Her death—my own at hand—the fiery gulf,
That flaming bound of wrath omnipotent !
It thunders ;—but it thunders to preserve ;
It strengthens what it strikes ; its wholesome dread
Averts the dreaded pain ; its hideous groans
Join heaven's sweet hallelujahs in thy praise,
Great source of good alone ! how kind in all !
In vengeance kind ! pain, death, gehenna, save.

Thus, in thy world material, mighty mind !
Not that alone which solaces, and shines,
The rough and gloomy, challenges our praise.
The winter is as needful as the spring ;
The thunder, as the sun ; a stagnate mass
Of vapours breeds a pestilential air :
Nor more propitious the Favonian breeze
To nature's health, than purifying storms ;

[1] Lucia.

The dread volcano ministers to good.
Its smother'd flames might undermine the world.
Loud Ætnas fulminate in love to man;
Comets good omens are, when duly scann'd;
And, in their use, eclipses learn to shine.
   Man is responsible for ills receiv'd;
Those we call wretched are a chosen band,
Compell'd to refuge in the right, for peace.
Amid my list of blessings infinite,
Stand this the foremost, " That my heart has bled."
'Tis heaven's last effort of good-will to man;
When pain can't bless, heaven quits us in despair.
Who fails to grieve, when just occasion calls,
Or grieves too much, deserves not to be 'blest;
Inhuman, or effeminate, his heart;
Reason absolves the grief, which reason ends.
May heaven ne'er trust my friend with happiness,
Till it has taught him how to bear it well,
By previous pain; and made it safe to smile!
Such smiles are mine, and such may they remain;
Nor hazard their extinction, from excess.
My change of heart a change of style demands;
The consolation cancels the complaint,
And makes a convert of my guilty song.
   As when o'er-labour'd, and inclin'd to breathe,
A panting traveller, some rising ground,
Some small ascent, has gain'd, he turns him round,
And measures with his eye the various vales,
The fields, woods, meads, and rivers, he has past;
And, satiate of his journey, thinks of home,
Endear'd by distance, nor affects more toil;
Thus I, though small, indeed, is that ascent
The muse has gain'd, review the paths she trod;
Various, extensive, beaten but by few;

And, conscious of her prudence in repose,
Pause ; and with pleasure meditate an end,
Though still remote ; so fruitful is my theme.
Through many a field of moral, and divine,
The muse has stray'd ; and much of sorrow seen
In human ways ; and much of false and vain ;
Which none, who travel this bad road, can miss.
O'er friends deceas'd full heartily she wept ;
Of love divine the wonders she display'd ;
Prov'd man immortal ; show'd the source of joy ;
The grand tribunal rais'd ; assign'd the bounds
Of human grief : in few, to close the whole,
The moral muse has shadow'd out a sketch,
Though not in form, nor with a Raphael-stroke,
Of most our weakness needs believe, or do,
In this our land of travel, and of hope,
For peace on earth, or prospect of the skies.
    What then remains ? much ! much ! a mighty
            debt   [thine ;
To be discharg'd : these thoughts, O night ! are
From thee they came, like lovers' secret sighs,
While others slept. So, Cynthia (poets feign)
In shadows veil'd, soft sliding from her sphere,
Her shepherd cheer'd ; of her enamour'd less,
Than I of thee.—And art thou still unsung,
Beneath whose brow, and by whose aid, I sing ?
Immoral silence ! where shall I begin ?
Where end ? or how steal music from the spheres,
To soothe their goddess ?
                        O majestic Night !
Nature's great ancestor ! day's elder-born !
And fated to survive the transient sun !
By mortals, and immortals, seen with awe !
A starry crown thy raven brow adorns,

An azure zone thy waist; clouds, in heaven's loom
Wrought through varieties of shape and shade,
In ample folds of drapery divine,
Thy flowing mantle form; and, heaven throughout,
Voluminously pour thy pompous train.
Thy gloomy grandeurs (nature's most august,
Inspiring aspect!) claim a grateful verse;
And, like a sable curtain starr'd with gold,
Drawn o'er my labours past, shall close the scene.
  And what, O man! so worthy to be sung?
What more prepares us for the songs of heaven?
Creation, of archangels is the theme!
What, to be sung, so needful? What so well
Celestial joys prepare us to sustain?
The soul of man, His face design'd to see,
Who gave these wonders to be seen by man,
Has here a previous scene of objects great,
On which to dwell; to stretch to that expanse
Of thought, to rise to that exalted height
Of admiration, to contract that awe,
And give her whole capacities that strength,
Which best may qualify for final joy.
The more our spirits are enlarg'd on earth,
The deeper draught shall they receive of heaven
    Heaven's King! whose face unveil'd consum-
        mates bliss;
Redundant bliss! which fills that mighty void,
The whole creation leaves in human hearts!
Thou, who didst touch the lip of Jesse's son,
Rapt in sweet contemplation of these fires,
And set his harp in concert with the spheres;
While of thy works material the supreme
I dare attempt, assist my daring song.
Loose me from earth's inclosure, from the sun's

Contracted circle set my heart at large ;
Eliminate my spirit, give it range
Through provinces of thought yet unexplored ;
Teach me, by this stupendous scaffolding,
Creation's golden steps, to climb to thee.
Teach me with art great nature to control,
And spread a lustre o'er the shades of night.
Feel I thy kind assent ? and shall the sun
Be seen at midnight, rising in my song ?   [heart,
    Lorenzo! come, and warm thee: thou, whose
Whose little heart, is moor'd within a nook
Of this obscure terrestrial, anchor weigh.
Another ocean calls, a nobler port ;
I am thy pilot, I thy prosp'rous gale.
Gainful thy voyage through yon azure main ;
Main, without tempest, pirate, rock, or shore ;
And whence thou mayst import eternal wealth ;
And leave to beggar'd minds the pearl and gold.
Thy travels dost thou boast o'er foreign realms ?
Thou stranger to the world ! thy tour begin ;
Thy tour through nature's universal orb.
Nature delineates her whole chart at large ;
On soaring souls, that sail among the spheres ;
And man how purblind, if unknown the whole !
Who circles spacious earth, then travels here,
Shall own, he never was from home before !
Come, my [1] Prometheus, from thy pointed rock
Of false ambition if unchain'd, we'll mount ;
We'll, innocently, steal celestial fire,
And kindle our devotion at the stars ;
A theft, that shall not chain, but set thee free.
    Above our atmosphere's intestine wars,

---

[1] Night viii.

Rain's fountain-head, the magazine of hail;
Above the northern nests of feather'd snows,
The brew of thunders, and the flaming forge
That forms the crooked lightning; 'bove the caves
Where infant tempests wait their growing wings,
And tune their tender voices to that roar,
Which soon, perhaps, shall shake a guilty world;
Above misconstru'd omens of the sky,
Far-travell'd comets' calculated blaze;
Elance thy thought, and think of more than man.
Thy soul, till now, contracted, wither'd, shrunk,
Blighted by blasts of earth's unwholesome air,
Will blossom here; spread all her faculties
To these bright ardours; every power unfold,
And rise into sublimities of thought.
Stars teach, as well as shine. At nature's birth,
Thus their commission ran—" Be kind to man."
Where art thou, poor benighted traveller!   [fail.
The stars will light thee; though the moon should
Where art thou, more benighted! more astray!
In ways immoral? The stars call thee back;
And, if obey'd their counsel, set thee right.
    This prospect vast, what is it?—Weigh'd aright,
'Tis nature's system of divinity,
And every student of the night inspires.
'Tis elder scripture, writ by God's own hand:
Scripture authentic! uncorrupt by man.
Lorenzo! with my radius (the rich gift
Of thought nocturnal!) I'll point out to thee
Its various lessons; some that may surprise
An unadept in mysteries of night;
Little, perhaps, expected in her school,
Nor thought to grow on planet, or on star.
Bulls, lions, scorpions, monsters here we feign;

Ourselves more monstrous, not to see what here
Exists indeed ;—a lecture to mankind.

What read we here ?—Th' existence of a God ?
Yes ; and of other beings, man above ;
Natives of ether ! Sons of higher climes !
And, what may move Lorenzo's wonder more,
Eternity is written in the skies.
And whose eternity ?—Lorenzo ! thine ;
Mankind's eternity.   Nor faith alone,
Virtue grows here ; here springs the sov'reign cure
Of almost every vice ; but chiefly thine ;
Wrath, pride, ambition, and impure desire.

Lorenzo ! thou canst wake at midnight too,
Though not on morals bent : ambition, pleasure !
Those tyrants I for thee so[1] lately fought,
Afford their harass'd slaves but slender rest.
Thou, to whom midnight is immoral noon,
And the sun's noontide blaze, prime dawn of day ;
Not by thy climate, but capricious crime,
Commencing one of our Antipodes !
In thy nocturnal rove, one moment halt,
'Twixt stage and stage, of riot, and cabal ;
And lift thine eye, (if bold an eye to lift,
If bold to meet the face of injur'd heaven)
To yonder stars : for other ends they shine,
Than to light revellers from shame to shame,
And, thus, be made accomplices in guilt.

Why from yon arch, that infinite of space,
With infinite of lucid orbs replete,
Which set the living firmament on fire,
At the first glance, in such an overwhelm
Of wonderful, on man's astonish'd sight,

---

[1] Night viii.

Rushes Omnipotence ?—To curb our pride;
Our reason rouse, and lead it to that power,
Whose love lets down these silver chains of light;
To draw up man's ambition to himself,
And bind our chaste affections to his throne.
Thus the three virtues, least alive on earth,
And welcom'd on heaven's coast with most applause,
An humble, pure, and Heavenly-minded heart,
Are here inspir'd :—and canst thou gaze too long?

Nor stands thy wrath depriv'd of its reproof,
Or unupbraided by this radiant choir.
The planets of each system represent
Kind neighbours ; mutual amity prevails ;
Sweet interchange of rays, receiv'd, return'd ;
Enlight'ning, and enlighten'd ! All, at once,
Attracting, and attracted ! Patriot like,
None sins against the welfare of the whole ;
But their reciprocal, unselfish aid,
Affords an emblem of millennial love.
Nothing in nature, much less conscious being,
Was e'er created solely for itself :
Thus man his sov'reign duty learns in this
Material picture of benevolence.

And know, of all our supercilious race,
Thou most inflammable ! thou wasp of men !
Man's angry heart, inspected, would be found
As rightly set, as are the starry spheres ;
'Tis Nature's structure, broke by stubborn will,
Breeds all that uncelestial discord there.
Wilt thou not feel the bias nature gave?
Canst thou descend from converse with the skies,
And seize thy brother's throat ?—For what—a clod,
An inch of earth ? the planets cry, " Forbear,"
They chase our double darkness ; Nature's gloom,

And (kinder still!) our intellectual night.
   And see, day's amiable sister sends
Her invitation, in the softest rays
Of mitigated lustre; courts thy sight,
Which suffers from her tyrant brother's blaze.
Night grants thee the full freedom of the skies,
Nor rudely reprimands thy lifted eye;
With gain, and joy, she bribes thee to be wise.
Night opes the noblest scenes, and sheds an awe,
Which gives those venerable scenes full weight,
And deep reception, in th' intender'd heart;
While light peeps through the darkness, like a spy;
And darkness shows its grandeur by the light.
Nor is the profit greater than the joy,
If human hearts at glorious objects glow,
And admiration can inspire delight.
   What speak I more, than I, this moment, feel?
With pleasing stupor first the soul is struck:
(Stupor ordain'd to make her truly wise!)
Then into transport starting from her trance,
With love, and admiration, how she glows!
This gorgeous apparatus! this display!
This ostentation of creative power!
This theatre!—what eye can take it in?
By what divine enchantment was it rais'd,
For minds of the first magnitude to launch
In endless speculation, and adore?
One sun by day, by night ten thousand shine;
And light us deep into the Deity;
How boundless in magnificence and might!
O what a confluence of ethereal fires,
Form urns unnumber'd, down the steep of heaven,
Streams to a point, and centres in my sight!
Nor tarries there; I feel it at my heart.

My heart, at once, it humbles, and exalts;
Lays it in dust, and calls it to the skies.
Who sees it unexalted? or unaw'd?
Who sees it, and can stop at what is seen?
Material offspring of Omnipotence!
Inanimate, all animating birth!
Work worthy Him who made it! worthy praise!
All praise! praise more than human! nor denied
Thy praise divine!—But tho' man, drown'd in sleep,
Withholds his homage, not alone I wake;
Bright legions swarm unseen, and sing, unheard
By mortal ear, the glorious Architect,
In this his universal temple .hung
With lustres, with innumerable lights,
That shed religion on the soul; at once,
The temple, and the preacher! O how loud
It calls devotion! genuine growth of night!
   Devotion! daughter of astronomy!
An undevout astronomer is mad.
True; all things speak a God; but in the small,
Men trace out him; in great, he seizes man;
Seizes, and elevates, and wraps, and fills
With new inquiries, mid associates new.
Tell me, ye stars! ye planets! tell me, all
Ye starr'd and planeted inhabitants! what is it?
What are these sons of wonder? say, proud arch,
(Within those azure palaces they dwell)
Built with divine ambition! in disdain
Of limit built! built in the taste of heaven!
Vast concave! ample dome! wast thou design'd
A meet apartment for the Deity?—
Not so; that thought alone thy state impairs,
Thy lofty sinks, and shallows thy profound,
And straitens thy diffusive; dwarfs the whole,

And makes a universe an orrery.

But when I drop mine eye, and look on man,
Thy right regain'd, thy grandeur is restor'd,
O nature ! wide flies off th' expanding round.
As when whole magazines, at once, are fir'd,
The smitten air is hollow'd by the blow ;
The vast displosion dissipates the clouds ;
Shock'd ether's billows dash the distant skies ;
Thus (but far more) th' expanding round flies off,
And leaves a mighty void, a spacious womb,
Might teem with new creation ; reinflam'd
Thy luminaries triumph, and assume
Divinity themselves. Nor was it strange,
Matter high-wrought to such surprising pomp,
Such godlike glory, stole the style of gods,
From ages dark, obtuse, and steep'd in sense ;
For, sure, to sense, they truly are divine,
And half absolv'd idolatry from guilt ;
Nay, turn'd it into virtue. Such it was
In those, who put forth all they had of man
Unlost, to lift their thought, nor mounted higher ;
But, weak of wing, on planets perch'd ; and thought
What was their highest, must be their ador'd.

But they how weak, who could no higher mount ?
And are there, then, Lorenzo ! those, to whom
Unseen, and unexistent, are the same ?
And if incomprehensible is join'd,
Who dare pronounce it madness, to believe ?
Why has the mighty Builder thrown aside
All measure in his work ; stretch'd out his line
So far, and spread amazement o'er the whole ?
Then (as he took delight in wide extremes),
Deep in the bosom of his universe,
Dropt down that reasoning mite, that insect, man,

To crawl, and gaze, and wonder at the scene ?——
That man might ne'er presume to plead amazement
For disbelief of wonders in himself.
Shall God be less miraculous, than what
His hand has form'd ? Shall mysteries descend
From unmysterious ? Things more elevate,
Be more familiar ? uncreated lie
More obvious than created, to the grasp
Of human thought ? The more of wonderful
Is heard in him, the more we should assent.
Could we conceive him, God he could not be ;
Or he not God, or we could not be men.
A God alone can comprehend a God ;
Man's distance how immense ! On such a theme,
Know this, Lorenzo ! (seem it ne'er so strange)
Nothing can satisfy, but what confounds ;
Nothing, but what astonishes, is true.
The scene thou seest, attests the truth I sing,
And every star sheds light upon thy creed.
These stars, this furniture, this cost of heaven,
If but reported, thou hadst ne'er believ'd ;
But thine eye tells thee, the romance is true.
The grand of nature is th' Almighty's oath,
In reason's court, to silence unbelief.

How my mind, opening at this scene, imbibes
The moral emanations of the skies,
While nought, perhaps, Lorenzo less admires !
Has the Great Sov'reign sent ten thousand worlds
To tell us, he resides above them all,
In glory's unapproachable recess ?
And dare earth's bold inhabitants deny
The sumptuous, the magnific embassy
A moment's audience ? Turn we, nor will hear
From whom they come, or what they would impart

For man's emolument; sole cause that stoops
Their grandeur to man's eye ? Lorenzo ! rouse ;
Let thought, awaken'd, take the lightning's wing,
And glance from east to west, from pole to pole.
Who sees, but is confounded, or convinc'd ?
Renounces reason, or a God adores ?
Mankind was sent into the world to see :
Sight gives the science needful to their peace ;
That obvious science asks small learning's aid.
Wouldst thou on metaphysic pinions soar ?
Or wound thy patience amid logic thorns ?
Or travel history's enormous round ?
Nature no such hard task enjoins : she gave
A make to man directive of his thought ;
A make set upright, pointing to the stars,
As who shall say, " Read thy chief lesson there."
Too late to read this manuscript of heaven,
When, like a parchment-scroll, shrunk up by flames,
It folds Lorenzo's lesson from his sight.
   Lesson how various ! Not the God alone,
I see his ministers ; I see, diffus'd
In radiant orders, essences sublime,
Of various offices, of various plume,
In heavenly liveries, distinctly clad,
Azure, green, purple, pearl, or downy gold,
Or all commix'd ; they stand, with wings outspread,
List'ning to catch the master's least command,
And fly through nature, ere the moment ends ;
Numbers innumerable !—Well conceiv'd
By pagan, and by christian ! O'er each sphere
Presides an angel, to direct its course,
And feed, or fan, its flames ; or to discharge
Other high trusts unknown. For who can see
Such pomp of matter and imagine, mind,

For which alone inanimate was made,
More sparingly dispens'd ? That nobler son,
Far liker the great sire !—'tis thus the skies
Inform us of superiors numberless,
As much, in excellence, above mankind,
As above earth, in magnitude, the spheres.
These, as a cloud of witnesses, hang o'er us ;
In a throng'd theatre are all our deeds ;
Perhaps, a thousand demigods descend
On ev'ry beam we see, to walk with men.
Awful reflection ! Strong restraint from ill !
    Yet, here, our virtue finds still stronger aid
From these ethereal glories sense surveys.
Something, like magic, strikes from this blue vault;
With just attention is it view'd ? We feel
A sudden succour, unimplor'd, unthought ;
Nature herself does half the work of man.
Seas, rivers, mountains, forests, desarts, rocks,
The promontory's height, the depth profound
Of subterranean, excavated grots,
Black brow'd, and vaulted high, and yawning wide
From nature's structure, or the scoop of time ;
If ample of dimension, vast of size,
Ev'n these an aggrandizing impulse give ;
Of solemn thought enthusiastic heights
Ev'n these infuse.—But what of vast in these ?
Nothing ;—or we must own the skies forgot.
Much less in art.—Vain art ! thou pigmy power !
How dost thou swell and strut, with human pride,
To show thy littleness ! What childish toys,
Thy watery columns squirted to the clouds !
Thy basin'd rivers, and imprison'd seas !
Thy mountains moulded into forms of men .
Thy hundred-gated capitals ! or those

Where three days' travel left us much to ride;
Gazing on miracles by mortals wrought,
Arches triumphal, theatres immense,
Or nodding gardens pendent in mid-air!
Or temples proud to meet their gods half-way!
Yet these affect us in no common kind.
What then the force of such superior scenes?
Enter a temple, it will strike an awe:
What awe from this the Deity has built?
A good man seen, though silent, counsel gives:
The touch'd spectator wishes to be wise:
In a bright mirror his own hands have made,
Here we see something like the face of God.
Seems it not then enough, to say, Lorenzo!
To man abandon'd, " Hast thou seen the skies?"

    And yet, so thwarted nature's kind design
By daring man, he makes her sacred awe
(That guard from ill) his shelter, his temptation
To more than common guilt, and quite inverts
Celestial art's intent.   The trembling stars
See crimes gigantic, stalking through the gloom
With front erect, that hide their head by day,
And making night still darker by their deeds.
Slumb'ring in covert, till the shades descend,
Rapine and murder, link'd, now prowl for prey.
The miser earths his treasure; and the thief,
Watching the mole, half-beggars him ere morn.
Now plots, and foul conspiracies, awake;
And, muffling up their horrors from the moon,
Havock and devastation they prepare,
And kingdoms tott'ring in the field of blood.
Now sons of riot in mid-revel rage.
What shall I do?—Suppress it? or proclaim?—
Why sleeps the thunder? Now Lorenzo! now,

His best friend's couch the rank adulterer
Ascends secure; and laughs at gods and men.
Prepost'rous madmen, void of fear or shame,
Lay their crimes bare to these chaste eyes of heaven;
Yet shrink, and shudder, at a mortal's sight.
Were moon, and stars, for villains only made?
To guide, yet screen them, with tenebrious light?
No; they were made to fashion the sublime
Of human hearts, and wiser make the wise.

 Those ends were answer'd once; when mortals
Of stronger wing, of acquiline ascent [liv'd
In theory sublime. O how unlike
Those vermin of the night, this moment sung,
Who crawl on earth, and on her venom feed!
Those ancient sages, human stars! they met
Their brothers of the skies, at midnight hour;
Their counsel ask'd; and, what they ask'd, obey'd.
The Stagirite, and Plato, he who drank
The poison'd bowl, and he of Tusculum,
With him of Corduba (immortal names!)
In these unbounded, and Elysian, walks,
An area fit for gods, and godlike men,
They took their nightly round, through radiant paths
By seraphs trod; instructed, chiefly, thus,
To tread in their bright footsteps here below;
To walk in worth still brighter than the skies.
There they contracted their contempt of earth;
Of hopes eternal kindled, there, the fire;
There, as in near approach, they glow'd, and grew
(Great visitants!) more intimate with God,
More worth to men, more joyous to themselves.
Through various virtues, they, with ardour, ran
The zodiac of their learn'd, illustrious lives.

 In christian hearts, O for a pagan zeal!

A needful, but opprobrious prayer! As much
Our ardour less, as greater is our light.
How monstrous this in morals! Scarce more strange
Would this phenomenon in nature strike,
A sun, that froze her, or a star, that warm'd.
What taught these heroes of the moral world?
To these thou giv'st thy praise, give credit too.
These doctors ne'er were pension'd to deceive thee;
And pagan tutors are thy taste.—They taught,
That, narrow views betray to misery:
That, wise it is to comprehend the whole:
That, virtue, rose from nature, ponder'd well,
The single base of virtue built to heaven:
That God, and nature, our attention claim:
That, nature is the glass reflecting God,
As, by the sea, reflected is the sun,
Too glorious to be gaz'd on in his sphere:
That, mind immortal loves immortal aims:
That, boundless mind affects a boundless space:
That vast surveys, and the sublime of things,
The soul assimilate, and make her great:
That, therefore, heaven her glories, as a fund
Of inspiration, thus spreads out to man.
Such are their doctrines; such the night inspir'd
  And what more true? What truth of greater
      weight?
The soul of man was made to walk the skies;
Delightful outlet of her prison here!
There, disencumber'd from her chains, the ties
Of toys terrestrial, she can rove at large,
There, freely can respire, dilate, extend,
In full proportion let loose all her powers;
And, undeluded, grasp at something great.
Nor, as a stranger, does she wander there;

But, wonderful herself, through wonder strays;
Contemplating their grandeur, finds her own;
Dives deep in their economy divine,
Sits high in judgment on their various laws,
And, like a master, judges not amiss.
Hence greatly pleas'd, and justly proud, the soul
Grows conscious of her birth celestial; breathes
More life, more vigour, in her native air;
And feels herself at home amongst the stars;
And, feeling, emulates her country's praise.
    What call we, then, the firmament, Lorenzo?—
As earth the body, since, the skies sustain
The soul with food, that gives immortal life,
Call it, the noble pasture of the mind;
Which there expatiates, strengthens, and exults,
And riots through the luxuries of thought.
Call it, the garden of the Deity,
Blossom'd with stars, redundant in the growth
Of fruit ambrosial; moral fruit to man.
Call it, the breastplate of the true High priest,
Ardent with gems oracular, that give,
In points of highest moment, right response;
And ill neglected, if we prize our peace.
    Thus, have we found a true astrology;
Thus, have we found a new, and noble sense,
In which alone stars govern human fates.
O that the stars (as some have feign'd) let fall
Bloodshed, and havock, on embattled realms,
And rescued monarchs from so black a guilt!
Bourbon! this wish how gen'rous in a foe!
Wouldst thou be great, wouldst thou become a God,
And stick thy deathless name among the stars,
For mighty conquests on a needle's point?
Instead of forging chains for foreigners,

Bastile thy tutor : grandeur all thy aim ?
As yet thou know'st not what it is : how great,
How glorious, then, appears the mind of man,
When in it all the stars, and planets, roll !
And what it seems, it is : great objects make
Great minds, enlarging as their views enlarge ;
Those still more godlike, as these more divine.

    And more divine than these, thou canst not see.
Dazzled, o'erpower'd, with the delicious draught
Of miscellaneous splendours, how I reel
From thought to thought, inebriate, without end !
An Eden, this ! a paradise unlost !
I meet the Deity in ev'ry view,
And tremble at my nakedness before him !
O that I could but reach the tree of life !
For here it grows, unguarded from our taste ;
No flaming sword denies our entrance here ;
Would man but gather, he might live for ever.

    Lorenzo ! much of moral hast thou seen.
Of curious arts art thou more fond ? Then mark
The mathematic glories of the skies,
In number, weight, and measure, all ordain'd.
Lorenzo's boasted builders, chance, and fate,
Are left to finish his aerial towers ;
Wisdom and choice, their well-known characters
Here deep impress ; and claim it for their own.
Though splendid all, no splendour void of use ;
Use rivals beauty ; art contends with power ;
No wanton waste, amid effuse expense ;
The great Economist adjusting all
To prudent pomp, magnificently wise.
How rich the prospect ! and for ever new !
And newest to the man that views it most ;
For newer still in infinite succeeds.

Then, these aerial racers, O how swift !
How the shaft loiters from the strongest string !
Spirit alone can distance the career.
Orb above orb ascending without end !
Circle in circle, without end, inclos'd !
Wheel within wheel; Ezekiel ! like to thine !
Like thine, it seems a vision or a dream ;
Though seen, we labour to believe it true !
What involution ! what extent ! what swarms
Of worlds, that laugh at earth ! immensely great !
Immensely distant from each other's spheres !
What, then, the wondrous space thro' which they
At once it quite ingulfs all human thought;   [roll?
'Tis comprehension's absolute defeat.

  Nor think thou seest a wild disorder here ;
Through this illustrious chaos to the sight,
Arrangement neat, and chastest order, reign.
The path prescrib'd, inviolably kept,
Upbraids the lawless sallies of mankind.
Worlds, ever thwarting, never interfere ;
What knots are tied ! how soon are they dissolv'd,
And set the seeming married planets free !
They rove for ever, without error rove ;
Confusion unconfus'd ! nor less admire
This tumult untumultuous ; all on wing !
In motion, all ! yet what profound repose !
What fervid action, yet no noise ! as aw'd
To silence, by the presence of their Lord ;
Or hush'd by His command, in love to man,
And bid let fall soft beams on human rest,
Restless themselves.   On yon cærulean plain,
In exultation to their God, and thine,
They dance, they sing eternal jubilee,
Eternal celebration of His praise.

But, since their song arrives not at our ear,
Their dance perplex'd exhibits to the sight
Fair hieroglyphic of his peerless power.
Mark, how the Labyrinthian turns they take,
The circles intricate, and mystic maze,
Weave the grand cypher of omnipotence;
To gods, how great! how legible to man!

Leaves so much wonder greater wonder still?
Where are the pillars that support the skies?
What more than Atlantean shoulder props
Th' incumbent load? What magic, what strange art,
In fluid air these pond'rous orbs sustains?
Who would not think them hung in golden chains?—
And so they are; in the high will of heaven,
Which fixes all; makes adamant of air,
Or air of adamant; makes all of nought,
Or nought of all; if such the dread decree.

Imagine from their deep foundations torn
The most gigantic sons of earth, the broad
And towering Alps, all tost into the sea;
And, light as down, or volatile as air,
Their bulks enormous, dancing on the waves,
In time, and measure, exquisite; while all
The winds, in emulation of the spheres,
Tune their sonorous instruments aloft;
The concert swell, and animate the ball.
Would this appear amazing? What, then, worlds,
In a far thinner element sustain'd,
And acting the same part, with greater skill,
More rapid movement, and for noblest ends?

More obvious ends to pass, are not these stars
The seats majestic, proud imperial thrones,
On which angelic delegates of heaven,
At certain periods, as the Sov'reign nods,

Discharge high trusts of vengeance, or of love;
To clothe, in outward grandeur, grand design,
And acts most solemn still more solemnize?
Ye citizens of air! what ardent thanks,
What full effusion of the grateful heart,
Is due from man indulg'd in such a sight!
A sight so noble! and a sight so kind!
It drops new truths at every new survey!
Feels not Lorenzo something stir within,
That sweeps away all period? As these spheres
Measure duration, they no less inspire
The godlike hope of ages without end.
The boundless space, thro' which these rovers take
Their restless roam, suggests the sister thought
Of boundless time. Thus, by kind nature's skill,
To man unlabour'd, that important guest,
Eternity, finds entrance at the sight:
And an eternity, for man ordain'd,
Or these his destin'd midnight counsellors
The stars, had never whisper'd it to man.
Nature informs, but ne'er insults, her sons
Could she then kindle the most ardent wish
To disappoint it?—that is blasphemy.
Thus, of thy creed a second article,
Momentous, as the existence of a God,
Is found (as I conceive) where rarely sought;
And thou mayst read thy soul immortal, here.

Here, then, Lorenzo! on these glories dwell,
Nor want the gilt, illuminated, roof,
That calls the wretched gay to dark delights.
Assemblies?—this is one divinely bright;
Here, unendanger'd in health, wealth, or fame,
Range through the fairest, and the sultan scorn,
He, wise as thou, no crescent holds so fair,

As that, which on his turbant awes a world;
And thinks the moon is proud to copy him.
Look on her, and gain more than worlds can give,
A mind superior to the charms of power.
Thou muffled in delusions of this life !
Can yonder moon turn ocean in his bed,
From side to side, in constant ebb, and flow,
And purify from stench his watery realms ?
And fails her moral influence ? wants she power
To turn Lorenzo's stubborn tide of thought
From stagnating on earth's infected shore,
And purge from nuisance his corrupted heart ?
Fails her attraction when it draws to heaven ?
Nay, and to what thou valu'st more, earth's joy ?
Minds elevate, and panting for unseen,
And defecate from sense, alone obtain
Full relish of existence undeflower'd,
The life of life, the zest of worldly bliss :
All else on earth amounts—to what ? to this :
" Bad to be suffer'd; blessings to be left :"
Earth's richest inventory boasts no more.
　　Of higher scenes be, then, the call obey'd.
O let me gaze !—of gazing there's no end.
O let me think !—thought too is wilder'd here ;
In mid-way flight imagination tires ;
Yet soon re-prunes her wing to soar anew,
Her point unable to forbear, or gain ;
So great the pleasure, so profound the plan !
A banquet, this, where men, and angels, meet,
Eat the same manna, mingle earth and heaven.
How distant some of these nocturnal suns !
So distant (says the sage) 'twere not absurd
To doubt, if beams, set out at nature's birth,
Are yet arriv'd at this so foreign world ;

Though nothing half so rapid as their flight.
An eye of awe and wonder let me roll,
And roll for ever: who can satiate sight
In such a scene? in such an ocean wide
Of deep astonishment? where depth, height, breadth,
Are lost in their extremes; and where to count
The thick-sown glories in this field of fire,
Perhaps a seraph's computation fails.
Now, go, ambition! boast thy boundless might
In conquest, o'er the tenth part of a grain.

And yet Lorenzo calls for miracles,
To give his tott'ring faith a solid base.
Why call for less than is already thine?
Thou art no novice in theology;
What is a miracle?—'Tis a reproach,
'Tis an implicit satire, on mankind;
And while it satisfies, it censures too.
To common sense, great nature's course proclaims
A Deity: when mankind falls asleep,
A miracle is sent, as an alarm;
To wake the world, and prove him o'er again,
By recent argument, but not more strong.
Say, which imports more plenitude of power,
Or nature's laws to fix, or to repeal?
To make a sun, or stop his mid career?
To countermand his orders, and send back
The flaming courier to the frighted east,
Warm'd, and astonish'd, at his ev'ning ray?
Or bid the moon, as with her journey tir'd,
In Ajalon's soft, flowery vale repose?
Great things are these; still greater, to create.
From Adam's bower look down thro' the whole train
Of miracles;—resistless is their pow'r?
They do not, can not, more amaze the mind,

Than this, call'd un-miraculous survey,
If duly weigh'd, if rationally seen,
If seen with human eyes. The brute, indeed,
Sees nought but spangles here; the fool, no more.
Say'st thou, " The course of nature governs all?"
The course of nature is the art of God.
The miracles thou call'st for, this attest;
For say, could nature nature's course control?

But miracles apart, who sees him not,
Nature's controller, author, guide, and end?
Who turns his eye on nature's midnight face,
But must inquire—" What hand behind the scene,
What arm Almighty, put these wheeling globes
In motion, and wound up the vast machine?
Who rounded in his palm these spacious orbs?
Who bowl'd them flaming thro' the dark profound
Num'rous as glitt'ring gems of morning dew,
Or sparks from populous cities in a blaze,
And set the bosom of old night on fire?
Peopled her desart, and made horror smile?"
Or, if the military style delights thee,
(For stars have fought their battles, leagu'd with
   man)   [names?
" Who marshals this bright host? Enrolls their
Appoints their posts, their marches, and returns,
Punctual, at stated periods? who disbands
These vet'ran troops, their final duty done,
If e'er disbanded?"—He, whose potent word,
Like the loud trumpet, levied first their powers
In night's inglorious empire, where they slept
In beds of darkness: arm'd them with fierce flames
Arrang'd, and disciplin'd, and cloth'd in gold;
And call'd them out of chaos to the field,
Where now they war with vice and unbelief.

O let us join this army! joining these,
Will give us hearts intrepid, at that hour,
When brighter flames shall cut a darker night;
When these strong demonstrations of a God
Shall hide their heads, or tumble from their spheres,
And one eternal curtain cover all!

   Struck at that thought, as new awak'd, I lift
A more enlighten'd eye, and read the stars
To man still more propitious; and their aid
(Though guiltless of idolatry) implore;
Nor longer rob them of their noblest name.
O ye dividers of my time! Ye bright
Accomptants of my days, and months, and years,
In your fair kalendar distinctly mark'd!
Since that authentic, radiant register,   [him;
Though man inspects it not, stands good against
Since you, and years, roll on, tho' man stands still;
Teach me my days to number, and apply
My trembling heart to wisdom; now beyond
All shadow of excuse for fooling on.
Age smooths our path to prudence; sweeps aside
The snares keen appetite, and passion, spread
To catch stray souls; and woe to that gray head,
Whose folly would undo what age has done;
Aid then, aid, all ye stars!—Much rather, thou,
Great artist! thou, whose finger set aright
This exquisite machine, with all its wheels,
Though intervolv'd, exact; and pointing out
Life's rapid, and irrevocable flight,
With such an index fair, as none can miss,
Who lifts an eye, nor sleeps till it is clos'd.
Open mine eye, dread Deity! to read
The tacit doctrine of thy works; to see
Things as they are, unalter'd through the glass

Of worldly wishes.   Time, eternity!
('Tis these, mismeasur'd, ruin all mankind)
Set them before me; let me lay them both
In equal scale, and learn their various weight.
Let time appear a moment, as it is;
And let eternity's full orb, at once,
Turn on my soul, and strike it into heaven.
When shall I see far more than charms me now?
Gaze on creation's model in thy breast
Unveil'd, nor wonder at the transcript more?
When this vile, foreign, dust, which smothers all
That travel earth's deep vale, shall I shake off?
When shall my soul her incarnation quit,
And, re-adopted to thy blest embrace,
Obtain her apotheosis in thee?

　Dost think, Lorenzo, this is wand'ring wide?
No, 'tis directly striking at the mark;
To wake thy dead devotion[1] was my point;
And how I bless night's consecrating shades,
Which to a temple turn a universe;
Fill us with great ideas, full of heaven,
And antidote the pestilential earth!
In ev'ry storm, that either frowns, or fails,
What an asylum has the soul in prayer!
And what a fane is this, in which to pray!
And what a God must dwell in such a fane!
O what a genius must inform the skies!
And is Lorenzo's salamander-heart
Cold, and untouch'd, amid these sacred fires?
O ye nocturnal sparks! ye glowing embers,
On heaven's broad hearth! who burn, or burn no more,
Who blaze, or die, as great Jehovah's breath

---

[1] Page 244.

Or blows you, or forbears; assist my song;
Pour your whole influence; exorcise his heart,
So long possest; and bring him back to man.
　　And is Lorenzo a demurrer still?
Pride in thy parts provokes thee to contest
Truths, which, contested, put thy parts to shame.
Nor shame they more Lorenzo's head than heart,
A faithless heart, how despicably small!
Too strait, aught great, or gen'rous, to receive!
Fill'd with an atom! fill'd, and foul'd, with self!
And self mistaken! Self, that lasts an hour!
Instincts and passions, of the nobler kind,
Lie suffocated there; or they alone,
Reason apart, would wake high hope; and open,
To ravish'd thought, that intellectual sphere,
Where, order, wisdom, goodness, providence,
Their endless miracles of love display,
And promise all the truly great desire.
The mind that would be happy, must be great;
Great, in its wishes; great, in its surveys.
Extended views a narrow mind extend;
Push out its corrugate, expansive make,
Which, ere long, more than planets shall embrace,
A man of compass makes a man of worth;
Divine contemplate, and become divine.
　　As man was made for glory, and for bliss,
All littleness is in approach to woe;
Open thy bosom, set thy wishes wide,
And let in manhood; let in happiness;
Admit the boundless theatre of thought
From nothing, up to God; which makes a man.
Take God from nature, nothing great is left;
Man's mind is in a pit, and nothing sees;
Man's heart is in a jakes, and loves the mire.

Emerge from thy profound; erect thine eye;
See thy distress! how close art thou besieg'd!
Besieg'd by nature, the proud sceptic's foe!
Inclos'd by these innumerable worlds,
Sparkling conviction on the darkest mind,
As in a golden net of Providence.
How art thou caught, sure captive of belief!
From this thy blest captivity, what art,
What blasphemy to reason, sets thee free!
This scene is heaven's indulgent violence:
Canst thou bear up against this tide of glory?
What is earth bosom'd in these ambient orbs,
But, faith in God impos'd, and press'd on man?
Dar'st thou still litigate thy desp'rate cause,
Spite of these num'rous, awful, witnesses,
And doubt the deposition of the skies?
O how laborious is thy way to ruin!

    Laborious! 'tis impracticable quite;
To sink beyond a doubt, in this debate,
With all his weight of wisdom and of will,
And crime flagitious, I defy a fool.
Some wish they did; but no man disbelieves.
God is a spirit; spirit cannot strike
These gross, material organs; God by man
As much is seen, as man a God can see,
In these astonishing exploits of power.
What order, beauty, motion, distance, size!
Concertion of design, how exquisite!
How complicate, in their divine police!
Apt means! great ends! consent to gen'ral good!—
Each attribute of these material gods,
So long (and that with specious pleas) ador'd,
A sep'rate conquest gains o'er rebel thought;
And leads in triumph the whole mind of man.

Lorenzo! this may seem harangue to thee;
Such all is apt to seem, that thwarts our will.
And dost thou, then, demand a simple proof
Of this great master moral of the skies,
Unskill'd, or disinclin'd, to read it there?
Since 'tis the basis, and all drops without it,
Take it, in one compact, unbroken chain.
Such proof insists on an attentive ear;
'Twill not make one amid a mob of thoughts,
And, for thy notice, struggle with the world.
Retire;—the world shut out;—thy thoughts call
Imagination's airy wing repress;—— [home;—
Lock up thy senses;—let no passion stir;—
Wake all to reason;—let her reign alone;
Then, in thy soul's deep silence, and the depth
Of Nature's silence, midnight, thus inquire,
As I have done; and shall inquire no more.
In nature's channel, thus the questions run.
   " What am I? and from whence?—I nothing
           know,
But that I am; and, since I am, conclude
Something eternal: had there e'er been nought,
Nought still had been: eternal there must be.—
But what eternal?—Why not human race?
And Adam's ancestors without an end?—
That's hard to be conceiv'd; since every link
Of that long-chain'd succession is so frail;
Can every part depend, and not the whole?
Yet grant it true; new difficulties rise;
I'm still quite out at sea; nor see the shore.
Whence earth, and these bright orbs?—Eternal
           too?—
Grant matter was eternal; still these orbs
Would want some other father;—much design

Is seen in all their motions, all their makes;
Design implies intelligence, and art;
That can't be from themselves—or man; that art
Man scarce can comprehend, could man bestow?
And nothing greater yet allow'd than man.—
Who, motion, foreign to the smallest grain,
Shot through vast masses of enormous weight?
Who bid brute matter's restive lump assume
Such various forms, and gave it wings to fly?
Has matter innate motion? then each atom,
Asserting its indisputable right
To dance, would form a universe of dust:
Has matter none? then whence these glorious forms
And boundless flights, from shapeless, and repos'd?
Has matter more than motion? has it thought,
Judgment, and genius? is it deeply learn'd
In mathematics? has it fram'd such laws,
Which but to guess, a Newton made immortal?—
If so, how each sage atom laughs at me,
Who think a clod inferior to a man!
If art, to form; and counsel, to conduct;
And that with greater far, than human skill;
Resides not in each block;—a Godhead reigns.—
Grant, then, invisible, eternal, mind;
That granted, all is solv'd.—But, granting that,
Draw I not o'er me a still darker cloud?
Grant I not that which I can ne'er conceive?
A being without origin, or end!—
Hail, human liberty! there is no God—
Yet, why? on either scheme that knot subsists;
Subsist it must, in God, or human race;
If in the last, how many knots beside,
Indissoluble all?—Why choose it there,
Where, chosen, still subsist ten thousand more?

Reject it, where, that chosen, all the rest
Dispers'd, leave reason's whole horizon clear?
This is not reason's dictate; reason says,
Close with the side where one grain turns the scale;
What vast preponderance is here! can reason
With louder voice exclaim—Believe a God?
And reason heard, is the sole mark of man.
What things impossible must man think true,
On any other system! and how strange
To disbelieve, through mere credulity!"
   If, in this chain, Lorenzo finds no flaw,
Let it for ever bind him to belief.
And where the link, in which a flaw he finds?
And, if a God there is, that God how great!
How great that Power, whose providential care
Thro' these bright orbs' dark centres darts a ray!
Of nature universal threads the whole!
And hangs creation, like a precious gem,
Though little, on the footstool of his throne!
   That little gem, how large! a weight let fall
From a fixt star, in ages can it reach
This distant earth! say, then, Lorenzo! where,
Where, ends this mighty building? where, begin
The suburbs of creation? where, the wall
Whose battlements look o'er into the vale
Of non-existence! Nothing's strange abode!
Say, at what point of space Jehovah dropp'd
His slacken'd line, and laid his balance by;
Weigh'd worlds, and measur'd infinite, no more?
Where, rears his terminating pillar high
Its extra-mundane head? and says, to gods,
In characters illustrious as the sun,
     " I stand, the plan's proud period; I pronounce
    The work accomplish'd; the creation clos'd:

Shout, all ye gods! nor shout ye gods alone;
Of all that lives, or, if devoid of life,
That rests, or rolls, ye heights, and depths re-
        sound!   [sound!"
Resound! resound! ye depths, and heights, re-
Hard are those questions!—Answer harder still.
Is this the sole exploit, the single birth,
The solitary son of power divine?
Or has th' Almighty Father, with a breath,
Impregnated the womb of distant space?
Has he not bid, in various provinces,
Brother-creations the dark bowels burst
Of night primeval; barren, now, no more?
And he the central sun, transpiercing all
Those giant-generations, which disport
And dance, as motes, in his meridian ray;
That ray withdrawn, benighted, or absorb'd,
In that abyss of horror, whence they sprung;
While chaos triumphs, repossest of all
Rival creation ravish'd from his throne?
Chaos! of nature both the womb, and grave!
    Think'st thou my scheme, Lorenzo, spreads too
Is this extravagant?—No; this is just;   [wide?
Just, in conjecture, though 'twere false in fact.
If 'tis an error, 'tis an error sprung
From noble root, high thought of the Most High.
But wherefore error? who can prove it such?—
He that can set Omnipotence a bound.
Can man conceive beyond what God can do?
Nothing, but quite impossible is hard.
He summons into being, with like ease,
A whole creation, and a single grain.
Speaks he the word? a thousand worlds are born!
A thousand worlds? there's space for millions more:

And in what space can his great fiat fail?
Condemn me not, cold critic! but indulge
The warm imagination: why condemn?
Why not indulge such thoughts, as swell our hearts
With fuller admiration of that power,   [swell?
Who gives our hearts with such high thoughts to
Why not indulge in his augmented praise?
Darts not his glory a still brighter ray,
The less is left to chaos, and the realms
Of hideous night, where fancy strays aghast;
And, though most talkative, makes no report?

Still seems my thought enormous? think again;—
Experience 'self shall aid thy lame belief.
Glasses (that revelation to the sight!)
Have they not led us in the deep disclose
Of fine-spun nature, exquisitely small,
And, though demonstrated, still ill-conceived?
If, then, on the reverse, the mind would mount
In magnitude, what mind can mount too far,
To keep the balance, and creation poise?
Defect alone can err on such a theme;
What is too great, if we the cause survey?
Stupendous Architect! thou, thou art all!
My soul flies up and down in thoughts of thee,
And finds herself but at the centre still!
I Am, thy name! existence, all thine own!
Creation's nothing; flatter'd much, if styl'd
" The thin, the fleeting atmosphere of God."

O for the voice—of what? of whom?—what
Can answer to my wants, in such ascent,   [voice
As dares to deem one universe too small?
Tell me, Lorenzo! (for now fancy glows,
Fir'd in the vortex of Amighty power)
Is not this home creation, in the map

Of universal nature, as a speck,
Like fair Britannia in our little ball;
Exceeding fair, and glorious, for its size,
But, elsewhere, far out-measur'd, far outshone?
In fancy (for the fact beyond us lies)
Canst thou not figure it, an isle, almost
Too small for notice, in the vast of being;
Sever'd by mighty seas of unbuilt space
From other realms; from ample continents
Of higher life, where nobler natives dwell;
Less northern, less remote from Deity,
Glowing beneath the line of the supreme;
Where souls in excellence make haste, put forth
Luxuriant growths; nor the late autumn wait
Of human worth, but ripen soon to gods?
    Yet why drown fancy in such depths as these?
Return, presumptuous rover! and confess
The bounds of man; nor blame them, as too small
Enjoy we not full scope in what is seen?
Full ample the dominions of the sun!
Full glorious to behold! How far, how wide,
The matchless monarch, from his flaming throne
Lavish of lustre, throws his beams about him,
Farther, and faster, than a thought can fly,
And feeds his planets with eternal fires!
This Heliopolis, by greater far,
Than the proud tyrant of the Nile, was built;
And he alone, who built it, can destroy.
Beyond this city, why strays human thought?
One wonderful, enough for man to know!
One infinite! enough for man to range!
One firmament, enough for man to read!
O what voluminous instruction here!
What page of wisdom is denied him? none;

If learning his chief lesson makes him wise.
Nor is instruction, here, our only gain;
There dwells a noble pathos in the skies,
Which warms our passions, proselytes our hearts.
How eloquently shines the glowing pole!
With what authority it gives its charge,
Remonstrating great truths in style sublime,
Though silent, loud! heard earth around; above
The planets heard; and not unheard in hell;
Hell has her wonder, though too proud to praise.
Is earth, then, more infernal? has she those,
Who neither praise (Lorenzo!) nor admire?
    Lorenzo's admiration, preengag'd,
Ne'er ask'd the moon one question; never held
Least correspondence with a single star;
Ne'er rear'd an altar to the Queen of Heaven
Walking in brightness; or her train ador'd.
Their sublunary rivals have long since
Engross'd his whole devotion; stars malign,
Which made the fond astronomer run mad;
Darken his intellect, corrupt his heart;
Cause him to sacrifice his fame and peace
To momentary madness, call'd delight.
Idolater, more gross than ever kiss'd
The lifted hand to Luna, or pour'd out
The blood to Jove!--O thou, to whom belongs
All sacrificè! O thou Great Jove unfeign'd!
Divine instructor! thy first volume, this,
For man's perusal; all in capitals!
In moon, and stars (heaven's golden alphabet!)
Emblaz'd to seize the sight; who runs, may read;
Who reads, can understand.   'Tis unconfin'd
To Christian land, or Jewry; fairly writ,
In language universal, to mankind:

A language, lofty to the learn'd : yet plain
To those that feed the flock, or guide the plough,
Or, from his husk, strike out the bounding grain.
A language, worthy the Great Mind, that speaks!
Preface, and comment, to the sacred page!
Which oft refers its reader to the skies,
As pre-supposing his first lesson there,
And scripture self a fragment, that unread.
Stupendous book of wisdom, to the wise!
Stupendous book! and open'd, night! by thee.
    By thee much open'd, I confess, O night!
Yet more I wish; but how shall I prevail?
Say, gentle night? whose modest, maiden beams
Give us a new creation, and present
The world's great picture soften'd to the sight;
Nay, kinder far, far more indulgent still,
Say, thou, whose mild dominion's silver key
Unlocks our hemisphere, and sets to view
Worlds beyond number; worlds conceal'd by day
Behind the proud, and envious star of noon!
Canst thou not draw a deeper scene?—and show
The mighty potentate, to whom belong
These rich regalia pompously display'd
To kindle that high hope? Like him of Uz,
I gaze around; I search on every side—
O for a glimpse of him my soul adores!
As the chas'd hart, amid the desart waste,
Pants for the living streams; for him who made her,
So pants the thirsty soul, amid the blank
Of sublunary joys. Say, goddess! where? [throne?
Where, blazes his bright court? where burns his
Thou know'st; for thou art near him; by thee, round
His grand pavilion, sacred fame reports
The sable curtain drawn. If not, can none

Of thy fair daughter-train, so swift of wing,
Who travel far, discover where he dwells?
A star his dwelling pointed out below.
Ye pleiades! Arcturus! Mazaroth!
And thou, Orion! of still keener eye!
Say ye, who guide the wilder'd in the waves,
And bring them out of tempest into port!
On which hand must I bend my course to find him?
These courtiers keep the secret of their king;
I wake whole nights, in vain, to steal it from them.

I wake; and, waking, climb night's radiant scale,
From sphere to sphere; the steps by nature set
For man's ascent; at once to tempt and aid;
To tempt his eye, and aid his towering thought;
Till it arrives at the great goal of all.

In ardent contemplation's rapid car,
From earth, as from my barrier, I set out.
How swift I mount! diminish'd earth recedes;
I pass the moon; and, from her farther side,
Pierce heaven's blue curtain; strike into remote;
Where, with his lifted tube, the subtle sage
His artificial, airy journey takes,
And to celestial lengthens human sight.
I pause at ev'ry planet on my road,
And ask for him who gives their orbs to roll,
Their foreheads fair to shine. From Saturn's ring,
In which, of earths an army might be lost,
With the bold comet, take my bolder flight,
Amid those sov'reign glories of the skies,
Of independent, native lustre, proud;
The souls of systems! and the lords of life,
Thro' their wide empires!—What behold I now?
A wilderness of wonder burning round;
Where larger suns inhabit higher spheres;

Perhaps the villas of descending gods ;
Nor halt I here ; my toil is but begun ;
'Tis but the threshold of the Deity ;
Or, far beneath it, I am grovelling still.
Nor is it strange ; I built on a mistake ;
The grandeur of his works, whence folly sought
For aid, to reason sets his glory higher ;   [Him)
Who built thus high for worms (mere worm   to
O where, Lorenzo ! must the builder dwell ?
    Pause, then ; and, for a moment, here respire—
If human thought can keep its station here. [thou,
Where am I ?—where is earth ?—nay, where art
O sun ?—is the sun turn'd recluse ?—and are
His boasted expeditions short to mine ?—
To mine, how short ! On nature's Alps I stand,
And see a thousand firmaments beneath !
A thousand systems ! as a thousand grains !
So much a stranger, and so late arriv'd,
How can man's curious spirit not enquire,
What are the natives of this world sublime,
Of this so foreign, un-terrestrial sphere,
Where mortal, untranslated, never stray'd ?
    " O ye, as distant from my little home,
As swiftest sunbeams in an age can fly !
Far from my native element I roam,
In quest of new, and wonderful, to man.
What province this, of his immense domain,
Whom all obeys ? Or mortals here, or gods ?
Ye bord'rers on the coasts of bliss ! what are you ?
A colony from heaven ? or, only rais'd,
By frequent visit from heaven's neighbouring realms,
To secondary gods, and half divine ?—
Whate'er your nature, this is past dispute,
Far other life you live, far other tongue

You talk, far other thought, perhaps, you think,
Than man.   How various are the works of God!
But say, what thought? is reason here inthron'd,
And absolute? or sense in arms against her?
Have you two lights? or need you no reveal'd?
Enjoy your happy realms their golden age?
And had your Eden an abstemious Eve?
Our Eve's fair daughters prove their pedigree,
And ask their Adams—' Who would not be wise?'
Or, if your mother fell, are you redeem'd?
And if redeem'd—is you Redeemer scorn'd?
Is this your final residence? if not,
Change you your scene, translated? or by death?
And if by death; what death?—Know you disease?
Or horrid war?—with war, this fatal hour,
Europa groans (so call we a small field,
Where kings run mad). In our world, death deputes
Intemperance to do the work of age;
And hanging up the quiver nature gave him,
As slow of execution, for dispatch
Sends forth imperial butchers; bids them slay
Their sheep (the silly sheep they fleec'd before),
And toss him twice ten thousand at a meal.
Sit all your executioners on thrones?
With you, can rage for plunder make a god?
And bloodshed wash out ev'ry other stain?—
But you, perhaps, can't bleed: from matter gross
Your spirits clean, are delicately clad
In fine-spun ether, privileg'd to soar,
Unloaded, uninfected; how unlike
The lot of man! how few of human race
By their own mud unmurder'd! How we wage
Self-war eternal!---Is your painful day
Of hardy conflict o'er? or, are you still

Raw candidates at school? and have you those
Who disaffect reversions, as with us ?—
But what are we ? you never heard of man ;
Or earth, the bedlam of the universe !
Where reason (undiseas'd with you) runs mad,
And nurses folly's children as her own ;
Fond of the foulest.   In the sacred mount
Of holiness, where reason is pronounc'd
Infallible ; and thunders, like a god ;
Ev'n there, by saints, the demons are outdone ;
What these think wrong, our saints refine to right;
And kindly teach dull hell her own black arts ;
Satan, instructed, o'er their morals smiles.---
But this, how strange to you, who know not man!
Has the least rumour of our race arriv'd ?
Call'd here Elijah in his flaming car ?
Past by you the good Enoch, on his road
To those fair fields, whence Lucifer was hurl'd ;
Who brush'd, perhaps, your sphere in his descent,
Stain'd your pure crystal ether, or let fall
A short eclipse from his portentous shade ?
O ! that the fiend had lodg'd on some broad orb
Athwart his way ; nor reach'd his present home,
Then blacken'd earth with footsteps foul'd in hell,
Nor wash'd in ocean, as from Rome he past
To Britain's isle ; too, too, conspicuous there ?"

But this is all digression : where is he,
That o'er heaven's battlements the felon hurl'd
To groans, and chains, and darkness? Where is he,
Who sees creation's summit in a vale ?
He, whom, while man is man, he can't but seek ;
And if he finds, commences more than man ?
O for a telescope his throne to reach !
Tell me, ye learn'd on earth ! or blest above !

Ye searching, ye Newtonian angels ! tell,
Where, your great Master's orb ? his planets, where ?
Those conscious satellites, those morning stars,
First-born of Deity ! from central love,
By veneration most profound, thrown off ;
By sweet attraction, no less strongly drawn ;
Aw'd, and yet raptur'd ; raptur'd, yet serene ;
Past thought illustrious, but with borrow'd beams ;
In still approaching circles, still remote,
Revolving round the sun's eternal sire ?
Or sent, in lines direct, on embassies
To nations—in what latitude ?—Beyond
Terrestrial thought's horizon !—And on what
High errands sent ?—Here human effort ends ;
And leaves me still a stranger to his throne.

    Full well it might ! I quite mistook my road.
Born in an age more curious than devout ;
More fond to fix the place of heaven, or hell,
Than studious this to shun, or that secure.
'Tis not the curious, but the pious path,
That leads me to my point : Lorenzo ! know,
Without or star, or angel, for their guide,
Who worship God, shall find him.   Humble love,
And not proud reason, keeps the door of heaven ;
Love finds admission, where proud science fails.
Man's science is the culture of his heart ;
And not to lose his plummet in the depths
Of nature, or the more profound of God.
Either to know, is an attempt that sets
The wisest on a level with the fool.
To fathom nature (ill-attempted here !)
Past doubt is deep philosophy above ;
Higher degrees in bliss archangels take,
As deeper learn'd ; the deepest, learning still.

For, what a thunder of omnipotence
(So might I dare to speak) is seen in all!
In man! in earth! in more amazing skies!
Teaching this lesson, pride is loth to learn——
" Not deeply to discern, not much to know,
Mankind was born to wonder, and adore."
    And is there cause for higher wonder still,
Than that which struck us from our past surveys?
Yes; and for deeper adoration too.
From my late airy travel unconfin'd,
Have I learn'd nothing?—Yes, Lorenzo! this;
Each of these stars is a religious house;
I saw their altars smoke, their incense rise;
And heard hosannas ring thro' ev'ry sphere,
A seminary fraught with future gods.
Nature all o'er is consecrated ground,
Teeming with growths immortal, and divine.
The great proprietor's all bounteous hand
Leaves nothing waste; but sows these fiery fields
With seeds of reason, which to virtues rise
Beneath his genial ray; and, if escap'd
The pestilential blasts of stubborn will,
When grown mature, are gather'd for the skies.
And is devotion thought too much on earth,
When beings, so superior, homage boast,
And triumph in prostrations to the throne?
    But wherefore more of planets, or of stars?
Ethereal journeys, and, discover'd there,
Ten thousand worlds, ten thousand ways devout,
All nature sending incense to the throne,
Except the bold Lorenzos of our sphere?
Op'ning the solemn sources of my soul,
Since I have pour'd, like feign'd Eridanus,
My flowing numbers o'er the flaming skies,

Nor see, of fancy, or of fact, what more
Invites the muse.———Here turn we, and review
Our past nocturnal landscape wide :—then say,
Say, then, Lorenzo ! with what burst of heart,
The whole, at once, revolving in his thought,
Must man exclaim, adoring, and aghast ?
" O what a root ! O what a branch, is here !
O what a father ! What a family !
Worlds ! systems ! and creations !—And creations,
In one agglomerated cluster, hung,
[1] Great vine ! On thee, on thee the cluster hangs ;
The filial cluster ! infinitely spread
In glowing globes, with various being fraught ;
And drinks (nectareous draught !) immortal life.
Or, shall I say (for who can say enough ?)
A constellation of ten thousand gems,
(And, O ! of what dimension ! of what weight !)
Set in one signet, flames on the right hand
Of majesty divine ! The blazing seal,
That deeply stamps, on all created mind,
Indelible, his sovereign attributes,
Omnipotence, and love ! that, passing bound :
And this, surpassing that.   Nor stop we here,
For want of pow'r in God, but thought in man.
Ev'n this acknowledg'd, leaves us still in debt :
If greater aught, that greater all is thine,
Dread sire !—Accept this miniature of thee ;
And pardon an attempt from mortal thought,
In which archangels might have fail'd, unblam'd."
    How such ideas of th' Almighty's pow'r,
And such ideas of th' Almighty's plan,
(Ideas not absurd) distend the thought

[1] John, xv. 1.

Of feeble mortals ! nor of them alone !
The fulness of the deity breaks forth
In inconceivables to men, and gods.
Think, then, O think ; nor ever drop the thought;
How low must man descend, when gods adore !
Have I not, then, accomplish'd my proud boast ?
Did I not tell thee, " [1] We would mount, Lorenzo !
And kindle our devotion at the stars ?"
    And have I fail'd ? and did I flatter· thee ?
And art all adamant ? and dost confute
All urg'd, with one irrefragable smile ?
Lorenzo ! mirth how miserable here !
Swear by the stars, by him who made them, swear,
Thy heart, henceforth, shall be as pure as they :
Then thou, like them, shalt shine; like them, shalt
From low to lofty ; from obscure to bright ; [rise
By due gradation, nature's sacred law.
The stars, from whence ?—Ask chaos—he can tell.
These bright temptations to idolatry,
From darkness, and confusion, took their birth ;
Sons of deformity ! from fluid dregs
Tartarean, first they rose to masses rude ;
And then, to spheres opaque ; then dimly shone ;
Then brighten'd ; then blaz'd out in perfect day.
Nature delights in progress ; in advance
From worse to better : but, when minds ascend,
Progress, in part, depends upon themselves.
Heaven aids exertion ; greater makes the great ;
The voluntary little lessens more.
O be a man ! and thou shalt be a god !
And half self-made !—Ambition how divine !
    O thou, ambitious of disgrace alone !

[1] Page 243.

Still undevout? unkindled?—Though high-taught,
School'd by the skies, and pupil of the stars ;
Rank coward to the fashionable world !
Art thou asham'd to bend thy knee to heaven ?
Curst fume of pride, exhal'd from deepest hell !
Pride in religion is man's highest praise.
Bent on destruction ! and in love with death !
Not all these luminaries, quench'd at once,
Were half so sad, as one benighted mind,
Which gropes for happiness, and meets despair.
How, like a widow in her weeds, the night,
Amid her glimm'ring tapers, silent sits !
How sorrowful, how desolate, she weeps
Perpetual dews, and saddens nature's scene !
A scene more sad sin makes the darken'd soul,
All comfort kills, nor leaves one spark alive.
    Tho' blind of heart, still open is thine eye :
Why such magnificence in all thou seest ?
Of matter's grandeur, know, one end is this,
To tell the rational, who gazes on it—
" Tho' that immensely great, still greater he,
Whose breast, capacious, can embrace, and lodge,
Unburden'd, nature's universal scheme ;
Can grasp creation with a single thought ;
Creation grasp ; and not exclude its sire"—
To tell him farther—" It behoves him much
To guard th' important, yet depending, fate
Of being, brighter than a thousand suns :
One single ray of thought outshines them all."—
And if man hears obedient, soon he ! soar
Superior heights, and on his purple wing,
His purple wing bedropp'd with eyes of gold,
Rising, where thought is now denied to rise,
Look down triumphant on these dazzling spheres.

Why then persist?—No mortal ever liv'd
But, dying, he pronounc'd (when words are true)
The whole that charms thee, absolutely vain ;
Vain, and far worse?—Think thou, with dying men ;
O condescend to think as angels think !
O tolerate a chance for happiness !
Our nature such, ill choice ensures ill fate ;
And hell had been, tho' there had been no God.
Dost thou not know, my new astronomer !
Earth, turning from the sun, brings night to man?
Man, turning from his God, brings endless night ;
Where thou canst read no morals, find no friend,
Amend no manners, and expect no peace.
How deep the darkness ! and the groan, how loud !
And far, how far, from lambent are the flames !—
Such is Lorenzo's purchase ! such his praise !
The proud, the politic, Lorenzo's praise !
Tho' in his ear, and levell'd at his heart,
I've half read o'er the volume of the skies

  For think not thou hast heard all this from me ;
My song but echoes what great nature speaks.
What has she spoken ? Thus the goddess spoke,
Thus speaks for ever :—" Place, at nature's head,
A sov'reign, which o'er all things rolls his eye,
Extends his wing, promulgates his commands,
But, above all, diffuses endless good ;
To whom, for sure redress, the wrong'd may fly ;
The vile, for mercy ; and the pain'd, for peace ;
By whom, the various tenants of these spheres,
Diversified in fortunes, place, and powers,
Rais'd in enjoyment, as in worth they rise,
Arrive at length (if worthy such approach)
At that blest fountain-head, from which they stream ;
Where conflict past redoubles present joy ;

And present joy looks forward on increase;
And that, on more; no period! every step
A double boon! a promise, and a bliss."
How easy sits this scheme on human hearts!
It suits their make; it soothes their vast desires;
Passion is pleas'd; and reason asks no more;
'Tis rational! 'tis great!—But what is thine?
It darkens! shocks! excruciates! and confounds!
Leaves us quite naked, both of help, and hope,
Sinking from bad to worse; few years, the sport
Of fortune; then the morsel of despair.

Say, then, Lorenzo! (for thou know'st it well)
What's vice?—Mere want of compass in our thought
Religion, what?—The proof of common sense.
How art thou hooted, where the least prevails!
Is it my fault, if these truths call thee fool?
And thou shalt never be miscall'd by me.
Can neither shame, nor terror, stand thy friend;
And art thou still an insect in the mire?
How, like thy guardian angel, have I flown!
Snatch'd thee from earth; escorted thee thro' all
Th' ethereal armies; walkt thee, like a God,
Thro' splendours of first magnitude, arrang'd
On either hand; clouds thrown beneath thy feet;
Close-cruis'd on the bright paradise of God;
And almost introduc'd thee to the throne!
And art thou still carousing, for delight,
Rank poison; first, fermenting to mere froth,
And then subsiding into final gall?
To beings of sublime, immortal make,
How shocking is all joy, whose end is sure!
Such joy, more shocking still, the more it charms!
And dost thou choose what ends ere well-begun;
And infamous, as short?   And dost thou choose

(Thou, to whose palate glory is so sweet)
To wade into perdition, thro' contempt,
Not of poor bigots only, but thy own?
For I have peep'd into thy cover'd heart,
And seen it blush beneath a boastful brow;
For, by strong guilt's most violent assault,
Conscience is but disabled, not destroy'd.

 O thou most awful Being; and most vain!
Thy will, how frail! how glorious is thy power!
Though dread eternity has sown her seeds
Of bliss, and woe, in thy despotic breast;
Though heaven, and hell, depend upon thy choice;
A butterfly comes cross, and both are fled.
Is this the picture of a rational?
This horrid image, shall it be most just?
Lorenzo! no: it cannot,—shall not, be,
If there is force in reason; or, in sounds
Chaunted beneath the glimpses of the moon,
A magic, at this planetary hour,
When slumber locks the gen'ral lip, and dreams
Through senseless mazes hunt souls uninspir'd.
Attend—the sacred mysteries begin——
My solemn night-born adjuration hear;
Hear, and I'll raise thy spirit from the dust;
While the stars gaze on this inchantment new;
Inchantment, not infernal, but divine!

 " By silence, death's peculiar attribute;
By darkness, guilt's inevitable doom;
By darkness, and by silence, sisters dread!
That draw the curtain round night's ebon throne,
And raise ideas, solemn as the scene!
By night, and all of awful, night presents
To thought, or sense (of awful much, to both,
The goddess brings)! By these her trembling fires,

Like Vesta's, ever-burning; and, like hers,
Sacred to thoughts immaculate, and pure!
By these bright orators, that prove, and praise,
And press thee to revere, the Deity;
Perhaps, too, aid thee, when rever'd awhile,
To reach his throne; as stages of the soul,
Through which, at different periods, she shall pass,
Refining gradual, for her final height,
And purging off some dross at every sphere!
By this dark pall thrown o'er the silent world!
By the world's kings, and kingdoms, most renown'd,
From short ambition's zenith set for ever;
Sad presage to vain boasters, now in bloom!
By the long list of swift mortality,
From Adam downward to this evening knell,
Which midnight waves in fancy's startled eye;
And shocks her with a hundred centuries,
Round death's black banner throng'd, in human
        thought!
By thousands, now, resigning their last breath,
And calling thee—wert thou so wise to hear!
By tombs o'er tombs arising; human earth
Ejected, to make room for—human earth;
The monarch's terror! and the sexton's trade!
By pompous obsequies that shun the day,
The torch funereal, and the nodding plume,
Which makes poor man's humiliation proud;
Boast of our ruin! triumph of our dust!
By the damp vault that weeps o'er royal bones;
And the pale lamp that shows the ghastly dead,
More ghastly, through the thick incumbent gloom!
By visits (if tnere are) from darker scenes,
The gliding spectre! and the groaning grave!
By groans, and graves, and miseries that groan

For the grave's shelter ! By desponding men,
Senseless to pains of death, from pangs of guilt !
By guilt's last audit ! By yon moon in blood,
The rocking firmament, the falling stars,
And thunder's last discharge, great nature's knell !
By second chaos ; and eternal night"—
Be wise—Nor let Philander blame my charm ;
But own not ill-discharg'd my double debt,
Love to the living ; duty to the dead.

  For know I'm but executor ; he left
This moral legacy ; I make it o'er
By his command ; Philander hear in me ;
And heaven in both.—If deaf to these, Oh ! hear
Florello's tender voice ; his weal depends
On thy resolve ; it trembles at thy choice ;
For his sake—love thyself : example strikes
All human hearts ; a bad example more ;
More still a father's ; that ensures his ruin.
As parent of his being, wouldst thou prove
Th' unnatural parent of his miseries,
And make him curse the being which thou gav'st ?
Is this the blessing of so fond a father ?
If careless of Lorenzo ! spare, oh ! spare
Florello's father, and Philander's friend !
Florello's father ruin'd, ruins him ;
And from Philander's friend the world expects
A conduct, no dishonour to the dead.
Let passion do, what nobler motive should ;
Let love, and emulation, rise in aid
To reason ; and persuade thee to be—blest.

  This seems not a request to be denied ;
Yet (such th' infatuation of mankind !)
'Tis the most hopeless, man can make to man.
Shall I then rise, in argument, and warmth ?

And urge Philander's posthumous advice,
From topics yet unbroach'd?——
But oh! I faint! my spirits fail!—Nor strange!
So long on wing, and in no middle clime!
To which my great Creator's glory call'd:
And calls—but, now, in vain. Sleep's dewy wand
Has strok'd my drooping lids, and promises
My long arrear of rest; the downy god
(Wont to return with our returning peace)
Will pay, ere long, and bless me with repose.
Haste, haste, sweet stranger! from the peasant's
            cot,
The ship-boy's hammock, or the soldier's straw,
Whence sorrow never chas'd thee; with thee bring,
Not hideous visions, as of late; but draughts
Delicious of well tasted, cordial, rest;
Man's rich restorative; his balmy bath,
That supples, lubricates, and keeps in play
The various movements of this nice machine,
Which asks such frequent periods of repair.
When tir'd with vain rotations of the day,
Sleep winds us up for the succeeding dawn;
Fresh we spin on, till sickness clogs our wheels,
Or death quite breaks the spring, and motion ends.
When will it end with me?
                    ——" Thou only know'st,
Thou, whose broad eye the future, and the past,
Joins to the present; making one of three
To moral thought! Thou know'st, and thou alone,
All-knowing!—all unknown!—and yet well-
            known!
Near, tho' remote! and, tho' unfathom'd, felt!
And, tho' invisible, for ever seen!
And seen in all! the great and the minute:

Each globe above, with its gigantic race,
Each flower, each leaf, with its small people swarm'd,
(Those puny vouchers of Omnipotence !)   [clare
To the first thought, that asks, ' From whence ?' de-
Their common source. Thou fountain, running o'er
In rivers of communicated joy !
Who gav'st us speech for far, far humbler themes !
Say, by what name shall I presume to call
Him I see burning in these countless suns,
As Moses, in the bush ? Illustrious mind !
The whole creation, less, far less, to thee,
Than that to the creation's ample round.
How shall I name Thee ?—How my labouring soul
Heaves underneath the thought, too big for birth !
    " Great system of perfections ! Mighty cause
Of causes mighty ! Cause uncaus'd ! Sole root
Of nature, that luxuriant growth of God !
First Father of effects ! that progeny
Of endless series ; where the golden chain's
Last link admits a period, who can tell ?
Father of all that is or heard, or hears !
Father of all that is or seen, or sees !
Father of all that is, or shall arise !
Father of this immeasurable mass
Of matter multiform ; or dense, or rare ;
Opaque, or lucid ; rapid, or at rest ;
Minute, or passing bound ! in each extreme
Of like amaze, and mystery, to man.
Father of these bright millions of the night !
Of which the least full godhead had proclaim'd,
And thrown the gazer on his knee—or, say,
Is appellation higher still, thy choice ?
Father of matter's temporary lords !
Father of spirits ! nobler offspring ! sparks

Of high paternal glory; rich endow'd
With various measures, and with various modes
Of instinct, reason, intuition; beams
More pale, or bright from day divine, to break
The dark of matter organiz'd (the ware
Of all created spirit); beams, that rise
Each over other in superior light,
Till the last ripens into lustre strong,
Of next approach to godhead.   Father fond
(Far fonder than e'er bore that name on earth)
Of intellectual beings! beings blest
With powers to please thee; not of passive ply
To laws they know not; beings lodg'd in seats
Of well-adapted joys, in different domes
Of this imperial palace for thy sons;
Of this proud, populous, well-policied,
Though boundless habitation, plann'd by thee:
Whose several clans their several climates suit;
And transposition, doubtless, would destroy.
Or, oh! indulge, immortal King, indulge
A title, less august indeed, but more
Endearing; ah! how sweet in human ears!
Sweet in our ears, and triumph in our hearts!
Father of immortality to man!
A theme that[1] lately set my soul on fire—
And thou the next! yet equal! thou, by whom
That blessing was convey'd; far more! was bought;
Ineffable the price! by whom all worlds
Were made; and one redeem'd! illustrious light
From light illustrious! Thou, whose regal power
Finite in time, but infinite in space,

---

[1] Nights vi. and vii.

On more than adamantine basis fix'd,
O'er more, far more, than diadems, and thrones,
Inviolably reigns; the dread of gods!
And oh! the friend of man! beneath whose foot,
And by the mandate of whose awful nod,
All regions, revolutions, fortunes, fates,
Of high, of low of mind, and matter, roll
Through the short channels of expiring time,
Or shoreless ocean of eternity,
Calm, or tempestuous (as thy spirit breathes),
In absolute subjection!—And, O thou
The glorious Third! Distinct, not separate!
Beaming from both! with both incorporate;
And (strange to tell!) incorporate with dust!
By condescension, as thy glory, great,
Enshrin'd in man! Of human hearts, if pure,
Divine inhabitant! The tie divine
Of heaven with distant earth! by whom, I trust,
(If not inspir'd) uncensur'd this address
To thee, to them—to whom?—Mysterious power!
Reveal'd—yet unreveal'd! Darkness in light;
Number in unity! our joy! our dread!
The triple bolt that lays all wrong in ruin!
That animates all right, the triple sun!
Sun of the soul! her never-setting sun!
Triune, unutterable, unconceiv'd,
Absconding, yet demonstrable, great God!
Greater than greatest! better than the best!
Kinder than kindest! with soft pity's eye,
Or (stronger still to speak it) with thine own,
From thy bright home, from that high firmament,
Where thou, from all eternity, hast dwelt;
Beyond archangels' unassisted ken;

From far above what mortals highest call :
From elevation's pinnacle ; look down,
Through—what? Confounding interval! Thro' all
And more than lab'ring fancy can conceive ;
Through radiant ranks of essences unknown ;
Through hierarchies from hierarchies detach'd
Round various banners of Omnipotence,
With endless change of rapturous duties fir'd ;
Through wondrous beings interposing swarms,
All clustering at the call, to dwell in thee ;
Through this wide waste of worlds! this vista vast,
All sanded o'er with suns ; suns turn'd to night
Before thy feeblest beam—look down—down—
On a poor breathing particle in dust,   [down,
Or, lower, an immortal in his crimes.
His crimes forgive! forgive his virtues, too !
Those smaller faults, half-converts to the right.
Nor let me close these eyes, which never more
May see the sun (though night's descending scale
Now weighs up morn), unpitied, and unblest !
In thy displeasure dwells eternal pain ;
Pain, our aversion ; pain, which strikes me now ;
And, since all pain is terrible to man,
Though transient, terrible ; at thy good hour,
Gently, ah gently, lay me in my bed,
My clay-cold bed ! by nature, now, so near ;
By nature, near ; still nearer by disease !
Till then, be this, an emblem of my grave :
Let it out-preach the preacher ; every night
Let it out-cry the boy at Philip's ear ;
That tongue of death ! that herald of the tomb !
And when (the shelter of thy wing implor'd)
My senses, sooth'd, shall sink in soft repose,

O sink this truth still deeper in my soul,
Suggested by my pillow, sign'd by fate,
First, in fate's volume, at the page of man—
Man's sickly soul, though turn'd and toss'd for ever,
From side to side, can rest on nought but thee :
Here, in full trust, hereafter, in full joy ;
On thee, the promis'd, sure, eternal down
Of spirits, toil'd in travel through this vale.
Nor of that pillow shall my soul despond ;
For—love almighty ! love almighty ! (sing,
Exult, creation !) Love almighty, reigns !
That death of death ! that cordial of despair !
And loud eternity's triumphant song !

  " Of whom, no more :—For, O thou patron God !
Thou God and mortal ! thence more God to man !
Man's theme eternal ! man's eternal theme !
Thou canst not 'scape uninjur'd from our praise.
Uninjur'd from our praise can he escape,
Who, disembosom'd from the father, bows
The heaven of heavens, to kiss the distant earth !
Breathes out in agonies a sinless soul !
Against the cross, death's iron sceptre breaks !
From famish'd ruin plucks her human prey !
Throws wide the gates celestial to his foes !
Their gratitude, for such a boundless debt,
Deputes their suff'ring brothers to receive !
And, if deep human guilt in payment fails ;
As deeper guilt prohibits our despair !
Injoins it, as our duty, to rejoice !
And (to close all) omnipotently kind,
[1] Takes his delights among the sons of men."

                    [1] Prov. chap. viii.

What words are these—And did they come from
    heaven ?
And were they spoke to man ? to guilty man ?
What are all mysteries to love like this ?
The songs of angels, all the melodies
Of choral gods, are wafted in the sound ;
Heal and exhilarate the broken heart ;
Though plung'd, before, in horrors dark as night :
Rich prelibation of consummate joy !
Nor wait we dissolution to be blest.

    This final effort of the moral muse,
How justly[1] titled ? Nor for me alone :
For all that read ; what spirit of support,
What heights of consolation, crown my song !

    Then farewell night! Of darkness, now, no more :
Joy breaks ; shines ; triumphs ; 'tis eternal day.
Shall that which rises out of nought complain
Of a few evils, paid with endless joys ?
My soul ! henceforth, in sweetest union join
The two supports of human happiness,
Which some, erroneous, think can never meet ;
True taste of life, and constant thought of death !
The thought of death, sole victor of its dread !
Hope, be thy joy ; and probity thy skill ;
Thy patron he, whose diadem has dropp'd
Yon gems of heaven ; eternity, thy prize :
And leave the racers of the world their own,
Their feather, and their froth, for endless toils :
They part with all for that which is not bread ;
They mortify, they starve, on wealth, fame, power ;
And laugh to scorn the fools that aim at more.

[1] The Consolation.

How must a spirit, late escap'd from earth,
Suppose Philander's, Lucia's, or Narcissa's,
The truth of things new-blazing in its eye,
Look back, astonish'd, on the ways of men,
Whose lives' whole drift is to forget their graves!
And when our present privilege is past,
To scourge us with due sense of its abuse,
The same astonishment will seize us all.
What then must pain us, would preserve us now.
Lorenzo! 'tis not yet too late; Lorenzo!
Seize wisdom, ere 'tis torment to be wise;
That is, seize wisdom, ere she seizes thee.
For what, my small philosopher! is hell?
'Tis nothing but full knowledge of the truth,
When truth, resisted long, is sworn our foe;
And calls eternity to do her right.

Thus, darkness aiding intellectual light,
And sacred silence whisp'ring truths divine,
And truths divine converting pain to peace,
My song the midnight raven has outwing'd,
And shot, ambitious of unbounded scenes,
Beyond the flaming limits of the world,
Her gloomy flight. But what avails the flight
Of fancy, when our hearts remain below?
Virtue abounds in flatterers, and foes;
'Tis pride, to praise her; penance, to perform.
To more than words, to more than worth of tongue,
Lorenzo! rise, at this auspicious hour;
An hour, when heaven's most intimate with man;
When, like a fallen star, the ray divine
Glides swift into the bosom of the just;
And just are all, determin'd to reclaim;
Which sets that title high within thy reach.

Awake, then : thy Philander calls : awake !
Thou, who shalt wake, when the creation sleeps
When, like a taper, all these suns expire ;
When time, like him of Gaza in his wrath,
Plucking the pillars that support the world,
In nature's ample ruins lies entomb'd ; _
And midnight, universal midnight ! reigns.

END OF THE NIGHT THOUGHTS.

CHISWICK PRESS:—PRINTED BY WHITTINGHAM AND WILKINS,
TOOKS COURT CHANCERY LANE.